Mauzy's *Depression Glass*

Barbara & Jim Mauzy

a Photographic
Reference

with Prices

Schiffer Publishing Ltd

4880 Lower Valley Road, Atglen, PA 19310 USA

Mauzy, Barbara E.
   [Depression glass]
   Mauzy's depression glass : a photographic reference with
prices / Barbara & Jim Mauzy.
      p. cm.
   Includes bibliographical references and index.
   ISBN 0-7643-0934-X (hardcover)
   1. Glassware--United States--History--20th century--
Collectors and collecting Catalogs. I. Mauzy, Jim II. Title.
   NK5112 .M375 1999
   748.2913'075--dc21   99-26379
                                                        CIP

Cover design by Bruce Waters
Book design by Blair Loughrey
Type set in Florens/Souvenir/Zurich

ISBN: 0-7643-0934-X
Printed in China
1 2 3 4

Published by Schiffer Publishing Ltd.
4880 Lower Valley Road
Atglen, PA 19310
Phone: (610) 593-1777; Fax: (610) 593-2002
E-mail: Schifferbk@aol.com
Please visit our web site catalog at
www.schifferbooks.com

This book may be purchased from the publisher.
Include $3.95 for shipping.
Please try your bookstore first.
We are interested in hearing from authors
with book ideas on related subjects.
You may write for a free catalog.

In Europe, Schiffer books are distributed by
Bushwood Books
6 Marksbury Rd.
Kew Gardens
Surrey TW9 4JF England
Phone: 44 (0)181 392-8585; Fax: 44 (0)181 392-9876
E-mail: Bushwd@aol.com

Dear Readers

We welcome you to the first edition of *Mauzy's Depression Glass: A Photographic Reference with Prices*. This exciting project we now joyously share with you. Our book is a celebration of the beautiful glass created primarily during the 1920s to the 1940s.

While working on this book we had the opportunity to photograph pieces and collections belonging to many generous individuals all of whom are listed in the Acknowledgments. There were times we felt like editors compiling the knowledge of dozens of intelligent, well-versed experts. Our results are presented for you, and we hope you are as pleased as we are. Every attempt has been made to add new pieces, even since the publication of *Mauzy's Comprehensive Handbook of Depression Glass Prices,* and, as you turn the pages, you will see pieces of glass never before documented. We have also added four new patterns bringing the total to 140!

Yet, despite our efforts, we know that several patterns need better coverage. We invite you to contact us if you can help and care to be a part of the second edition. As you flip through, please take notice of the many owners of glassware who are acknowledged throughout, as without the generosity of them and others this book would not exist. This book belongs to those who helped give it life. We invite you to make the second book even more lively, and in a real way, yours!

We hope to hear from you!

Barbara & Jim Mauzy

Contents

About the Prices

We have done everything possible to provide accurate prices. We have monitored the Internet, auctions, and trade papers, gone to shows, and consulted with collectors and dealers alike. We have also brought to this our years of buying, selling, and collecting glass.

This book is designed to be a tool and a reference for identification. Hopefully it is an invaluable one! Values vary immensely according to the condition of the piece, the location of the market, and the overall quality of the design and manufacture. Condition is always of paramount importance when assigning a value. The prices shown in this reference are for individual items that are in mint condition, but not packaged. Prices in the Midwest differ from those in the West or East, and those at specialty shows such as Depression Glass shows will vary from those at general shows. And, of course, being at the right place at the right time can make all the difference.

All of these factors make it impossible to create an absolutely accurate price list, but we can offer a guide. The values shown in this reference reflect what one could realistically expect to pay.

Neither the authors nor the publisher are responsible for any outcomes resulting from consulting this reference.

Acknowledgments

This book was a group effort, and without the contributions and collaboration of the following individuals this reference would still be a dream. Some of the people listed we have known for years and others were strangers until the moment they entered the studio. We feel a close relationship with all, as sharing a passion has a deep way of bonding us. It is this love of glass that joins us all in creating this presentation.

The efforts of these people were phenomenal. Some traveled great distances to bring van, car, and truckloads of treasures to the studio. Others opened their homes to us, along with either Bruce or Blair, our wonderful and skilled photographers. We had individuals running around to friends and families gathering items we needed. Friends even recruited dealers who were previously unknown to us from shows they attended!

Throughout all the months, miles, pieces, and slides, we all shared a common goal: we wanted to present the best possible reference on Depression Glass. This book belongs to all of the names listed below (plus a few silent partners) and to all of you readers, collectors, and dealers.

Deborah D. Albright
Sherelyn A. Ammon
David G. Baker
Donald G. and Juanita M. Becker
Bob and Cindy Bentley
Helen & Edward Betlow
Sylvia A. Brown
Donna L. Cehlarik
Ardell & George Conn
Charlie Diefenderfer
Diefenderfer's Collectibles & Antiques
Carol L. Ellis
Corky & Becky Evans
Kyle & Barbara Ewing
L.E. Fawber & Thomas Dibeler
Connie & Bill Hartzell
Dottie & Doug Hevener / The Quacker Connection
Bettye S. James
Brad and Tammy James
Bryan and Marie James
Michael and Kathleen Jones
Vic & Jean Laermans
Neil McCurdy - Hoosier Kubboard Glass
Maria McDaniel

Paula Apperson McNamara
Jane O'Brien
Kelly O'Brien-Hoch
Lucille and Joseph Palmieri
Tanya Poillucci
Paul Reichwein
Michael Rothenberger / Mike's Collectables
Verna Rothenberger
Staci and Jeff Shuck / Gray Goose Antiques
Jesse Speicher
Reta M. Stoltzfus
Marie Talone
Debora & Paul Torsiello, Debzie's Glass
Robert Tulanowski
Eunice A. Yohn
Don & Terry Yusko

We also need to acknowledge the world's best photographers, Blair Loughrey and Bruce Waters. Their patience and artistry made this reference possible. Blair also designed the book. Great job, Blair! And Bruce created the fabulous cover. We love it, Bruce! Special thanks to our editor, Jennifer Lindbeck, for all her help and insight.

Thank you all very, very much!

DEPRESSION GLASS

ADAM
Reproduced
(1932-1934 Jeannette Glass Company)

How appropriate that the name of the first man is the name of the first pattern! This has been a pattern well received even by people with limited knowledge of Depression Glass. The strong design features in terms of shape and style make it appealing to many.

Three items need to be noted. First is the butter dish, which has been reproduced, so check our information pertaining to this matter prior to making a purchase. Second is the more elusive Adam-Sierra combination butter dish. On the bottom of the butter dish will be either Adam or Sierra. The key is the top which has both the Adam motif and the Sierra motif. The Adam pattern is on the outside of the lid and the Sierra pattern is on the inside of the lid. If you locate one of these, consider yourself lucky indeed. Another piece worthy of your attention is the pitcher. It is most commonly seen with a square foot. The pricing reflects the fact that the round-footed pitcher is harder to locate, and we are pleased to present one here.

We purchased a set of Adam a few years ago that included cups and saucers. The cups were in a purplish-pink hue we had never seen before, and they didn't even look like they belonged on the pink saucers. We were relieved when the last set sold, and now we wish we had saved one set to photograph. Oh well!

Pitcher w/ round base. *Courtesy of Vic & Jean Laermans.*

Back row: platter, 4.5" ashtray; *front row:* creamer & sugar.

Back row: 9" dinner, 9" grill, 9" dinner, 7.75" salad; *front row:* 4.5" tumbler, platter, sherbet, pair of candlesticks. *Courtesy of Marie Talone & Paul Reichwein.*

Back row: sugar w/ lid & creamer; *front row:* shaker, sugar w/ lid, creamer, salt & pepper. *Courtesy of Vic & Jean Laermans.*

9" bowl w/ lid. *Courtesy of Bryan & Marie James.*

ADAM	Pink	Green	Qty
Ash tray, 4.5"	32	32	____
Bowl, 4.75" berry	25	25	____
Bowl, 5.75" cereal	47	47	____
Bowl, 7.75" berry	30	30	____
Bowl, 9" w/lid	70	80	____
Bowl, 10" oval vegetable	35	35	____
Butter dish base *R*	30	150	____
Butter dish lid *R*	70	250	____
Butter complete	100	400	____
Butter w/Adam bottom & Sierra/Adam lid	trtp*		____
Cake plate	30	30	____
Candlestick, ea.	45	50	____
Candy jar w/lid, 2.5"	125	125	____
Coaster	23	21	____
Creamer, 3"	24	24	____
Cup	20	22	____
Pitcher, round base	75		____
Pitcher, square base	50	60	____
Plate, 6" sherbet	10	12	____
Plate, 7.75" salad	16	16	____
Plate, 9" dinner	36	33	____
Plate, 9" grill	24	23	____
Platter, 11.75"	35	35	____
Relish, 8", 2-part	22	22	____
Salt & pepper	90	120	____
Saucer	7	7	____
Sherbet	30	35	____
Sugar base, 3.25"	24	24	____
Sugar lid	30	45	____
Tumbler, 4.5"	35	35	____
Tumbler, 7.5"	85	65	____
Vase	450	150	____

Reproduction information: New butter base: points aimed at corners rather than middle of side edges. New butter lid: leaf veins disjointed rather than touching center

Note: Delphite candlesticks: $150 each. Yellow cup: $100. **Round** 7.75" salad plate & saucer in pink or yellow: $100.

*trtp = too rare to price

AMERICAN PIONEER

(1931-1934 Liberty Works)

This pattern is one of those that supports how regional Depression Glass can be. American Pioneer is rare on the East Coast, but much more prevalent in the Midwest.

Here's a piece of information on the 9.25" bowl with a lid, pictured in pink. The lid and base seem to be about 1/4" 'off' from each other creating an ill-fitting combination. Without considerable care it would be easy for the lid to simply slide off and ultimately be chipped or broken. This poor fit lends itself to damage and lids are likely to be the piece of a two-part item to receive abuse anyway. If you are considering the purchase of this item, make note of the poor fit so you can rest assured that, yes, the top and bottom really do go together.

American Pioneer has a large variety of items with lids. This pattern offers the collector the aforementioned 9.5" covered bowl, plus a covered 8.75" bowl, two candy jars with lids, cologne bottles and a powder jar as part of the dresser set, and two pitchers/urns with lids. Glassware items with both a base and a cover that have survived time and use are usually of greater value than the other pieces in the pattern.

Back row: 8" plate; *front row:* 4" tumbler, cup & saucer, sugar & creamer. *Courtesy of Paul Reichwein.*

3.5" sherbet, 4" wine goblet, 4.75" sherbet. *Courtesy of Paul Reichwein.*

Back row: 8" plate, saucer; *front row:* cup, 4.75" stemmed sherbet, 3.5" coaster. *Courtesy of Staci & Jeff Shuck/Gray Goose Antiques.*

Back row: 8" plate, 11.5" plate/tray w/ 2 handles; *front:* cup & saucer. *Courtesy of Charlie Diefenderfer.*

9" footed bowl w/ lid.

AMERICAN PIONEER	Pink	Green	Qty
Bowl, 4.25" mayonnaise	65	100	____
Bowl, 5" w/2 handles	25	25	____
Bowl, 8.75" w/lid	120	140	____
Bowl, 9" w/2 handles	30	40	____
Bowl, 9" w/lid & foot	120	140	____
Bowl, 10.75" console	65	80	____
Candlestick, 6.5", ea.	40	50	____
Candy jar w/lid, 1 lb.	100	125	____
Candy jar w/lid, 1.5 lb.	125	150	____
Cheese & cracker 2-piece set	65	80	____
Coaster, 3.5"	35	35	____
Creamer, 2.75"	25	25	____
Creamer, 3.75"	25	25	____
Cup	12	12	____
Dresser set, 4-piece set	600	600	____
Cologne bottle, ea.	125	125	____
Powder jar w/indents	125	125	____
Tray, 7.5"	100	100	____
Goblet, 4" wine	50	50	____
Goblet, 6" water	50	50	____
Ice pail	60	75	____
Lamp, 5.5" round	80		____
Lamp, 8.5" tall (all glass)	125	125	____
Lamp, 9.5" tall (glass base, metal shaft)	60		____
Pitcher/urn, 5"	100	125	____
Pitcher lid for 5" urn	100	125	____
Pitcher/urn, 7"	125	125	____
Pitcher lid for 7" urn	125	125	____
Plate, 6"	15	15	____
Plate, 6" w/2 handles	15	15	____
Plate, 8"	15	15	____
Plate, 11.5" tray w/2 handles	25	25	____
Saucer	6	6	____
Sherbet, 4.5"	18	20	____
Sherbet, 4.75" w/stem	40	50	____
Sugar, 2.75"	25	25	____
Sugar, 3.5"	25	25	____
Tumbler, 2.25", 1 oz. whiskey	65	100	____
Tumbler, 5 oz. juice	35	45	____

Note: Crystal items half of pink.

AMERICAN SWEETHEART
(1930-1936 Macbeth-Evans Glass Company)

The name says it all. This is definitely in the top five patterns that our customers enthusiastically love and collect, and it is equally popular in both pink and monax. The delicate nature of both the glass and the design meld to create a truly appealing sweetheart of a pattern.

While working on this book, we had the good fortune to meet Vic and Jean Laermans. They have generously shared some fabulous, difficult-to-find examples of American Sweetheart in pieces and colors that are simply awesome. We hope you enjoy seeing them as much as we appreciated the opportunity to photograph them. If you are looking for ruby (Ruby Red) and cobalt (Ritz Blue), good luck!

Monax American Sweetheart has a tendency to "feather." (This is a term Barbara has been using for years!) Simply put, the glass on the outer edges seems to separate as barbs on a feather. Occasionally there is some chipping after the "feathering" develops. The feathering itself is not damage as the glass is conducive to this sort of aging effect. Obviously, each purchaser must make his or her own judgment on this matter, but keep in mind this glass is almost 70 years old.

The metal tray/plate is definitely an American Sweetheart design, but we have no information about it.

Back row: 10.25" dinner, 9.75" dinner; *front row:* 6" cereal bowl, 4.25" sherbet, cup & saucer. *Courtesy of David G. Baker.*

Above: 11" oval vegetable bowl, sugar & creamer, 2-tier tid-bit. *Courtesy of David G. Baker.*

Left: *Back row:* platter, 9" luncheon; *front:* salt & pepper, cream soup bowl on 6" bread & butter plate. *Courtesy of David G. Baker.*

Back row: 9.5" flat soup; *front row:* 6.75" bowl, sugar w/ lid. *Courtesy of Vic & Jean Laermans.*

Above: 11" plate/tray in metal. *Courtesy of Vic & Jean Laermans.*

Right: *Back row:* 8" plate, 15.5" plate; *front row:* creamer & sugar w/ platinum trim, sugar, cup. *Courtesy of Vic & Jean Laermans.*

Below: *Back:* 8" salad plate, 12" plate/base for tidbit; *front:* cup, creamer & sugar. *Courtesy of Vic & Jean Laermans.*

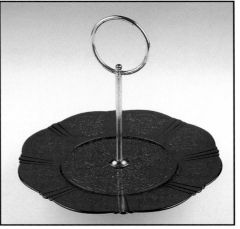

8" plate made into a server. *Courtesy of Debora & Paul Torsiello, Debzie's Glass.*

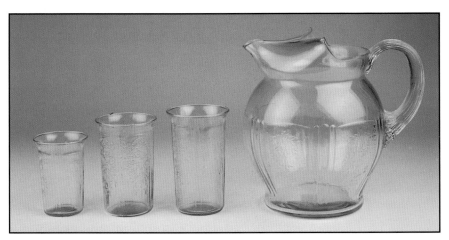

3.5" juice tumbler, 4.25" tumbler, 4.75" tumbler,
7.5" pitcher. *Courtesy of Vic & Jean Laermans.*

Salt & pepper. *Courtesy of
Vic & Jean Laermans.*

AMER. SWEET.	Pink	Monax	Red	Blue	Trimmed rim	Qty
Bowl, 3.75" flat berry	100					____
Bowl, cream soup	90	120				____
Bowl, 6" cereal	20	18			45	____
Bowl, 6.75"		trtp*				____
Bowl, 9" berry	50	65			250	____
Bowl, 9.5" flat soup	90	90			150	____
Bowl, 11" oval vegetable	75	95				____
Bowl, 18" console		600	1200	1400		____
Creamer	20	12	175	200	125	____
Cup	20	12	100	150	100	____
Lamp shade		500				____
Plate, 6" bread & butter	7	7			35	____
Plate, 8" salad	15	10	100	120	45	____
Plate, 9" luncheon		12			50	____
Plate, 9.75" dinner	40	28			120	____
Plate, 10.25" dinner		30				____
Plate, 11" chop plate		20				____
Plate, 12" salver	30	24	200	250	150	____
Plate, 15.5" server		300	400	500		____
Platter, 13"	65	70			250	____
Pitcher, 7.5", 60 oz	1000					____
Pitcher, 8", 80 oz.	850					____
Salt & pepper	650	500				____
Saucer	5	4	25	35	25	____
Sherbet, 3.75"	25					____
Sherbet, 4.25"	20	24			100	____
Sugar base	20	10	200	250	125	____
Sugar lid		600				____
Tid-bit, 2- tier (8" & 12" plates)	55	45	350	400		____
Tid-bit, 3-tier (8", 12", & 15.5" plates)		300	800	800		____
Tumbler, 3.5" juice	120					____
Tumbler, 4.25"	95					____
Tumbler, 4.75"	125					____

Note: Crystal sherbet in chrome base: $5. Cremax: 6" cereal, $15; 9"
berry, $45; cup, $500; lamp shade, $800.

*trtp = too rare to price

Back: 9.5" flat soup; *front:* 3.75" flat berry, cream
soup bowl. *Courtesy of Vic & Jean Laermans.*

2 sherbets: note the difference in size and color.
(Repro? Let us know!) *Courtesy of Jane O'Brien.*

2.5 oz. wine goblet. *Courtesy of Diefenderfer's Collectibles & Antiques.*

12.5" cake plate w/ 2 different metal lids. *Courtesy of Michael Rothenberger/Mike's Collectables.*

9" dinner, creamer.

ANNIVERSARY
(1947-1949 Pink...see note at bottom
Jeannette Glass Company)

There aren't many customers collecting this pattern, but when meeting with someone who does, he or she may be one of the more enthusiastic collectors around. Finding some of the pieces in this pattern can be a REAL challenge. We have had the opportunity to buy many collections through the years, but we have never been offered a set of Anniversary.

As with other patterns having iridescent pieces, Anniversary is sometimes mistaken for Carnival Glass. It is really one of the more recent offerings shown in this book. In fact, a few pieces in crystal and iridescent weren't made until 1972.

We were able to locate four different metal lids for the cake plate and picture two at this time. Collectors may want them all! We have read about a square cake plate but could not find one to present to you. If you have one, please let us know!

ANNIVERSARY	Pink	Crystal	Iridescent	Qty
Bowl, 4.75" berry	10	4	4	___
Bowl, 7.25" soup	20	8	8	___
Bowl, 9" fruit	27	12	14	___
Butter dish base	35	20		___
Butter dish lid	30	10		___
Butter complete	65	30		___
Candy jar w/lid	50	25		___
Cake plate, 12.5"	20	8		___
Cake plate cover (metal lid)	8			___
Candlestick, 4.75" ea.		10	14	___
Comport w/3 feet	18	5	8	___
Comport, ruffled w/3 feet		7		___
Creamer, 3.5"	12	5	8	___
Cup	8	3	4	___
Goblet, 2.5 oz. wine	20	8		___
Plate, 6.25" sherbet	5	1	2	___
Plate, 9" dinner	25	5	7	___
Plate, 12.5" sandwich	18	6	8	___
Relish, 8"	15	5	7	___
Relish, 4-part w/metal base		15		___
Saucer	4	1	2	___
Sherbet	10	3		___
Sugar base, 3.25"	12	5	8	___
Sugar lid	100	7	7	___
Tid-bit, 2-tier (made from 4.75" berry on top of 9" fruit bowl)		20		___
Tray/pickle dish, 9"	15	5	8	___
Vase, 6.5"	75	15		___
Vase, wall pin-up	35	15		___

Note: Crystal and Iridescent pieces made in 1960s & 1970s. Shell pink: cake plate & pin-up vase, $200 ea.

Back row: 12.5" sandwich plate, 6.5" vase; *front row:* cup & saucer, butter.

Candy jar w/ lid, butter. *Courtesy of Michael Rothenberger/Mike's Collectables.*

Cup & saucer, sugar w/ lid, creamer.

AUNT POLLY

(Late 1920s   U.S. Glass Company)

Once you own the 3.75" tumblers and sherbets, Aunt Polly becomes a challenge. The blue is a most appealing shade that many find attractive, while the green is much more difficult to locate.

U.S. Glass Company used the same blank for butter bottoms on Aunt Polly and other patterns including Cherryberry, Floral and Diamond Band, Strawberry, and U.S. Swirl. Other than a starburst pressed in the center of the base, the bottom is void of design, making the bases interchangeable.

We have added a new bowl to the Aunt Polly list since writing *Mauzy's Comprehensive Handbook of Depression Glass Prices*. Now included is a blue 4.5" bowl that is 2.75" deep, photographed by itself.

Back row: 6.5" vase, 8" luncheon plate, 6" sherbet plate, 7.75" berry bowl; front row: 3.75" tumbler, 4.75" bowl, 7.25" oval pickle w/ 2 handles, sherbet, sugar w/ lid. Courtesy of Charlie Diefenderfer.

4.5", 2.75" deep bowl.

AUNT POLLY	Blue	Green	Qty
Bowl, 4.5", 2.75" deep	65		____
Bowl, 4.75" berry, shallow	20	10	____
Bowl, 4.75", 2" deep		20	____
Bowl, 5.5" w/1 handle	28	18	____
Bowl, 7.25"oval pickle w/2 handles	45	18	____
Bowl, 7.75" berry	55	25	____
Bowl, 8.25"oval	145	60	____
Butter dish base	150	75	____
Butter dish lid	100	200	____
Butter complete	250	275	____
Candy base w/2 handles	50	25	____
Candy/sugar lid	200	75	____
Creamer	50	40	____
Pitcher, 8"	200		____
Plate, 6" sherbet	15	10	____
Plate, 8" luncheon	22		____
Salt & pepper	275		____
Sherbet	16	12	____
Sugar base	40	30	____
Sugar/candy lid	200	75	____
Tumbler, 3.75"	32		____
Vase, 6.5"	55	35	____

Note: Iridescent items 1/2 of Green EXCEPT for these: butter complete, $250; pitcher, $200.

Sugar w/ lid, butter. *Courtesy of Marie Talone.*

AURORA
(1937-1938 Hazel-Atlas Company)

Cobalt glass lovers are often drawn to Aurora—what a shame it is such a limited pattern! With a 6.5" plate as the only plate, this line is limited to desserts rather than meals.

The 4.5" bowl, sometimes referred to as "the deep bowl," is the most treasured item in Aurora, and its price has steadily risen through the years. Sometimes as prices increase the availability of an item may improve. Pieces perceived as more valuable have a way of showing up in the marketplace as individuals seek to take advantage of a higher price by selling something they own. Even with the upward pricing of the 4.5" bowl, these items are no more available than they were ten years ago.

Cobalt is the easiest of all the colors to collect. Here is an example of supply and demand controlling the market. One would assume that since the other colors are more elusive they would be worth more. In some cases this would be true, but Aurora is primarily a cobalt collector's pattern and the color in most demand.

Back row: 6.5" plate, 4.75" tumbler; *front row:* cup & saucer, 5.25" cereal bowl, creamer.

4.5" deep bowl. *Courtesy of Diefenderfer's Collectibles & Antiques.*

AURORA	Cobalt & Pink	Qty
Bowl, 4.5" deep	80	____
Bowl, 5.25" cereal	18	____
Creamer	25	____
Cup	15	____
Plate, 6.5"	10	____
Saucer	8	____
Tumbler, 4.75"	28	____

Note: Green and Crystal items 1/2 those in Cobalt and Pink.

AVOCADO
Reproduced
(1923-1933...see note at bottom of page 20
Indiana Glass Company)

Avocado was made with a mold edge along the rim. This thin line of extra glass is frequently nicked, and some collectors agonize over the condition of a piece to the point of rejecting items with damage to the extra glass. As always, the decision to make a purchase is totally up to the buyer.

Another feature of Avocado is the plain glass inside each piece of fruit. Often there are scratches and wear marks within the avocados negatively affecting an item's value. Take the time to hold a piece of Avocado up to the light prior to making a purchase and examine the bottom carefully.

The pitcher is a challenge to find accounting for why the price is much higher than most of the other pieces in this pattern.

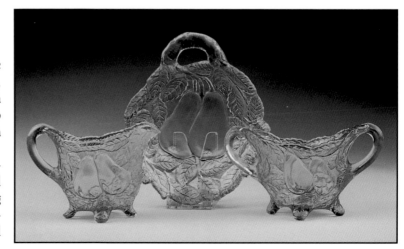

Creamer, 7" preserve bowl w/ 1 handle, sugar.
Courtesy of Diefenderfer's Collectibles & Antiques.

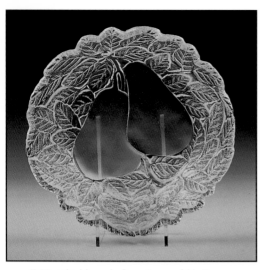

7.5" salad bowl. *Courtesy of Neil McCurdy - Hoosier Kubboard Glass.*

Back row: 6.25" cheese plate, 8.25" salad plate, 7" preserve w/ 1 handle; *front row:* cup & saucer, 6.25" bowl w/ 3 feet, 7.5" salad bowl. *Courtesy of Neil McCurdy - Hoosier Kubboard Glass.*

Sugar. *Courtesy of Vic & Jean Laermans.*

Back row: 10.25" cake plate w/ 2 handles, 9.5" salad bowl; *front row:* 5.25" olive bowl w/ 2 handles, 9" oval bowl w/ 2 handles, creamer & sugar. *Courtesy of Neil McCurdy - Hoosier Kubboard Glass.*

AVOCADO	Green	Pink	Crystal	Qty
Bowl, 5.25" olive w/2 handles	38	28	10	____
Bowl, 6.25" relish w/3 feet	30	28	10	____
Bowl, 7" preserve w/1 handle	28	24	10	____
Bowl, 7.5" salad	60	45	15	____
Bowl, 9" oval w/2 handles	35	28	12	____
Bowl, 9.5" salad	175	124	25	____
Creamer, 3.75"	35	35	15	____
Cup, 2 styles	40	35		____
Pitcher, 64 oz.	trtp*	1000	375	____
Plate, 6.25" cheese	20	18	8	____
Plate, 8.25" salad	25	10	8	____
Plate, 10.25" cake w/2 handles	70	50	15	____
Saucer	25	25		____
Sherbet/Sundae	65	65		____
Sugar, 3" at lowest pt.	35	35	15	____
Tumbler	300	200		____

Reproduction information: The following are new colors so everything in these colors is new: amethyst, blue, frosted pink, red, yellow, darker green, pink with an orange tint.

Note: Milk glass items made in 1950s. Milk white pitcher, $400; tumbler, $40; bowl, $30. Luncheon plate w/apple design, $10.

*trtp = too rare to price

BEADED BLOCK
(1927-1930s...see note bottom of page 22
Imperial Glass Company)

Collectors of Beaded Block may have mixed emotions with our pricing of their pattern; however, we feel these prices truly reflect the marketplace. If you have attempted to buy any Beaded Block on the Internet auctions, then you know how accurate our prices are. For collectors who already own many pieces, congratulations on a great investment! For those of you working on a collection, you may not appreciate seeing the higher prices in print; though you know that to buy Beaded Block (other than stumbling upon that occasionally underpriced treasure), you are already paying these prices.

Several new items have been added to the list. There are three Lily Bowls with distinctly different dimensions. Shown is the syrup, unique to this pattern. The foot was manufactured with a turned-up rim to act as a reservoir to collect drips that might trickle from the spout. Also presented are three comports in two different sizes.

The 6" vase is not Beaded Block, but many people include it in their collection. You can see how they were originally marketed with pry-off lids and consumable contents.

Back: 7.75" plate; *front:* 4.75" jelly w/ 2 handles, creamer. *Courtesy of Michael Rothenberger/Mike's Collectables.*

Right: 5.5" square bowl, 5.25" pitcher, 6" "go along" vase. *Courtesy of Michael Rothenberger/Mike's Collectables.*

Below: Assortment of creamers & sugars. *Courtesy of Neil McCurdy - Hoosier Kubboard Glass.*

Assortment of jelly bowls. *Courtesy of Neil McCurdy - Hoosier Kubboard Glass.*

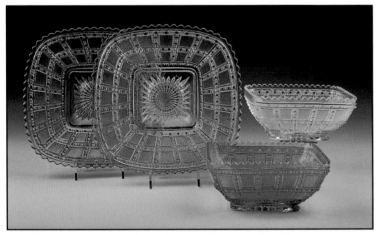

Two 7.75" square plates & two 5.5" square bowls.

Back: lily bowl—3" tall w/ 5" opening & 3.5" base; *front:* lily bowl—2.5" tall w/ 3" base, lily bowl—3" tall w/ 4.5" opening & 3.5" base. *Courtesy of Neil McCurdy - Hoosier Kubboard Glass.*

BEADED BLOCK	Amber,Green, Iridescent, & Pink	Opalescent	Crystal	Qty
Bowl, lily, 2.5" tall, 3" base	50	50	50	____
Bowl, lily, 3" tall, 3.5" base, 4.5" opening	50	50	50	____
Bowl, lily, 3" tall, 3.5" base, 5" opening	50	50	50	____
Bowl, 4.5" round lily	35	50	20	____
Bowl, 4.75-5" jelly w/2 handles (looks like a cream soup)	35	45	20	____
Bowl, 5.25" round lily			35	____
Bowl, 5.5" square	70	80	20	____
Bowl, 5.5" w/1 handle	35	45	20	____
Bowl, 6" round	50	60	20	____
Bowl, 6" square w/ ruffled rim			75	____
Bowl, 6.25" round	50	60	20	____
Bowl, 6.5" round	50	60	20	____
Bowl, 6.5" pickle w/2 handles	60	70	20	____
Bowl, 6.75" round	50	60	20	____
Bowl, 7.25" round & flared	60	70	20	____
Bowl, 7.5" round	60	70	20	____
Bowl, 7.75" round w/fluted rim	60	70	20	____
Bowl, 8.5" celery	80	90	25	____
Candy jar, pear-shaped	300	300	300	____
Comport, 4.5" tall, 5" diam.			50	____
Comport, 4.75" tall, 4.5" diam.	50		50	____
Creamer	25	35	15	____
Jelly, 4.5" stemmed	65	75	20	____
Jelly, 4.5" stemmed & flared	65	75	20	____
Pitcher, 5.25"	175	200	100	____
Plate, 7.75" square	35	45	20	____
Plate, 8" round	45			____
Plate, 8.75" round	40	50	20	____
Sugar, 4.25"	25	35	15	____
Syrup, 4.25"			150	____
Vase, 6", (go along)	25			____

Note: White made in 1950s. Later issued pieces in other colors from 1970s & 1980s marked "IG" for Imperial Glass. Yellow pear-shaped candy jar, $300.

Back row: 8.5" celery bowl, 8.75" round plate, 8" round plate; *front row:* 6.5" pickle bowl w/ 2 handles, 8.5" celery bowl. *Courtesy of Neil McCurdy - Hoosier Kubboard Glass.*

Back row: 6.25" round bowl, two 5.25" pitchers; *front row:* square 6" bowl w/ ruffled rim, 7.75" round bowl w/ fluted rim. *Courtesy of Neil McCurdy - Hoosier Kubboard Glass.*

6" "go along" vase originally packaged w/ red pepper.

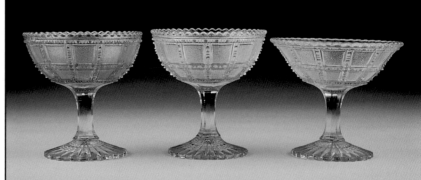

Above: Two 4.75" comports w/ 4.5" diameters & one 4.5" comport w/ 5" diameter. *Courtesy of Neil McCurdy - Hoosier Kubboard Glass.*

Left: 4.25" syrup. *Courtesy of Neil McCurdy - Hoosier Kubboard Glass.*

BLOCK OPTIC
(1929-1933 Hocking Glass Company)

For years Block Optic has been a very popular pattern. It is readily available, there are many items from which to select, and the prices are relatively reasonable. The clean lines are geometric without making the strong statement of patterns such as Pyramid and Tea Room.

Green is by far the most popular color. The luncheon plates, sherbets, cups, and saucers are plentiful and very inexpensive, making it easy to start a Block Optic collection with a minimal investment.

The 6" sherbet plate is often used as a saucer, but true saucers with cup rings do exist. They are harder to find than the sherbet plates; however they are not impossible to find by any means. Please note that the cups were made in four styles and two are shown. Often customers who wish to add to a collection are unable to determine which cup they have if faced with varying designs. Other choices include multiple designs of shakers, sherbets, creamers, and sugars. The tumbler options are numerous, too. Tumblers are flat, footed, with and without gold trim, and on rare occasions have black feet.

The Block Optic mug is not often seen. Note that the handle is solid glass and one is unable to reach a finger through it.

Above: *Back row:* 11.75" console bowl w/ rolled edge, 6.25" candy jar w/ lid; *front row:* mayonnaise comport, sherbet on 6" sherbet plate. *Courtesy of Reta M. Stoltzfus*

Below: *Back row:* 12.75" plate, ice bucket w/ metal handle; *front row:* sugar & creamer in 2 styles. *Courtesy of Reta M. Stoltzfus.*

BLOCK OPTIC	Green	Pink	Yellow	Qty
Bowl, 4.25", 1.25" deep	12	12		____
Bowl, 4.5", 1.5" deep	30	30		____
Bowl, 5.25" cereal	15	30		____
Bowl, 7.25" salad	165	165		____
Bowl, 8.5" berry	35	35		____
Bowl, 11.75" console w/rolled edge	100	100		____
Butter dish base	50			____
Butter dish lid	25			____
Butter complete, 3" x 5" rectangle	75			____
Candlestick, ea.	60	50		____
Candy jar w/lid, 2.25" tall	65	65	65	____
Candy jar w/lid, 6.25" tall	70	140		____
Creamer, 5 varieties	14	14	16	____
Cup, 4 styles	8	8	8	____
Goblet, 3.5" wine	trtp*		trtp*	____
Goblet, 4" cocktail	45	45		____
Goblet, 4.5" wine	45	45		____
Goblet, 5.75"	35	35		____
Goblet, 7.25"			45	____
Ice bucket w/metal handle	50	80		____
Ice/butter tub w/2 tab handles	80	120		____
Mayonnaise comport, 4" across	65	80		____
Mug	65			____
Pitcher, 7.5", 54 oz.	85	150		____
Pitcher, 8", 80 oz.	100	100		____
Pitcher, 8.5", 54 oz.	70	70		____
Pitcher, 9"	100			____
Plate, 6" sherbet	4	4	4	____
Plate, 8" salad	6	6	7	____
Plate, 9" dinner	30	40	40	____
Plate, 9" grill	35	45	45	____
Plate, 10.25" sandwich	25	25		____
Plate, 12.75"	30		30	____
Salt & pepper, short	125			____
Salt & pepper, tall w/foot	45	80	95	____
Sandwich server w/center handle	75	75		____

BLOCK OPTIC (Cont.)	Green	Pink	Yellow	Qty
Saucer, 5.75"	8	8		____
Saucer, 6.25"	8	8		____
Sherbet, cone-shaped	6			____
Sherbet, 3.25" round	7	8	10	____
Sherbet, 4.75" stemmed sundae	20	20	24	____
Sugar, 3 styles	14	14	16	____
Tumbler, 1.5", 1 oz. whiskey	40	45		____
Tumbler, 2.25", 2 oz. whiskey	34	34		____
Tumbler, 2.5", 3 oz.	25	25		____
Tumbler, 3.25", 3 oz. w/foot	30	30		____
Tumbler, 3.5", 5 oz. 3.75"	25	25		____
Tumbler, 3.75", 9.5 oz. flat	18	18		____
Tumbler, 4.75", 12 oz. flat	30	30		____
Tumbler, 5", 10 or 11 oz. flat	25	20		____
Tumbler, 5.25", 15 oz. flat	45	40		____
Tumbler, 6", 10 oz. w/foot	35	35		____
Tumbler, 9 oz. w/foot	20	18	28	____
Tumble-up night set	100			____
Bottle	15			____
Tumbler, 3"	85			____
Vase, 5.75"	350			____

*trtp = too rare to price

Note: Amber: 11.75" rolled edge console bowl, $75; candlesticks, $40 ea. Rectangular butter: green clambroth, $300; blue, $500; crystal, $100.

5.75" goblet, 4.75" stemmed sherbet/sundae, 9 oz. footed tumbler w/ gold rim, two 10 oz. footed tumblers, one w/ black foot. *Courtesy of Reta M. Stoltzfus.*

3" x 5" rectangular butter, 9" dinner, 2.25" candy jar w/ lid, ice/ butter tub w/ 2 tab handles. *Courtesy of Reta M. Stoltzfus.*

Back row: 10.25" sandwich plate, 4.25" bowl; *front row:* 5.25" cereal bowl, 8.5" berry bowl, 7.25" salad bowl. *Courtesy of Reta M. Stoltzfus.*

Sandwich server w/ center handle, cup & saucer, 8" salad plate, candlesticks, cup. *Courtesy of Reta M. Stoltzfus.*

Salt & pepper in both styles. *Courtesy of Reta M. Stoltzfus.*

Mug.

7.5" 54 oz. pitcher
& 8" 80 oz. pitcher.
*Courtesy of Reta
M. Stoltzfus.*

9" pitcher &
8.5" 54 oz. pitcher.
*Courtesy of Reta M.
Stoltzfus.*

3.75" flat tumbler, 5.25" flat tumbler, tumble-up night set. *Courtesy of Reta M. Stoltzfus*.

Two of the various handle styles on cups. *Courtesy of Reta M. Stoltzfus*.

2.25" candy jar w/ lid. *Courtesy of Michael Rothenberger/Mike's Collectables*.

Right: 7.25" goblet. *Courtesy of Diefenderfer's Collectibles & Antiques*.

Far right: 12.75" plate, 11.75" console bowl w/ rolled edge.

BOWKNOT
(Late 1920s ?   Manufacturer ?)

For what Bowknot lacks in the number of pieces made, it makes up for in its delicate and charming design. As there is no dinner plate, this pattern is relegated to luncheons and desserts, but what a lovely table setting it presents!

The 5.5" cereal bowl has become scarce. The footed tumbler is found more frequently than the flat one as reflected in the price difference. Interestingly, there is no saucer for the cup.

BOWKNOT	Green	Qty
Bowl, 4.5" berry	20	____
Bowl, 5.5" cereal	28	____
Cup	9	____
Plate, 7" salad	14	____
Sherbet	20	____
Tumbler, 5" flat	28	____
Tumbler, 5" w/foot	25	____

Back row: 7" salad plate, 5" flat tumbler;
front row: cup, sherbet, 5" tumbler w/ foot.

BUBBLE
(1934-1965   Hocking Glass Company)

We enjoy sharing the fact that one of our daughters has chosen blue Bubble as her pattern!

Jim also has his own connection with this pattern. As a child in the 1950s, he spent the summers on his Uncle Charlie's farm where his Aunt Verna used blue Bubble bowls for berries and cereal.

Blue Bubble is not difficult to collect except for the elusive 4" berry bowl. The other bowls can still be found, but locating a perfect one is a challenge. Be sure to take the time to run your fingernail along each of the humps of the individual bubbles as damage is sometimes not apparent.

It is actually easier to find Bubble in blue than any other color, even crystal. It does seem that the crystal collectors are few and far between. Many Royal Ruby collectors are interested in red Bubble. Forest Green collectors seem devoted to either Charm, Sandwich, or Bubble, and don't mix and match as often as Ruby collectors. The stems with clear feet continue to be in high demand in both colors. The labels on the boxed sets refer to these tumblers as "Inspiration."

The 8.25" Jade-ite bowl has risen in price as Jade-ite collectors seek a myriad of interesting examples of this glass. Likewise, collectors of pink often reach for the 8.25" pink bowl.

A crystal 5.25" cereal bowl is shown with a hammered aluminum rim. This is a truly unique Bubble item.

Back row: 8.25" pitcher, 9.25" dinner plate; *front:* 4.5"
12 oz. iced tea tumbler, 4.5" fruit bowl, cup & saucer.
Courtesy of L. E. Fawber & Thomas Dibeler.

4.5" fruit bowl, 9.25" dinner plate, 4" berry bowl, 7.75" flat soup bowl. *Courtesy of Donald G. & Juanita M. Becker.*

5.25" cereal bowl, 4.5" fruit bowl, 9.25" dinner plate, cup. *Courtesy of Donald G. & Juanita M. Becker.*

8.25" berry bowl in 3 colors. *Courtesy of Donald G. & Juanita M. Becker.*

Back: 5.25" cereal bowl in hammered aluminum rim ($25); *front:* candlestick, 4" fruit bowl.

BUBBLE	Blue	Green	Red	Crystal	Qty
Bowl, 4" berry	30			5	____
Bowl, 4.5" fruit	12	10	12	5	____
Bowl, 5.25" cereal	14	14		5	____
Bowl, 7.75" flat soup	18			7	____
Bowl, 8.25" berry	18	15	20	7	____
Bowl, 9" flanged	trtp*				____
Candlestick, ea.		25	25	8	____
Creamer	35	14		7	____
Cup	5	8	10	3	____
Lamp, 3 styles				40	____
Pitcher, 8.25"			60	60	____
Plate, 6.75" bread & butter	4	18		2	____
Plate, 9.25" dinner	8	28	25	5	____
Plate, 9.25" grill	20				____
Platter, 12"	18			9	____
Saucer	1	5	5	1	____
Stem, 3.5 oz. cocktail		14	12	3	____
Stem, 4 oz. juice		14	12	3	____
Stem, 4.5 oz. cocktail		14	14	3	____
Stem, 5.5 oz. juice		14	14	3	____
Stem, 6 oz. sherbet		12	12	3	____
Stem, 9 oz. water		14	14	5	____
Stem, 9.5 oz. water		14	14	5	____
Stem, 14 oz. iced tea		20		7	____
Sugar	20	14		7	____
Tidbit, 2-tier				50	____
Tumbler, 6 oz. juice			10	3	____
Tumbler, 3.25", 8 oz. old fashioned			16	3	____
Tumbler, 9 oz. water			12	3	____
Tumbler, 4.5", 12 oz. iced tea			15	6	____
Tumbler, 6", 16 oz. lemonade			20	8	____

Note: Pink: 8.25" berry bowl, $20; cup, $100; saucer, $50. Jade-ite 8.25" berry bowl, $30. Dark blue: cup & saucer, $125 for set; 6.75" bread & butter plate, $45. Iridescent: 8.25" berry bowl, $10.

*trtp = too rare to price

5.5 oz. juice stem as originally packaged. *Courtesy of Charlie Diefenderfer.*

6 oz. sherbet stem as originally packaged. *Courtesy of Charlie Diefenderder.*

6.5" candy
jar w/ lid.
*Courtesy
of David
G. Baker.*

CAMEO
Reproduced
(1930-1934   Hocking Glass Company)

If you desire dinnerware with many options and pieces, particularly in green, this pattern is worthy of your consideration. Also known as "Ballerina" and "Dancing Girl," this very attractive glass is quite popular and relatively available with the exception of some of the higher priced items.

As with Block Optic, Cameo provides multiple items to collect. There are two candy jars, two creamers, two sherbets, two sugars, and so on. There is a plethora of bowls, plates, and tumblers from which to select. The 8.5" square salad plate is the most elusive plate of all, and uniquely it is the only square plate in a family of round ones.

Actually early pieces of Cameo came from Block Optic molds. Examining the creamer, sugar, candy jar with lid, and additional items verifies their connection. Hocking Glass Company further developed Cameo with additional pieces such as the cookie jar and console bowl. The Cameo mold was then used by Hocking Glass Company in 1940 to create the "Philbe" line. You can read about this pattern by looking under Philbe. It is fascinating to see how the companies cleverly arrived at their diverse array of dinnerware designs.

Back row: 9" soup bowl, 10" cake plate; *front row:* salt & pepper, candlestick, 5" mayonnaise comport. *Courtesy of David G. Baker.*

Back row: 7.5" 3-part relish,
12" platter w/ tab handles;
front row: 11" console bowl
w/ 3 feet, 4" candy jar w/ lid.
Courtesy of David G. Baker.

Back row: 10" sandwich
plate, 8.5" square plate; *front
row:* cup & saucer, cream
soup bowl, jam jar w/ lid.
Courtesy of David G. Baker.

Back row: 10.5" plate w/
tab handles, 10" oval
vegetable bowl; *front row:*
3.25" sugar, 4.25" sugar,
3.25" creamer. *Courtesy of
David G. Baker.*

5.5" cereal bowl, 7.25" salad bowl, 8.25" berry bowl.
Courtesy of David G. Baker.

3.75" juice tumbler, 4" water tumbler, 5" tumbler.
Courtesy of David G. Baker.

CAMEO	Green	Yellow	Pink	Crystal (Platinum trim)	Qty
Bottle, water/ Whitehouse Vinegar (dark green)	20				____
Bowl, 4.25" sauce				8	____
Bowl, cream soup	150				____
Bowl, 5.5" cereal	35	35	200	8	____
Bowl, 7.25" salad	60				____
Bowl, 8.25" berry	45		200		____
Bowl, 9" soup	100		150		____
Bowl, 10" oval vegetable	35	45			____
Bowl, 11" console w/3 feet	85	120	65		____
Butter dish base	100				____
Butter dish lid	150				____
Butter dish complete	250	trtp*			____
Cake plate, 10" w/ 3 feet	30				____
Cake plate, 10.5" no feet (same as rimmed 10.5" dinner)	125		250		____
Candlestick, ea.	70				____
Candy jar w/lid, 4" tall	100	120	500		____
Candy jar w/lid, 6.5" tall	225				____
Cocktail shaker w/metal lid, 11.25"				1000	____
Comport, 5" mayonnaise	65		250		____
Cookie jar/lid	65				____
Creamer, 3.25"	25	25			____
Creamer, 4.25"	30		150		____
Cup, styles	15	8	100	8	____
Decanter w/stopper, 10.25"	200			225	____
Decanter w/stopper, 10.25" frosted	50				____
Domino tray, 7" w/ 3" indent	200				____
Domino tray, 7", no indent			350	200	____
Goblet, 3.5" wine	1500		1000		____
Goblet, 4" wine	90		250		____
Goblet, 5.75" water	65		200		____
Ice bowl/Open butter, 3" tall x 5.5" wide	200		850	300	____
Jam jar w/lid	200			175	____
Pitcher, 5.75" milk or syrup, 20 oz.	375	trtp*			____
Pitcher, 6" juice, 36 oz.	70				____
Pitcher, 8.5" water, 56 oz.	75		trtp*	500	____
Plate, 6" sherbet	6	5	100	4	____
Plate, 7" salad				5	____
Plate, 8.25" luncheon	14	12	35	4	____

6" juice pitcher, 8.5" water pitcher.
Courtesy of David G. Baker.

CAMEO (Cont.)	Green	Yellow	Pink	Crystal (Platinum trim)	Qty
Plate, 8.5" square	75	300			____
Plate, 9.5" dinner	25	15	100		____
Plate, 10" sandwich	20		50		____
Plate, 10.5" dinner, rimmed (same as 10.5" cake plate)	125		250		____
Plate, 10.5" grill no handles	12	8	50		____
Plate, 10.5" grill w/tab handles	75	10			____
Plate, 10.5" w/tab handles	15	15			____
Platter, 12" w/tab handles	30	45			____
Relish, 7.5", 3-part w/3 feet	30			160	____
Salt & pepper *R*	100		1000		____
Sandwich server w/center handle	trtp*				____
Saucer	200				____
Sherbet, 3.25", blown	25		75		____
Sherbet, 3.25" molded	18	40	80		____
Sherbet, 4.75" w/tall stem	35	50	100		____
Sugar, 3.25"	25	25			____
Sugar, 4.25"	30		150		____
Tray, Domino sugar, 7" w/indent	200				____
Tray, Domino sugar, no indent			350	200	____
Tumbler, 3 oz. juice w/foot	75		150		____
Tumbler, 3.75" juice, 5 oz.	45		100		____
Tumbler, 4" water, 9 oz.	40		80	10	____
Tumbler, 4.75", 10 oz. no foot	40		100		____
Tumbler, 5", 9 oz., w/foot	40	20	120		____
Tumbler, 5", 11 oz., no foot	50	60	100		____
Tumbler, 5.25"	90		140		____
Tumbler, 5.75"	80		140		____
Tumbler, 6.25"	750				____
Vase, 5.75"	400				____
Vase, 8"	65				____

Reproduction information: All miniatures are new. Salt & pepper reproduced in blue, green, & pink; glass is too thick, green is too dark.

*trtp = too rare to price

Cookie jar, 8" vase. *Courtesy of David G. Baker.*

5.75" water goblet, 4.75" sherbet w/ tall stem. *Courtesy of Charlie Diefenderfer.*

7" domino tray w/ 3" indent. *Courtesy of Vic and Jean Laermans.*

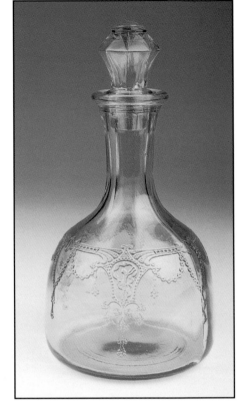

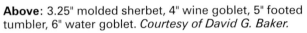

Above: 3.25" molded sherbet, 4" wine goblet, 5" footed tumbler, 6" water goblet. *Courtesy of David G. Baker.*

Right: 10.5" decanter. *Courtesy of Charlie Diefenderfer.*

Back row: 8.25" berry bowl, 8.25" luncheon plate; *front row:* 3.25" molded sherbet, 4" 9 oz. water tumbler, 3.75" 5 oz. juice tumbler. *Courtesy of Staci & Jeff Shuck/Gray Goose Antiques.*

Back row: 9.5" dinner, 10.5" grill w/ no handles; *front row:* 3.25" molded sherbet, 3.25" sugar, cup & saucer.

Cocktail shaker, 4" 9 oz. water tumbler. *Courtesy of Neil McCurdy - Hoosier Kubboard Glass and Staci & Jeff Shuck/Gray Goose Antiques.*

11" console bowl w/ 3 feet. *Courtesy of Donna L. Cehlarik & Jane O'Brien.*

CHERRY BLOSSOM
Reproduced
(1930-1939 Jeannette Glass Company)

Here is one pattern collected equally in all colors with universal appeal. The strong, attractive design is recognizable even to a novice collector, lending itself to often being selected by someone just entering the world of Depression Glass collecting. Cherry Blossom must have had a large distribution area when introduced in the 1930s as people from all over the country tell us how they remember Cherry Blossom in Grandma's house.

The earliest footed pieces have round bases. Later changes to molds include creating scalloped bases. Pink was made throughout the entire time Jeannette produced Cherry Blossom, but green was terminated around 1935, which leaves us with more pink than green.

A sure sign of a pattern's popularity is when it is reproduced. The list of items that fall under this category is long, so do take care to review our explanations prior to purchasing a piece that has been reproduced. Look for an *R* to determine the pieces that need this extra attention.

We have never seen the cookie jar, but it was confirmed for us by someone who had one and sold it. If you are the lucky owner, we would love to hear from you. The shakers are equally as elusive. Collectors with the 9" platter are indeed lucky, and whenever we meet someone who has found a mug they are elated! (By the way, be sure to check the Dealer Directory in the back of this book. These fine people may be able to help you on your quest to locate quality Depression Glass.)

Cherry Blossom 4.75" berry bowls and 5.75" cereal bowls were made with a "hard edge." This definitive line where the rim interfaces with the curve of the bowl is subject to damage when stacking the bowls or using them. Most Cherry Blossom collectors are a bit forgiving of this rim. Actually, 100% perfect rims may have been repaired. These bowls are just prone to imperfections after the passage of time.

Above: 7 oz. mug. *Courtesy of Marie Talone.*

Right: *Back row:* 7" salad plate, 10.25" cake plate, 9" dinner plate; *middle row:* 8" flat pitcher w/ pattern only at top, 8.5" berry bowl, 4.25" tumbler w/ no foot, sherbet, 6.75" pitcher w/ round base; *front row:* 11" platter, sugar w/ lid, creamer. *Courtesy of Marie Talone & Paul Reichwein*.

Top Right: 5" tumbler, no foot & pattern only at top. *Courtesy of Charlie Diefenderfer*.

Top Left: Butter dish. *Courtesy of Marie Talone & Paul Reichwein.*

Center: 6.75" pitcher w/ round base & 6.75" pitcher w/ scalloped base. *Courtesy of Michael Rothenberger/Mike's Collectables.*

Bottom: *Back row:* 9" grill plate, 10.5" sandwich tray w/ 2 handles, 13" divided platter; *middle row:* 5.75" cereal bowl, 3.5" tumbler w/ no foot, cup & saucer, 9" oval vegetable bowl; *front row:* 3.75" tumbler w/ foot, 4.75" berry bowl. *Courtesy of Marie Talone & Paul Reichwein.*

Delphite Cherry Blossom. *Back row:* 11" platter, 6.75" pitcher w/ scalloped foot; *front row:* 4.75" berry bowl, 9" bowl w/ 2 handles. *Courtesy of Bob & Cindy Bentley.*

Delphite Cherry Blossom. *Back row:* 9" dinner plate, 6" sherbet plate; *front row:* cup & saucer, sherbet. *Courtesy of Bob & Cindy Bentley.*

Delphite Cherry Blossom. *Back:* 10.5" sandwich plate w/ 2 handles; *front:* 4.5" tumbler w/ round foot, sugar, 9" oval vegetable bowl, creamer. *Courtesy of Bob & Cindy Bentley.*

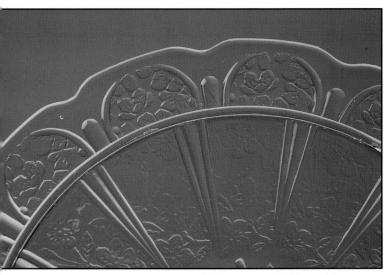

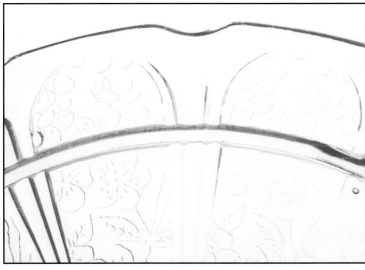

Close-up of edge of reproduction cake plate. Note that the design along the outside rim does not accurately line up with the rest of the design along the plate. *Courtesy of Charlie Diefenderfer.*

Close-up of edge of original cake plate. Compare this to the repro cake plate and see how much more closely the design lines up as it crosses the outside rim. *Courtesy of Charlie Diefenderfer.*

CHERRY BLOSSOM	Pink	Green	Delphite	Qty
Bowl, 4.75" berry	25	25	20	____
Bowl, 5.75" cereal *R*	65	50		____
Bowl, 7.75" flat soup	95	90		____
Bowl, 8.5" berry *R*	55	55	60	____
Bowl, 9" oval vegetable	65	55	60	____
Bowl, 9" w/2 handles	55	70	35	____
Bowl, 10.5" fruit w/3 feet	100	100		____
Butter dish base *R*	20	30		____
Butter dish lid *R*	80	90		____
Butter complete *R*	100	120		____
Cake plate, 10.25" *R*	35	45		____
Coaster, 3.25"	18	16		____
Cookie Jar	trtp*			____
Creamer	20	20	25	____
Cup *R*	22	22	20	____
Mug, 7 oz.	500	300		____
Pitcher, 6.75", scalloped base w/pattern all over	65	65	90	____
Pitcher, 6.75", round base w/pattern all over	75	75		____
Pitcher, 8" footed w/pattern only at top	80	75		____
Pitcher, 8" flat w/pattern only at top	80	70		____
Plate, 6" sherbet	10	10	10	____
Plate, 7" salad	25	28		____
Plate, 9" dinner *R*	30	30	25	____
Plate, 9" grill	35	30		____
Plate, 10" grill		100		____
Platter, 9"	1000	1200		____
Platter, 11"	50	50	50	____
Platter, 13" & 13" divided *R*	100	100		____
Salt & pepper *R*	trtp*	trtp*		____
Saucer *R*	6	6	6	____
Sherbet, 2.75" tall	20	25	20	____
Sugar base, 3"	20	20	25	____
Sugar lid	28	30		____
Tray, 10.5" sandwich w/2 handles	40	40	35	____
Tumbler, 3.5" no foot, pattern only at top	25	30		____
Tumbler, 3.75" w/foot, pattern all over	20	25	30	____

CHERRY BLOS. (Cont.)	Pink	Green	Delphite	Qty
Tumbler, 4.25" no foot, pattern only at top	20	25		____
Tumbler, 4.5" w/round foot, pattern all over	42	42	38	____
Tumbler, 4.5" scalloped foot, pattern all over *R*	40	40	38	____
Tumbler, 5" no foot, pattern only at top	125	100		____

Note: Yellow: 10.5" 3-footed fruit bowl, $450. Translucent Green: grill plate, $400. Jade-ite: grill plate, $400; 10.5" 3-footed fruit bowl & dinner plate, $450 each.

Reproduction information: New colors: blue (transparent, cobalt, & delphite), iridescent, & red. Also reproduced in pink & green. 5.75" cereal bowl: *new* - 2" mold ring on bottom; *old* - 2 1/2" mold ring on bottom. 8.5" round berry bowl: *new* - smooth edges to leaves, veins same size; *old* - irregular veins, realistically shaped leaf. Butter dish lid: *new* - 1 molded line in smooth area near base; *old* - 2 molded lines. Butter dish base: *new* - branches without texture and end about 1/4" from outer edge, leaves unrealistic; *old* - textured branch that ends very close to outer edge, realistic leaves. *New* cake plate: from underside of plate the design along the outside rim does not accurately line up with the rest of the design inside the rim. Cup: *new* - pattern is sparse on bottom; *old* - 4 cherries & many leaves on bottom. 6.75" pitcher: *new* - 7 cherries on smooth bottom; *old* - 9 cherries on textured bottom. 9" dinner plate & saucer: *new* - crudely finished at outer edges so one can feel a ridge; *old* - smooth edges. 13" divided platter: *new* - too heavy & too thick, VERY DIFFICULT TO DISCERN; *old* - leaves still have more realistic design upon close examination. Salt & pepper: assume what you have found is new! 10.5" sandwich tray w/2 handles: *new* - if handles are at 9:00 & 3:00 center branch lines up horizontally; *old* - if handles are at 9:00 & 3:00 center branch with textures will be vertical. 4.5" tumbler with scalloped foot and pattern all over: *new* - 1 or 3 weak lines dividing pattern and smooth rim at top; *old* - 3 clearly distinct lines between pattern and rim at top.

Reproduction salt & pepper shakers.
Courtesy of Charlie Diefenderfer.

Reproduction tumblers do not have three distinct lines between the pattern design and the smooth rim at the top. *Courtesy of Charlie Diefenderfer.*

CHILD'S JUNIOR DINNER SET (Reproduced)	Pink	Delphite	Qty
Creamer	55	50	____
Cup *R*	55	45	____
Plate, 6"	20	15	____
Saucer *R*	12	8	____
Sugar	55	50	____
14-piece set	458	372	____
Box (for pink) in fairly reasonable condition: $35, mint condition: $50			

Reproduction information: Butter dish: all are new regardless of color! Cup: lopsided handle, cherries may be upside down & off-color. Saucer: design not centered.

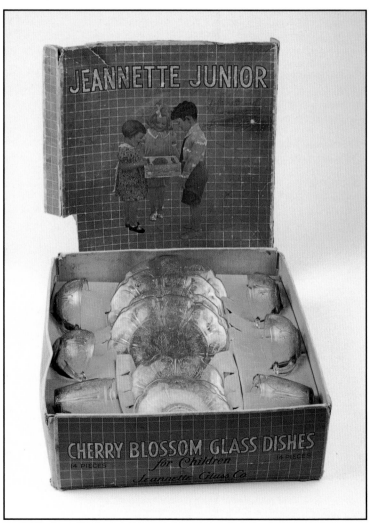

"Child's Junior Dinner Set" in original box.
Courtesy of Charlie Diefenderfer.

CHERRYBERRY

(1928-1931 U.S. Glass Company)

Depression Glass patterns that do not have dinner plates are often overlooked by collectors. Cherryberry, with its charming design, deserves more attention than it generally receives. Sherbets are abundant, but beyond that this is a pattern for the patient and persevering. However, don't misunderstand, it is worth the search!

Many of the rims on Cherryberry pieces have a ridged texture susceptible to damage. The rims need particular attention when choosing a selection to buy.

If you like this pattern, you may want to look at U.S. Glass Company's Strawberry pattern. The molds are the same and the designs are quite similar.

CHERRYBERRY	Pink & Green	Crystal & Iridescent	Qty
Bowl, 4" berry	12	6	____
Bowl, 6.25"	100	40	____
Bowl, 6.5" salad	30	15	____
Bowl, 7.5" berry	30	15	____
Butter dish base	75	30	____
Butter dish lid	150	70	____
Butter complete	225	100	____
Comport, 3.5" tall, 5.5" dia.	35	18	____
Creamer, small	25	14	____
Creamer, large, 4.5"	40	16	____
Olive dish, 5" w/1 handle	25	14	____
Pickle dish, 8.25" oval	25	14	____
Pitcher, 7.75"	200	100	____
Plate, 6" sherbet	10	5	____
Plate, 7.5" salad	20	6	____
Sherbet	10	5	____
Sugar, small	25	14	____
Sugar base, large	35	14	____
Sugar lid (fits large)	65	36	____
Tumbler, 3.25"	45	20	____

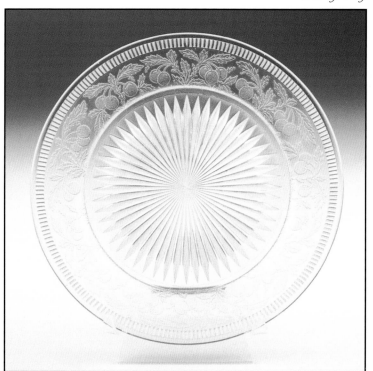

7.5" salad plate.

Comport.

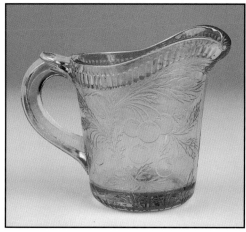

Above: 3" creamer. *Courtesy of Vic & Jean Laermans.*

Left: Sherbet & 6" sherbet plate. *Courtesy of Marie Talone & Paul Reichwein.*

Castle decoration dinners with two distinctly different shades of blue, values the same. *Courtesy of Charlie Diefenderfer.*

Castle decoration creamer & sugar.
Courtesy of Vic & Jean Laermans.

CHINEX CLASSIC
(Late 1930s-1942 Macbeth-Evans
Division Corning Glass Works)

Chinex Classic is most often collected with the castle design. We have met many men who particularly enjoy this pattern. The castle design was actually marketed as the Windsor design on Cremax, a line by Corning.

Through the years we have purchased several sets of Chinex Classic with the castle design. If we had known we would be doing this book, there are many items we would have photographed, such as the butter dish. The castle design is found only in the middle of the base. There is no design on the lid.

CHINEX CLASSIC	Castle	Floral	Plain	Qty
Bowl, 6" dessert	15	10	5	____
Bowl, 6.75" salad	13	20	10	____
Bowl, 7" vegetable	35	25	10	____
Bowl, 7.75" coupe soup	35	25	10	____
Bowl, 9" vegetable	35	25	10	____
Bowl, 11"	40	30	20	____
"Butter dish" base	30	20	15	____
"Butter dish" lid	120	60	35	____
"Butter" complete (actually a "covered utility dish")	150	80	50	____
Creamer	15	10	5	____
Cup	12	7	5	____
Plate, 6.25" bread & butter	8	4	3	____
Plate, 9.75" dinner	25	10	6	____
Plate, 11.5" salver	25	15	8	____
Saucer	6	4	3	____
Sherbet	20	10	7	____
Sugar	15	10	5	____

Castle decoration.
Back: 9" vegetable bowl, 7.75" coupe soup bowl; *front:* 6" dessert bowl.

Castle decoration. *Back row:* 11.5" salver, 9.75" dinner plate, 6.25" bread & butter plate; *front:* cup & saucer.

CHRISTMAS CANDY

(Late 1930s-early 1950s   Indiana Glass Company)

The teal color of Christmas Candy is one many ogle. As only a few patterns were made in teal or ultramarine, some people are intrigued upon first seeing it.

Once you make the connection between the pattern names and the designs, it becomes relatively easy to remember the names, as exemplified by this pattern. The outer rim of the glassware is reminiscent of the hard ribbon candy associated with Christmas lending itself to the name "Christmas Candy." Because the design is only on the rim and feet, there is a vast expanse of undecorated glass, making scratches easy to detect. Scratches do negatively impact the value of any glassware.

There aren't many pieces made in this pattern, particularly in teal, but the availability of dinner plates does allow one to create a reasonably complete table setting.

Above: Sugar & creamer. *Courtesy of Vic & Jean Laermans.*

Below: *Back row:* 8.25" luncheon plate, 11.25" sandwich plate, 9.5" dinner plate; *front:* 6" bread & butter plate, 7.25" soup bowl, cup & saucer. *Courtesy of Charlie Diefenderfer.*

CHRISTMAS CANDY	Teal	Crystal	Qty
Bowl, 5.75" fruit		5	____
Bowl, 7.25" soup	75	10	____
Bowl, 9.5" vegetable	trtp*		____
Creamer, 3.5"	35	10	____
Cup	35	5	____
Mayonnaise 3-pc. set		35	____
Mayo. comport		20	____
Mayo. ladle		10	____
Mayo. under plate		5	____
Plate, 6" bread & butter	15	5	____
Plate, 8.25" luncheon	30	8	____
Plate, 9.5" dinner	50	10	____
Plate, 11.25" sandwich	80	18	____
Saucer	15	5	____
Sugar, 3.25"	35	10	____
Tidbit, 2 tier		20	____

*trtp = too rare to price

CIRCLE
(1930s Hocking Glass Company)

New collectors sometimes have problems discerning the difference between Circle, Ring, and Block Optic. Circle has one grouping of ridges encircling each piece. Block Optic has a geometric block design, and Ring has multiple groupings of four rings each. All are made by Hocking Glass Company, so the colors and shapes do blend together well.

Green is much more prevalent than pink and is also the primary color sought by collectors. Items made with two colors of glass, e.g., the crystal sherbet with a green foot, are especially popular at this time.

Like Block Optic that has four cup styles, Circle has two. Hocking Glass Company was wonderful at providing options for their customers, but there is a difference between these items worth noting. One cup has a smaller bottom that fits the saucer. The other cup tapers in toward a base too wide to fit in the ring of the saucer and it will only work resting on the 6" sherbet plate like Princess, another Hocking pattern.

6" sherbet plate, 8.25" luncheon plate, cup.

3" sherbet, 5" flat iced tea tumbler.

3" sherbet w/ green foot, crystal bowl ($10).

CIRCLE	Green	Pink	Qty
Bowl, 4.5"	12		____
Bowl, 5" w/flared rim	20		____
Bowl, 5.25"	12		____
Bowl, 8"	25		____
Bowl, 9.25"	28		____
Creamer	12	12	____
Cup, 2 styles	6	6	____
Decanter, handled			
w/ stopper	65	65	____
Goblet, 4.5" wine	14	14	____
Goblet, 8 oz., water	14	14	____
Pitcher, 60 oz.	45		____
Pitcher, 80 oz.	45		____
Plate, 6" sherbet	5	5	____
Plate, 8.25" luncheon	8	8	____
Plate, 9.5" dinner	40	40	____
Plate, 10" sandwich	15	15	____
Reamer (fits top of 80 oz.			
pitcher)	25	25	____
Saucer	8		____
Sherbet, 3" w/stem	8	8	____
Sherbet, 4.75" w/ stem	10	10	____
Sugar	12	12	____
Tumbler, 3.5" juice, flat	12		____
Tumbler, 4" water, flat	10		____
Tumbler, 5" iced tea, flat	18		____
Tumbler, 15 oz., flat	25		____

Note: Crystal items 1/2 of those in green. Vase w/ shape similar to pitcher: crystal & iridescent, $35.

Left: 8 oz. water goblet. *Courtesy of Charlie Diefenderfer.*

Below: Creamer & sugar. *Courtesy of Vic & Jean Laermans.*

CLOVERLEAF

(1930-1936 Hazel-Atlas Glass Company)

New collectors have discovered Cloverleaf. No matter what the piece, even the relatively common sherbets, Cloverleaf is a hot commodity, with bowls being in the greatest demand. The 8" bowl is the most difficult to find, but any bowl is a prized possession.

Green Cloverleaf is the most popular color, but yellow and black are actively sought by many. Our teenage son has even expressed an interest in collecting black Cloverleaf. Pink seems to be the only color receiving minimal attention at this time. The fact that there is a limited selection of pink Cloverleaf may contribute to this.

Some pieces were made with the design imprinted on the inside and some were made with the design on the outside. Neither style is of greater value.

The same molds used to create Cloverleaf were also used on Ribbon, another pattern introduced in 1930.

Above: *Back:* 8" luncheon plate; *front row:* salt & pepper, cup & saucer, candy jar w/ lid. *Courtesy of Paula Apperson McNamara.*

Left: 3.75" tumbler, 4" tumbler, 5.75" tumbler w/ foot. *Courtesy of Paula Apperson McNamara.*

Back: 10.25" grill plate; *front row:* sherbet w/ pattern on outside, sherbet w/ pattern inside, creamer & sugar. *Courtesy of Paula Apperson McNamara.*

Back: 7" salad bowl; *front:* 5" cereal bowl, 4" dessert bowl, 8" bowl. *Courtesy of Paula Apperson McNamara.*

Cup & saucer. *Courtesy of Charlie Diefenderfer.*

Salts & peppers in 3 different colors. *Courtesy of Michael Rothenberger/Mike's Collectables.*

CLOVERLEAF	Green	Yellow	Black	Pink	Qty
Ash tray, 4"	65		65		___
Ash tray, 5.75"	85		85		___
Bowl, 4" dessert	28	30		18	___
Bowl, 5" cereal	35	40			___
Bowl, 7" salad	55	55			___
Bowl, 8"	85				___
Candy jar w/lid	65	120			___
Creamer	14	20	25		___
Cup	10	12	22	10	___
Plate, 6" sherbet	8	8	40		___
Plate, 8" luncheon	10	15	20	10	___
Plate, 10.25" grill	35	35			___
Salt & pepper	50	110	100		___
Saucer	5	5	8	5	___
Sherbet	10	12	25	8	___
Sugar	14	20	25		___
Tumbler, 3.75" flat	65				___
Tumbler, 4" flat	45			30	___
Tumbler, 5.75" w/foot	35	35			___

COLONIAL, "KNIFE & FORK"

(1934-1938 Hocking Glass Company)

There are few patterns with many different pieces made in several colors, but this is one of them. Pink and green seem to be collected fairly equally, with the least attention given to crystal.

Colonial has a very distinctive look that is not easily mixed with other patterns as there are no other patterns having a similar design. The green is not the same shade as many other green Depression Glass patterns. Green Colonial has a definite yellow tint to it.

Grill plates, divided dishes that separate the food on the plate, are much easier to find than dinner plates. We have never had a mug in any color and would love to photograph one—hint!

Here is a clarification on the tumblers and stems as this pattern has an assortment of both. Flat tumblers are like drinking glasses that have no foot and rest flat on a surface. Footed tumblers have a ball of glass and then a circular base or foot of glass. Just as it sounds, stems have a stem of glass separating the circular foot from the rest of the glass.

Keep in mind the sugar and spoon holder/celery are similar in design. The sugar base is 4.25" tall and the spoon holder is 5.5" tall. If you are shopping with *Mauzy's Comprehensive Handbook of Depression Glass Prices*, you can use the measure provided on the back cover of the book to verify what you are looking at.

Back row: 10" dinner plate, 8.5" luncheon plate; *middle row:* 6" sherbet plate/saucer, 7.25" low soup bowl; *front row:* 3" sherbet, 9" berry bowl, 7.75" pitcher. *Courtesy of Charlie Diefenderfer.*

Back row: 5.5" celery/spoon holder, 12" platter; *middle row:* 4.25" sugar base, 5.75" water goblet, 3" goblet, 7" pitcher; *front row:* 2.5" whiskey tumbler, 4" water tumbler. *Courtesy of Charlie Diefenderfer.*

5.75" water goblet, 4" water tumbler, 3" juice tumbler, 2.5" whiskey tumbler. *Courtesy of Charlie Diefenderfer.*

5" creamer/milk pitcher & sugar w/ lid.
Courtesy of Charlie Diefenderfer.

5.25" claret, 4" cocktail, 3.75" cordial, 3" goblet.
Courtesy of Charlie Diefenderfer.

4.75" cream soup bowl.

COLONIAL, "KNIFE & FORK"	Pink	Green	Crystal	Qty
Bowl, 3.75" berry	65			____
Bowl, 4.75" berry	20	20	10	____
Bowl, 4.75" cream soup	75	75	50	____
Bowl, 5.5" cereal	70	110	25	____
Bowl, 7.25" low soup	70	70	20	____
Bowl, 9" berry	35	35	20	____
Bowl, 10" oval vegetable	40	40	20	____
Butter dish base	500	40	25	____
Butter dish lid	200	20	15	____
Butter complete	700	60	40	____
Celery/spoon holder, 5.5"	135	135	60	____
Cheese dish		260		____
Creamer, 5" (same as 5" milk pitcher)	70	35	20	____
Cup	14	12	5	____
Goblet, 3", 2 oz.		30	10	____
Goblet, 3.75" cordial, 1 oz.		30	10	____
Goblet, 4" cocktail, 3 oz.		28	8	____
Goblet, 4.5" wine, 2.5 oz.		28	8	____
Goblet, 5.25" claret, 4 oz.		28	8	____
Goblet, 5.75" water, 8.5 oz.		32	15	____
Mug, 4.5"	600	800		____
Pitcher, 5" milk/creamer	70	35	20	____
Pitcher, 7" w/or w/out ice lip	60	60	30	____
Pitcher, 7.75" w/or w/out ice lip	75	85	30	____
Plate, 6" sherbet/saucer	8	8	4	____
Plate, 8.5" luncheon	10	10	4	____
Plate, 10" dinner	65	70	25	____
Plate, 10" grill	30	25	10	____
Platter, 12"	40	35	15	____
Salt & pepper	160	160	50	____
Saucer/sherbet plate	8	8	4	____
Sherbet, 3"	25			____
Sherbet, 3.25"	14	15	5	____
Spoon holder/celery, 5.5"	135	135	60	____
Sugar base, 4.25"	28	18	10	____
Sugar lid	60	30	15	____
Tumbler, 2.5" whiskey, 1.5 oz., flat	18	20	12	____
Tumbler, 3" juice, 5 oz., flat	25	25	10	____
Tumbler, 3.25", 3 oz. w/foot	20	25	10	____
Tumbler, 4" water, 9 oz., flat	20	20	10	____
Tumbler, 4", 5 oz. w/foot	35	45	15	____
Tumbler, 5", 11 oz., flat	36	45	15	____
Tumbler, 5.25", 10 oz. w/foot	50	50	20	____
Tumbler, 12 oz. iced tea, flat	55	55	20	____
Tumbler, 15 oz. lemonade, flat	70	80	40	____

Note: Beaded top pitcher, $1300. Ruby tumblers, $150.
White: cup, $5; saucer, $2.

Back row: 10" grill plate, 10" dinner plate, 8.5" luncheon plate; *front row:* 4.75" berry bowl, cup & saucer, 5.5" cereal bowl, 7.75" pitcher. *Courtesy of Charlie Diefenderfer.*

Back row: 2.5" whiskey tumbler, 4" water tumbler, 10" oval vegetable bowl; *front row:* butter, 9" berry bowl. *Courtesy of Charlie Diefenderfer.*

Back row: 5" creamer/milk pitcher, 12" platter; *front row:* sugar w/ lid, shaker, 5.5" spoon holder/celery. *Courtesy of Charlie Diefenderfer.*

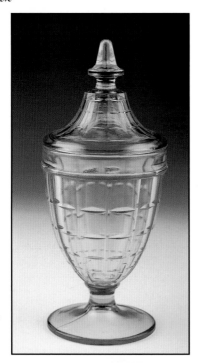

8.75" candy
jar w/ lid.

COLONIAL BLOCK
(1930s, White in 1950s Hazel-Atlas Glass Company)

Many dealers believe that overall pink is the most popular color of Depression Glass. Colonial Block is one of those patterns to dispute that position. Pink is not easily found, but not many are looking for it either, so the pink prices haven't risen . . . yet.

Hazel-Atlas advertised Colonial Block as having a "modernistic design." Colonial Block may have been a response to the Cubist movement in design and art; however, many collectors looking for a retro style lean toward Manhattan and Moderntone. Once again here is a pattern lacking dinner plates and for that matter plates of any kind. There are no cups and no saucers. Practically speaking it is necessary to mix this with other patterns in order to serve a meal.

Cobalt blue glassware decorated with Shirley Temple's face is quite collectible. The creamer shown is unique because it is a Colonial Block creamer with Shirley Temple.

Above: *Back row:* creamer, 7" bowl, butter; *front row:* sugar w/ lid, 7" bowl, sherbet. *Courtesy of Debora & Paul Torsiello, Debzie's Glass.*

Right: Creamer & sugar w/ lid.

COLONIAL BLOCK	Pink & Green	Qty
Bowl, 4"	10	___
Bowl, 7"	20	___
Butter dish base	20	___
Butter dish lid	40	___
Butter complete	60	___
Butter tub	60	___
Candy jar w/lid, 8.75"	40	___
Creamer	15	___
Goblet	12	___
Pitcher	75	___
Powder jar w/lid	40	___
Sherbet	10	___
Sugar base	15	___
Sugar lid	15	___
Tumbler, 5.25" juice	30	___

Note: White creamer, sugar base, $7; sugar lid, $8. Black powder jar w/lid, $40.

Above: 4" bowl. *Courtesy of Michael Rothenberger/Mike's Collectables.*

Left: Cobalt 4" creamer w/ Shirley temple motif. *Courtesy of Vic & Jean Laermans.*

COLONIAL FLUTED
(1928-1933 Federal Glass Company)

In 1928, Federal Glass Company entered the world of manufacturing the colored glass now referred to as Depression Glass with this pattern. The design was simple and later patterns with greater detail became more popular. Colonial Fluted was removed from production in 1933 before many pieces were created.

In 1930, Federal Glass Company advertised "The Bridgette Set:" a luncheon set of Colonial Fluted consisting of 6 cups, 6 saucers, 6 plates, 6 sherbets, a creamer, and a sugar with a lid, which were decorated in red or black with the four suits found on playing cards. You will find a similar set pictured if you look up Moderntone. Because these enameled embellishments were placed on top of the glass, abrasive cleaning will wear them away.

You can recognize Colonial Fluted, nicknamed "Rope," by the distinctive rope-like design near the outer rim of each piece.

Back row: 8" luncheon plate, 6" sherbet plate; *front row:* sherbet, creamer.

COLONIAL FLUTED	Green	Qty
Bowl, 4" berry	10	____
Bowl, 6" cereal	14	____
Bowl, 6.5" salad (deep)	25	____
Bowl, 7.5" berry	25	____
Creamer	10	____
Cup	5	____
Plate, 6" sherbet	5	____
Plate, 8" luncheon	8	____
Saucer	3	____
Sherbet	8	____
Sugar base	10	____
Sugar lid	25	____

Note: Crystal items worth 1/2 of those in green.

Above: Sugar w/ lid. *Courtesy of Vic & Jean Laermans.*

Above right: : Cup & saucer. *Courtesy of Charlie Diefenderfer.*

Back: 11" chop plate; *front:* butter, cup & saucer. *Courtesy of Marie Talone & Paul Reichwein.*

COLUMBIA
Reproduced
(1938-1942 Federal Glass Company)

Only a few patterns are more popular in crystal (clear) than other colors and Columbia is one of them. In all fairness to pink lovers, there are only four Columbia items made in pink and they are very difficult to find.

Often butter dishes are one of the most challenging items to locate in a given pattern. Columbia butter dishes are very common and remain an inexpensive commodity.

This pattern has become much more popular in the past five years. Once the pieces stood unnoticed, now collectors are frequently requesting Columbia. An increased interest may lead to an increase in value. It will be interesting to watch this pattern.

Snack plate, cup. *Courtesy of Michael Rothenberger/ Mike's Collectables.*

9.5" luncheon plate, saucer, 6" bread & butter plate. *Courtesy of Debora & Paul Torsiello, Debzie's Glass.*

COLUMBIA	Crystal	Pink	Qty
Bowl, 5" cereal	20		____
Bowl, 8" soup	25		____
Bowl, 8.5" salad	20		____
Bowl, 10.5" fruit w/ruffled rim	20		____
Butter dish base	6		____
Butter dish lid	14		____
Butter complete	20		____
Cup	8	25	____
Plate, 6" bread & butter	6	20	____
Plate, 9.5" luncheon	10	35	____
Plate, 11" chop	10		____
Saucer	3	10	____
Snack plate	25		____
Tumbler, 2.75", 4 oz. juice *R*	*30*		____
Tumbler, 9 oz. water	35		____

Note: Ruby flashed butter, $25. Other flashed or satinized butters, $20.

Reproduction information: Juice glasses marked "France" on bottom are new.

8.5" salad bowl. *Courtesy of Diefenderfer's Collectibles & Antiques.*

Sherbet & 7.75" pitcher. *Courtesy of Kyle & Barbara Ewing*.

8" berry bowl w/ 2 handles.

6" sherbet plate/saucer, sherbet, 5" tumbler.

CORONATION
(1936-1940 Hocking Glass Company)

Where is the green Coronation?

Ruby Coronation is very popular with Royal Ruby collectors. We have sold many a "berry set" of either a 6.5" bowl or an 8" bowl with four, six, or eight 4.25" bowls. These bowls are always easier to sell when grouped together especially when approaching the Christmas season.

Take note of the 5" tumbler. It is very similar to the Old Colony tumbler. Both have a scalloped foot; however Coronation has a vertical band of ribs above the middle of the tumbler. Old Colony tumblers have wider ribs in the bottom half of the tumbler. Recently collectors have begun to mix and match patterns and pieces based on availability and cost. The Coronation tumbler is a very acceptable substitute for Old Colony with a substantial savings.

CORONATION	Pink	Ruby	Green	Qty
Bowl, 4.25" berry w/2 handles	6	8		____
Bowl, 4.25" with no handles	80		50	____
Bowl, 6.5" w/2 handles	8	15		____
Bowl, 8" berry w/2 handles	12	20		____
Bowl, 8" with no handles	150		180	____
Cup	5	9		____
Pitcher, 7.75"	700			____
Plate, 6" sherbet/saucer	5			____
Plate, 8.5" luncheon	8	12	50	____
Saucer/6" sherbet plate	5			____
Sherbet	8		80	____
Tumbler, 5"	35		180	____

Note: Crystal saucer, $1.

CREMAX

(Late 1930s-early 1940s   Macbeth-Evans
Division Corning Glass Works)

Corning created a line of tableware called Cremax. The opaque glass was given dark fired-on rims and named "Bordette" and pastel rims and named "Rainbow." The Windsor design on Cremax is also known as Chinex Classic. When referring to this ivory color, Corning used the term "Chinex," as used on certain pieces of Dogwood Depression Glass. This glassware was created to compete with china and pottery. Advertisements touted the fact that this amazing dinnerware would not craze and would be difficult to chip.

Overall transparent glass has had the greatest following, but Cremax seems to be gaining in popularity. Perhaps the pastel colors of Rainbow are pleasing to those seeking to create a pastoral look. This will be a pattern worth watching as increased demand may result in higher prices.

Delphite Cremax was manufactured and distributed in Canada where it remains plentiful. Fortunately pieces are filtering south as they are very popular in America.

Above: Cup & saucer, demitasse cup & saucer.

Below: *Back row:* 12" salver, 6" dessert/cereal bowl; *front row:* 2 cups & saucers, 6" bread & butter plate.

CREMAX	Cremax	All other colors w/or w/out decorations	Qty
Bowl, 6" dessert/cereal	5	8	___
Bowl, 7" bowl	8	16	___
Bowl, 7.75" coupe soup	8	16	___
Bowl, 9" vegetable	8	16	___
Creamer	6	10	___
Cup	5	6	___
Cup, demitasse	15	15	___
Plate, 6" bread & butter	5	7	___
Plate, 9.75" dinner	8	12	___
Plate, 12" salver	8	10	___
Saucer	5	6	___
Saucer, demitasse	5	5	___
Sugar	6	10	___

Above: Princess decoration on 9.75" dinner plate.

Right: 7.75" coupe soup bowl. *Courtesy of Charlie Diefenderfer.*

Delphite Cremax creamers & sugar manufactured in Canada as "Pyrex Brand." *Courtesy of Vic & Jean Laermans.*

CROW'S FOOT
(1930s   Paden City Glass Company)

Paden City Glass Company produced wonderful pieces of excellent quality as exemplified by this pattern. The colors are brilliant and the shapes distinctive.

No pieces of Crow's Foot are common and the choices are many so collecting the entire set will be a hunt. Fortunately this is not a pattern prone to chipping, so if there is an absence of scratching, the item is probably in good condition.

Many people who collect Crow's Foot are interested in any piece, not a particular color as is the norm with most collectors of other patterns. Some collectors of Crow's Foot are actually Paden City Glass Company collectors and this is part of a larger search.

Red is a bit more common than black or blue, but don't misinterpret this comment as no color is easily found. The Internet has proven to be a good source for this pattern.

Many variations are available as Paden City used Crow's Foot blanks with other patterns and with overlays and embellishments. Crow's Foot molds were used to create Peacock Reverse.

Above: 4.5" vase, 5.75" candlestick. *Courtesy of Debora & Paul Torsiello, Debzie's Glass.*

Below: 11" oval bowl, 11.5" bowl w/ 3 feet, 11" square console bowl w/ rolled edge. *Courtesy of Debora & Paul Torsiello, Debzie's Glass.*

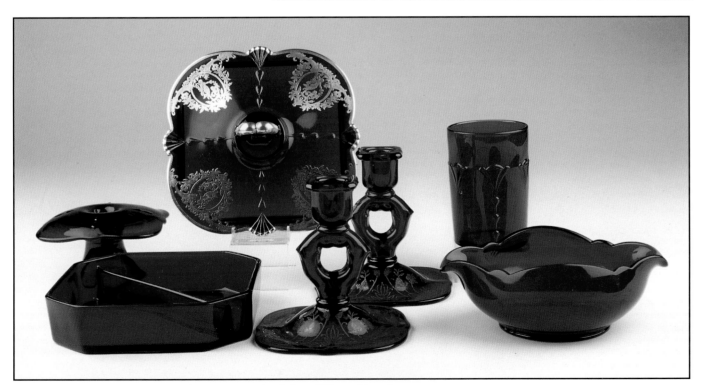

Back row: lid w/ silver overlay for 6.25" candy dish, 4.25" tumbler; *front row:* "mushroom" candlestick, base for 6.25" candy dish, pair of candlesticks, 6.5" bowl. *Courtesy of Debora & Paul Torsiello, Debzie's Glass.*

11.75" vase & 10.25" vase. *Courtesy of Debora & Paul Torsiello, Debzie's Glass.*

6.5" comport. *Courtesy of Debora & Paul Torsiello, Debzie's Glass.*

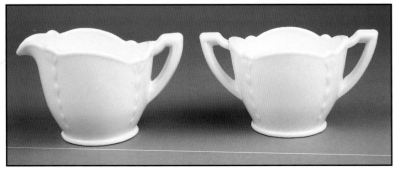

Creamer & sugar. *Courtesy of Vic & Jean Laermans.*

CROW'S FOOT	Red	Black, Blue & Amethyst	Other colors	Qty
Bowl, 4.75" square	30	35	15	____
Bowl, cream soup	25	30	14	____
Bowl, 6" round	30	35	15	____
Bowl, 6.5" round	50	60	25	____
Bowl, 8.5" square w/ 2 handles	50	60	30	____
Bowl, 8.75" square	50	60	30	____
Bowl, 10" w/foot	80	80	35	____
Bowl, 10" square w/2 handles	65	75	35	____
Bowl, 11" oval	35	45	20	____
Bowl, 11" square	65	75	35	____
Bowl, 11" square w/rolled edge	70	80	35	____
Bowl, 11.5" round w/3 feet	90	120	50	____
Bowl, 11.5" console	85	100	45	____
Bowl, Nasturtium w/3 feet	200	225	100	____
Bowl, whipped cream w/3 feet	60	70	30	____
Cake plate, square	85	100	45	____
Candlestick, round base, ea.	50	55	25	____
Candlestick, square "mushroom," ea.	20	25	15	____
Candlestick, 5.75" tall, ea.	20	25	15	____
Candy w/lid, 6.25" across	170	200	90	____
Candy w/ lid, 6.5" 3-sections, 2 styles	75	90	40	____
Cheese stand, 5"	30	40	20	____
Comport, 3.25" tall	30	40	18	____
Comport, 4.75" tall	60	75	40	____
Comport, 6.5" tall	70	90	40	____
Creamer, flat or footed	18	20	10	____
Cup, flat or footed	10	15	5	____
Gravy boat, flat	100	120	50	____
Gravy boat, pedestal	150	175	75	____
Mayonnaise, 3 feet	50	65	30	____
Plate, 5.75"	10	15	5	____
Plate, 8"	15	20	5	____
Plate, 8.5" square	15	20	8	____
Plate, 9.25" small dinner	40	50	20	____
Plate, 9.5" 2 handles	70	80	40	____
Plate, 10.25" round w/2 handles	55	65	25	____
Plate, 10.25" square w/2 handles	45	55	25	____
Plate, 10.5" dinner	100	125	50	____
Plate, 11" cracker	50	60	30	____
Plate, 12"	30	45	20	____
Relish, 11" 3 sections	100	120	50	____
Sandwich server, round w/center handle	70	80	40	____
Sandwich server, square w/center handle	50	60	20	____
Saucer, round	10	15	5	____
Saucer, square	12	17	7	____
Sugar, flat or footed	18	20	10	____
Tumbler, 4.25"	80	100	40	____
Vase, 4.5"	60	75	40	____
Vase, 10.25", curved in	100	120	50	____
Vase, 10.25", curved out	95	110	40	____
Vase, 11.75"	150	185	70	____

CUBE

(1929-1933 Jeannette Glass Company)

The Cube or Cubist 2.5" creamer and 2.5" sugar may be among the most recognizable pieces of Depression Glass. Although common, dealers report that they consistently sell! On the other end of the spectrum is the 8.75" pitcher. This is one of the most challenging Cube piece to locate, but equally easy to sell.

Coloring inconsistencies are very evident within this pattern. The greens run from dark to medium green and the pink is found in pale shades, medium shades, and orangish pink. Both green and pink are equally collected; however, green was discontinued prior to the end of production, so less green is now available.

The 7" 3-footed relish pictured is reportedly only one of two known to exist. If you have one, congratulations!

If you locate an item that doesn't match the measurements on the list, you might have one of the dozens of pieces of American by Fostoria Glass Company.

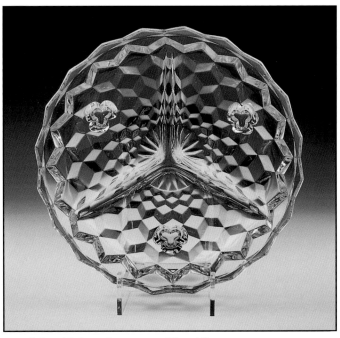

7" relish w/ 3 feet. *Courtesy of Staci & Jeff Shuck/Gray Goose Antiques.*

Back: 6.5" salad bowl; *front:* 4.5" dessert bowl, butter.
Courtesy of Diefenderfer's Collectibles & Antiques.

CUBE	Pink	Green	Qty
Bowl, 4.5" dessert, pointy rim	10	8	____
Bowl, 4.5" deep	10		____
Bowl, 6.5" salad	14	18	____
Butter dish base	30	30	____
Butter dish lid	50	50	____
Butter complete	80	80	____
Candy jar w/lid	40	45	____
Coaster, 3.25"	10	10	____
Creamer, 2.5"	4		____
Creamer, 3.75"	8	10	____
Cup	8	10	____
Pitcher, 8.75"	250	250	____
Plate, 6" sherbet	5	8	____
Plate, 8" luncheon	15	15	____
Powder jar w/lid, 3 feet	35	40	____
Relish, 7" w/3feet (like Windsor)	trtp*		____
Salt & pepper	50	50	____
Saucer	4	4	____
Sherbet	8	10	____
Sugar, 2.5"	4		____
Sugar base, 3"	8	10	____
Sugar lid/candy lid	20	20	____
Tumbler, 4"	85	85	____

*trtp = too rare to price

Note: Ultramarine: 4.5" bowl, $50; 6.5" bowl, $85. Amber: small cream & sugar, $10 ea. White: small cream & sugar, $3 ea. Crystal: tray for larger cream & sugar, $5; other items, $1.

Above: *Back row:* 3" sugar, 6" sherbet plate, candy jar w/ lid; *middle row:* 4" tumbler, powder jar w/ lid, 4.5" deep bowl; *front row:* cup, sherbet, 4.5" dessert. *Courtesy of Marie Talone & Paul Reichwein.*

Right: 3.25" coasters. *Courtesy of Charlie Diefenderfer.*

Above: Salt & pepper. *Courtesy of Michael Rothenberger/Mike's Collectables.*

Left: *Back:* 6.5" salad bowl; *front:* powder jar w/ lid, candy jar w/ lid. *Courtesy of Diefenderfer's Collectibles & Antiques.*

CUPID
(1930s Paden City Glass Company)

Cupid is another example of the fine quality of glassware manufactured by Paden City Glass Company. The distinctive etched design always shows two cupids facing one another.

The blue samovar is the rarest Cupid item and one of the rarest pieces of Depression Glass overall. Please note that the metal handles and spout are missing, but the glass is in perfect condition and clearly exhibits the beautiful Cupid design.

Cupid shapes and sizes are the same as Peacock and Rose by Paden City. Once again a glass company is able to get additional mileage from molds by utilizing them in more than one way.

11.25" cake stand, 8.5" oval bowl w/ foot. *Courtesy of Neil McCurdy - Hoosier Kubboard Glass.*

CUPID	Green & Pink	Qty
Bowl, 8.5" oval w/foot, 4.25" deep	300	___
Bowl, 9.25" fruit w/foot	300	___
Bowl, 9.25" w/center handle	300	___
Bowl, 10.25" fruit	225	___
Bowl, 10.5" w/rolled edge	225	___
Bowl, 11" console	225	___
Cake plate, 11.75"	200	___
Cake stand, 2" tall, 11.25" dia.	200	___
Candlestick, ea.	100	___
Candy jar w/lid, 5.25" tall	400	___
Candy dish w/lid, 3-part flat	300	___
Casserole w/lid	400	___
Comport, 6.25"	200	___
Creamer, no foot	175	___
Creamer, 4.25" w/foot	150	___
Creamer, 5" w/foot	150	___
Ice bucket, 6"	300	___
Ice tub, 4.75"	300	___
Lamp w/silver overlay	500	___
Mayonnaise, 3-piece set	250	___
Mayo. comport	150	___
Mayo. ladle	50	___
Mayo. under plate	50	___
Plate, 10.5"	175	___
Samovar	1000	___
Sugar, no foot	175	___
Sugar, 4.25" w/foot	150	___
Sugar, 5" w/foot	150	___
Tray, 10.75" w/center handle	200	___
Tray, 10.75" oval w/foot	250	___
Vase, 10.75" elliptical	600	___
Vase, fan-shaped	425	___
Vase, 10"	325	___

Note: Black: covered casserole, $650.
Peacock blue: comport, $250; mayonnaise, $375; 10.5" plate, $250; samovar, $2000.

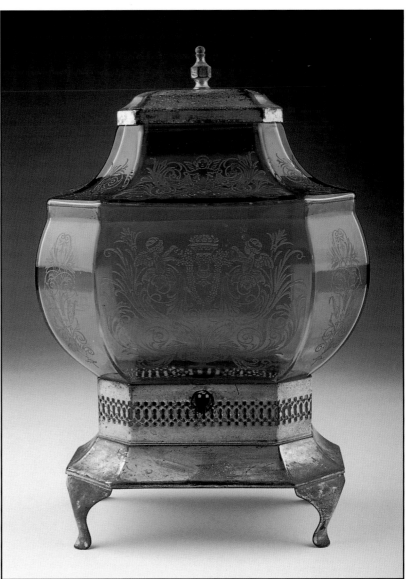

Samovar.

Back row: 8.25" luncheon plate, 9.25" dinner plate; front row: cup & saucer, cream soup bowl, 9 oz. tumbler. *Courtesy of Sherelyn A. Ammon.*

4.75" berry bowl. *Courtesy of Charlie Diefenderfer.*

Back row: 9.25" berry bowl, 11.5" cake/sandwich plate; front row: 7.25" berry bowl, 10" oval vegetable bowl on 10.75" platter. *Courtesy of Sherelyn A. Ammon.*

DAISY
(1933 crystal, 1940 amber, others till 1980s Indiana Glass Company)

Crystal Daisy was introduced in 1933, but production of this pattern continued for fifty more years in other colors. Pictured is the most commonly collected amber from 1940. Daisy has a deeper amber than many other Depression Glass patterns as it is a browner hue. Crystal Daisy will be featured in a future book.

Indiana's green, used in this pattern and shown on the sugar, was actually avocado. Do you remember this as a prolifically used decorating color in the 1960s and 1970s? Many of today's collectors are looking at the 1950s for their inspiration. Perhaps the 1960s will soon be a source of ideas. At that point green Daisy may become quite desirable. We'll see . . .

DAISY	Amber & Fired-on red	Green	Crystal	Qty
Bowl, 4.75" berry	10	8	5	____
Bowl, cream soup	12	6	5	____
Bowl, 6" cereal	35	15	8	____
Bowl, 7.25" berry	15	10	8	____
Bowl, 9.25" berry	35	18	14	____
Bowl, 10" oval vegetable, w/tab handles	18	15	10	____
Creamer, 4.25"	10	10	8	____
Cup	6	5	4	____
Plate, 6" sherbet	5	4	2	____
Plate, 7.25" salad	7	5	4	____
Plate, 8.5" luncheon	7	5	4	____
Plate, 9.25" dinner	10	10	6	____
Plate, 10.25" grill	9	8	5	____
Plate, 10.25" grill w/indent (fits cream soup)	20	20		____
Plate, 11.5" cake/sandwich	15	10	7	____
Platter, 10.75"	15	10	7	____
Relish, 7.5" 3-part w/3 feet	35		10	____
Saucer	5	4	2	____
Sherbet, 3"	10	8	5	____
Sugar, 4"	10	10	8	____
Tumbler, 9 oz., 4.75"	20	12	10	____
Tumbler, 12 oz., 6.5"	40	25	20	____

Note: White sugar, $10.

Above: Sherbet, 7.25" salad plate, 6" sherbet plate, creamer, sugar. *Courtesy of Sherelyn A. Ammon.*

Right: Sugar. *Courtesy of Vic & Jean Laermans.*

DELLA ROBBIA
(1928-1940s Westmoreland Glass Company)

This is one of the patterns that doesn't tend to chip but has its own unique form of damage. In order for a piece of Della Robbia to command the prices listed, the applied colors on the apples, grapes, and pears must be bold and free from wear.

Added to the list are the No. 1067 candlesticks and matching bowl. For lack of a better name, we are using "pyramid style" as they are formed by a pyramid-like stack of balls of glass colored in the same applied colors as the fruit. The No. 1067 bowl rests on three feet created by the same arrangement of balls of glass.

The prices are a good indication of the items that are easy to find and those that will create a challenge. The pitcher and punch bowl will be the most difficult to locate in good condition. The salt and pepper shakers are fairly common, but the lids are usually in terrible shape. The value indicated is for shakers with original tops in good condition.

Close-up of pattern.

8 oz. 6" water tumbler.

DELLA ROBBIA	Crystal w/applied colors	Qty
Basket, 9"	100	___
Basket, 12"	125	___
Bowl, 4.5"	20	___
Bowl, 5" finger	25	___
Bowl, 6"	25	___
Bowl, 6.5" w/1 handle	25	___
Bowl, 7.5"	30	___
Bowl, 8"	35	___
Bowl, 8" w/handles	40	___
Bowl, 8" heart w/1 handle	60	___
Bowl, 9"	45	___
Bowl, 12" w/foot	80	___
Bowl, 12", no. 1067	75	___
Bowl, 13" w/rolled edge	80	___
Bowl, 14" oval	100	___
Bowl, 14" punch	250	___
Bowl, 15"	100	___
Candlestick, no. 1067, pyramid style, ea.	40	___
Candlestick, 4" 1-light, ea.	20	___
Candlestick, 4" 2-light, ea.	35	___
Candy, chocolate, round & flat	50	___
Candy jar w/lid, scalloped edge	80	___
Comport, 6.5" mint, 3.5" tall	50	___
Comport, 8" sweetmeat	25	___
Comport, 12"	80	___
Comport, 13"	80	___
Creamer	18	___
Cup	15	___
Cup, punch	12	___
Pitcher	250	___
Plate, 6" liner for 5" finger bowl	8	___

DELLA ROBBIA (Cont.)	Crystal w/applied colors	Qty
Plate, 6.25" bread & butter	8	___
Plate, 7.25" salad	15	___
Plate, 9" luncheon	20	___
Plate, 10.5" dinner	75	___
Plate, 14" torte	50	___
Plate, 14" salver/cake w/foot	85	___
Plate, 18"	100	___
Plate, 18" liner for punch bowl w/upturned rim	150	___
Platter, 14"	100	___
Punch bowl	250	___
Punch bowl 15-piece set	600	___
Salt & pepper	60	___
Saucer	8	___
Stem, 3 oz. wine	25	___
Stem, 3.25 oz. cocktail	25	___
Stem, 5 oz. sherbet, 4.75"	20	___
Stem, 5 oz. champagne	25	___
Stem, 6 oz. champagne	25	___
Stem, 8 oz. water, 6"	25	___
Sugar	18	___
Tumbler, 5 oz. ginger ale, flat	25	___
Tumbler, 8 oz. w/foot	25	___
Tumbler, 8 oz. water, flat	25	___
Tumbler, 11 oz. iced tea w/foot	30	___
Tumbler, 12 oz. iced tea, flat	30	___
Tumbler, 12 oz. iced tea, w/foot	35	___
Tumbler, 12 oz. iced tea, 5.25" without usual "bell" or flare at rim	35	___

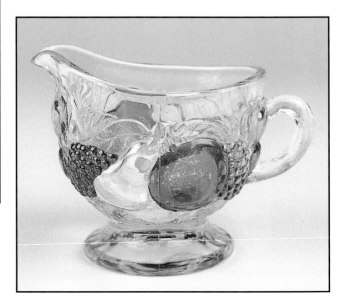

Above: Pair of 1067 pyramid style candlesticks, 12" three-footed 1067 bowl, 6.5" bowl w/ 1 handle.

Right: Creamer. *Courtesy of Vic & Jean Laermans.*

DIAMOND QUILTED
(Late 1920s-early 1930s Imperial Glass Company)

Here is a pattern found in really lovely pastel-like hues. Diamond Quilted blue is a bit like ice blue, but with a shade all its own. People unfamiliar with Depression Glass will stop and comment about the attractive color of a piece of blue Diamond Quilted that has caught their attention.

Diamond Quilted is not easily found on the East Coast; however, it is fairly abundant in the Midwest in pink, green, and amber. Different colors and patterns were originally distributed in different regions and this may be an example of that phenomenon. Red and black are the most difficult colors to find.

Above: *Back row:* 6.5" sherbet plate, 10.5" console bowl w/ rolled edge; *front row:* 3.5" tall sherbet, 7" footed rolled edge bowl.

Left: *Back row:* cup & saucer, 6.75" ruffled bowl, creamer; *front row:* sherbet, pair of low candlesticks, sugar. *Courtesy of Vic & Jean Laermans.*

Back row: 6.5" sherbet plate, 8" luncheon plate, 5.5" bowl w/ 1 handle; *front row:* 3.5" tall sherbet, 7" bowl. *Courtesy of Charlie Diefenderfer.*

Above: Creamers & sugars in a variety of colors. *Courtesy of Vic & Jean Laermans.*

Left: Floral motif painted on black creamer & sugar. *Courtesy of Vic & Jean Laermans.*

DIAMOND QUILTED	Pink, Green, & Amber	Blue & Black	Qty	DIAMOND QUILTED (Cont.)	Pink, Green, & Amber	Blue & Black	Qty
Bowl, cream soup	20	20	____	Mayonnaise, 3-pc. set	45	65	____
Bowl, 5" cereal	10	18	____	Mayo. comport	15	25	____
Bowl, 5.5" w/1 handle	10	18	____	Mayo. ladle	20	30	____
Bowl, 6.25" footed w/cover (resembles a stemmed candy)	50	50	____	Mayo. under plate	10	10	____
				Pitcher	60		____
Bowl, 7"	20		____	Plate, 6.5" sherbet w/indent	8	8	____
Bowl, 7" w/ crimped rim	15	20	____	Plate, 7" salad	10	10	____
Bowl, 7" footed, rolled edge (resembles a comport)	50	50	____	Plate, 8" luncheon	12	14	____
				Plate, 14" sandwich	20		____
				Punch bowl	400		____
Bowl, 7.5" footed, straight rim (resembles a comport)	50	50	____	Punch bowl foot (base)	250		____
				Salver, 8.25" (resembles a pedestal cake plate)	50	50	____
Bowl, 10.5" console w/rolled edge	30	60	____	Salver, 10" (resembles a pedestal cake plate)	50	50	____
Candlesticks, high and low, each	15	30	____	Sandwich server w/center handle	30	50	____
Candy jar w/lid, low w/3 feet	125		____	Saucer	5	5	____
				Sherbet, 3.5"	10	15	____
Compote, 3.5", 6.5" dia.	50	50	____	Sugar	10	18	____
Compote, 6" tall, 7.25" across	50		____	Tumbler, 1.5 oz. whiskey	15		____
				Tumbler, 6 oz. w/foot	10		____
Compote w/lid, 11.25"	120		____	Tumbler, 9 oz. water, flat	15		____
Creamer	10	18	____	Tumbler, 9 oz. water w/foot	15		____
Cup	10	18	____	Tumbler, 12 oz. iced tea, flat	18		____
Goblet, 1 oz. cordial	15		____				
Goblet, 2 oz. wine	15		____	Tumbler, 12 oz. iced tea w/foot	18		____
Goblet, 3 oz. wine	15		____	Vase	60	80	____
Goblet, 9 oz. champagne, 6"	12		____				
Ice bucket	60	90	____				

Note: Red items twice those in pink. Basket with metal bail in a variety of sizes, $25-65. Larger baskets command higher prices.

DIANA
(1937-1941 Federal Glass Company)

Pink is the most popular color among collectors of Diana. The 12.5" console bowl and 11.5" sandwich plate are the easiest pieces to locate in pink as well as in amber and crystal.

As with other patterns, Federal Glass Company incorporated a Diana mold into another pattern. The salt and pepper shakers in Diana are the same dimensions as the Sharon shakers.

The demitasse cups and saucers are not child's dinnerware because there are no child's pieces in this pattern. Six demitasse cups and saucers fit on a circular rack for display, but we were unable to photograph this arrangement. Demitasse cups and saucers are not common in Depression Glass dinnerware. You will, however, find other examples in Fire-King.

The Diana sherbet is often confused with other patterns as the ribs or texture of the swirls are larger than those found on other Diana pieces.

Back: 11.5" sandwich plate; *front:* 11" console bowl. *Courtesy of Charlie Diefenderfer*.

Demitasse cup & saucer, cream soup bowl, 3.5" coaster. *Courtesy of Marie Talone & Paul Reichwein.*

Above: Sherbet.

Left: *Back row:* 11" console bowl, 6" bread & butter plate; *front row:* 5" cereal bowl, demitasse cup & saucer, 5" cereal bowl. *Courtesy of Charlie Diefenderfer.*

Above: Shakers in two colors. *Courtesy of Michael Rothenberger/ Mike's Collectables.*

Right: Candy jar w/ lid. *Courtesy of Marie Talone.*

DIANA	Pink	Amber	Crystal	Qty
Ash tray, 3.5"	5		5	____
Bowl, 5" cereal	12	12	5	____
Bowl, cream soup	25	20	5	____
Bowl, 9" salad	30	20	10	____
Bowl, 11" console	40	30	10	____
Bowl, 12.5" console w/scalloped rim	35	25	15	____
Candy jar w/lid	50	50	15	____
Coaster, 3.5"	10	10	2	____
Creamer	12	12	5	____
Cup	20	10	3	____
Cup, demitasse, 2" tall	40		8	____
Plate, 6" bread & butter	8	5	2	____
Plate, 9.5" dinner	20	14	5	____
Plate, 11.5" sandwich	25	20	10	____
Platter, 12"	35	25	10	____
Rack (metal) to hold 6 demitasse sets	25			____
Salt & pepper	80	100	25	____
Saucer	8	5	2	____
Saucer, demitasse, 4.25"	10		4	____
Sherbet	12	12	3	____
Sugar	12	12	5	____
Tumbler, 4.25"	45	30	10	____

Note: Green ash tray, $10. Red demitasse cup, $12; saucer, $8.

DOGWOOD

(1930-1934 Macbeth-Evans Glass Company)

Dogwood is among the oldest and most popular of all the Depression Glass patterns. The design is appealing, and a wide variety of items was made. The dogwood blossom is the state flower for several states contributing to its popularity among collectors. Pink is the most desired color and the easiest to find; although, some items are quite elusive. Less people collect green and less green Dogwood is found. The green 8" luncheon plate is common, but beyond that most anything else becomes a challenge. Fortunately, few collectors are looking for Monax and Cremax as pieces in these colors are few and far between.

There are two creamers, two sugars, and two cups. The thick versus thin shapes are a bit different from each other beyond just the gauge of the glass. The thin ones are more difficult to find, seem to blend more consistently with other Dogwood pieces, and are in greater demand as reflected in the pricing.

Macbeth-Evans Glass Company used the same molds for both Dogwood and Thistle. More and more collectors are combining patterns to create an eclectic table setting. These two patterns do compliment each other.

Cup & saucer, 4.75" tumbler, 8" almost straight-sided pitcher. *Courtesy of Diefenderfer's Collectibles & Antiques.*

DOGWOOD	Pink	Green	Monax & Cremax	Qty
Bowl, 5.5" cereal	35	45	10	____
Bowl, rolled edge cereal	65	65		____
Bowl, 8.5" berry	65	130	40	____
Bowl, 10.25" fruit	600	300	150	____
Cake plate, 11"	1250			____
Cake plate, 13"	150	150	200	____
Coaster, 3.25"	trtp*			____
Creamer, 2.5" thin, no foot	30	50		____
Creamer, 3.25" thick, footed	22			____
Cup, thin	22	45		____
Cup, thick	18		45	____
Lamp shade (10.25" bowl w/hole)	125	125	50	____
Pitcher, 8", almost straight sided	275	575		____
Pitcher, 8", "fat" w/ice lip (similar to American Sweetheart pitcher)	650			____
Plate, 6" bread & butter	10	10	24	____
Plate, 8" luncheon	10	10		____
Plate, 9" dinner	40			____
Plate, 10.5" grill w/ pattern only on rim	25	25		____
Plate, 10.5" grill with pattern all over plate	30			____
Plate, 12" salver	35		20	____
Platter, 12"	800			____
Saucer	8	8	20	____
Sherbet, 2 styles	40	150		____
Sugar, 2.5" thin, no foot	30	45		____
Sugar, 3.25" thick, footed	22			____
Tumbler, 3.5"	400			____
Tumbler, 4"	50	120		____
Tumbler, 4.75"	60	125		____
Tumbler, 5"	95	140		____
Tumbler, molded w/decorated band near top	30			____

*trtp = too rare to price

Note: Yellow cereal and luncheon plate, $75 each.

Back row: 9" dinner plate, 8" luncheon plate, 4.75" tumbler; *front row:* thick cup & saucer, sherbet on 6" bread & butter plate. *Courtesy of David G. Baker.*

Monax 12" salver, Cremax 8.5" berry bowl.

10.25" fruit bowl.

Back row: 13" cake plate, 12" salver; *front:* 8.5" berry bowl, 5.5" cereal bowl, 3.25" sugar, 3.25" creamer, 2.5" creamer, thin cup. *Courtesy of David G. Baker.*

DORIC
(1935-1938 Jeannette Glass Company)

If there is one pattern a dealer can count on selling at a show, Doric is it. Pink and green customers are abundant and most of the pieces are relatively affordable.

Care needs to be taken prior to buying the 4.5" berry bowls. The glass along the rim is often nicked from use. A moment taken to run a fingernail along the edge may save one from purchasing a damaged item. Another item to watch is the salt shaker. Salt is notorious for damaging the original metal shaker lids on old glass. However, Doric is a softer glass and the salt shaker is often permanently cloudy, and we do mean permanently. Don't buy a cloudy shaker with the expectation of taking it home, washing it, and returning it to its original shine. This just won't happen.

If the Doric pattern appeals to you, be sure to check Doric and Pansy.

Top: 9" oval vegetable bowl, 8.25" berry bowl, 5" footed tumbler. *Courtesy of Diefenderfer's Collectibles & Antiques.*

Center: *Back row:* cup & saucer, 8" x 8" relish tray; *front row:* 4" x 8" relish tray, 4" x 4" relish tray. *Courtesy of Don & Terry Yusko.*

Bottom: 7.5" footed pitcher, 5.5" flat pitcher, 4" footed tumbler. *Courtesy of Michael Rothenberger/Mike's Collectables.*

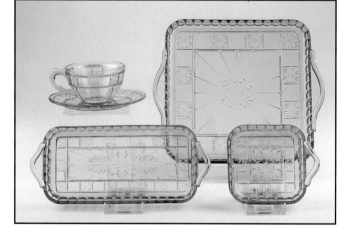

DORIC	Pink	Green	Delphite	Qt
Bowl, 4.5" berry	12	12	50	___
Bowl, 5" cream soup	500	500		___
Bowl, 5.5" cereal	80	100		___
Bowl, 8.25" berry	35	35	150	___
Bowl, 9" w/2 handles	25	25		___
Bowl, 9" oval vegetable	35	40		___
Butter dish base	25	35		___
Butter dish lid	55	65		___
Butter complete	80	100		___
Cake plate, 10.25"	30	30		___
Candy dish, 3 parts	15	15	18	___
Candy dish, 3 parts in Hammered aluminum tray	75	75	75	___
Candy jar w/lid, 8"	40	40		___
Coaster, 3"	20	20		___
Creamer	14	18		___
Cup	10	10		___
Pitcher, 5.5", flat	45	60	1400	___
Pitcher, 7.5", footed	700	1200		___
Plate, 6" sherbet	8	8		___
Plate, 7" salad	25	25		___
Plate, 9" dinner	25	25		___
Plate, 9" grill	25	28		___
Platter, 12"	25	28		___
Relish tray, 4" x 4"	10	10		___
Relish tray, 4" x 8"	12	20		___
Relish tray, 2-tier, 4" x 4" over 4" x 8"	75	75		___
Relish tray, 8" x 8"	40	40		___
Salt & pepper	45	40		___
Saucer	5	5		___
Sherbet	14	18	5	___
Sugar base	14	18		___
Sugar lid	20	32		___
Tray, 10" w/handles	20	20		___
Tumbler, 4", footed (foot is barely more than a ring of extra glass)	75	100		___
Tumbler, 4.5", flat	75	120		___
Tumbler, 5", footed (foot is barely more than a ring of extra glass)	90	150		___

Note: Yellow 7.5" pitcher, too rare to price. 3-part candy dish, iridescent from 1970s, Ultramarine, $30. Serrated 9" dinner, $200.

Back row: 10" tray w/ handles, 12" platter; *front row:* salt & pepper, sugar w/ lid & creamer. *Courtesy of Don & Terry Yusko.*

Back row: 9" dinner plate, 10" cake plate; *front row:* 8" candy jar w/ lid, 4.5" berry bowl, butter. *Courtesy of Don & Terry Yusko.*

DORIC AND PANSY
(1937-1938 Jeannette Glass Company)

Ultramarine Doric and Pansy was predominantly distributed in Canada and England making it difficult for Americans to find. As dealers travel and the Internet connects us all, more ultramarine Doric and Pansy is finding its way into the United States. Ultramarine is a color that appeals to many, even non-collectors. The beautiful design of Doric and Pansy is enhanced by this dramatic color. The pattern is so attractive that it also looks lovely in pink and crystal. However, there are few people collecting crystal, but many do buy pink.

Jeannette Glass Company manufactured this as well as Doric. These patterns work very well together, and Doric has offerings unavailable in Doric and Pansy. You may want to supplement your collection of pink with easier-to-find, generally less expensive Doric. If you are building an ultramarine collection, the tumblers will be the most difficult items of all. The 4.25" tumbler is very hard to find, and the 4.5" tumbler is virtually impossible to find.

8" berry bowl. *Courtesy of Diefenderfer's Collectibles & Antiques.*

Back: 9" bowl w/ handles; *middle:* butter & 6" sherbet plate; *front:* 8" berry bowl & 4.5" berry bowl. *Courtesy of Charlie Diefenderfer.*

Sugar, salt & pepper, creamer. *Courtesy of Vic & Jean Laermans.*

DORIC AND PANSY	Ultramarine	Pink	Qty
Bowl, 4.5" berry	25	15	____
Bowl, 8" berry	100	35	____
Bowl, 9" w/handles	40	25	____
Butter dish base	100		____
Butter dish lid	400		____
Butter complete	500		____
Creamer	130		____
Cup	25	15	____
Plate, 6" sherbet	20	13	____
Plate, 7" salad	45		____
Plate, 9" dinner	40		____
Salt & pepper	500		____
Saucer	10	8	____
Sugar	130		____
Tray, 10" sandwich w/2 open handles	40		____
Tumbler, 4.25", 10 oz.	125		____
Tumbler, 4.5", 9 oz.	trtp*		____

*trtp = too rare to price

Note: Crystal items 1/2 of ultramarine.

4.25" 10 oz. tumbler.

"Pretty Polly Party Dishes:" plate, creamer, cup & saucer.
Courtesy of Diefenderfer's Collectibles & Antiques.

"PRETTY POLLY PARTY DISHES" Child's Set	Ultramarine	Pink	Qty
Creamer	75	50	____
Cup	60	40	____
Plate	20	12	____
Saucer	15	10	____
Sugar	75	50	____
14-piece set	530	348	____

EMERALD CREST
called "GREEN CREST" in 1949

(1949-1955   Fenton Art Glass Company)

Emerald Crest was part of a series of "Crest" glassware. Aqua Crest was introduced in 1940, Crystal Crest in 1942, and then Emerald Crest. Other offerings included Ivory Crest and Peach Crest in 1940, Silver Crest in 1943, Rose Crest in 1944, and Snow Crest in 1950. One can see how successful these lovely pieces from the Fenton Art Glass Company were.

Some collectors specialize in one color, such as Emerald Crest, while others enjoy all versions. Still other collectors so appreciate Fenton's quality in craftsmanship and design that they buy anything Fenton. If it's Fenton glassware, they are interested!

Measurements were carefully made at the time of photographing these pieces in an attempt to accurately document this pattern. Prices reflect the availability of respective items. Baskets have delicate handles that are subject to damage. Those in perfect condition are worth considerably more than small plates. The green mayonnaise ladle is much harder to find than the crystal one. Candle holders are simply difficult to find.

Back: 10.25" dinner plate; *front row:* 3" sugar, 6" beaded melon pitcher, 3.25" creamer. *Courtesy of Vic & Jean Laermans.*

Back: 11.5" plate; *front row:* 4.5" fan vase, cup & saucer, 4" vase w/ crimped rim. *Courtesy of Vic & Jean Laermans.*

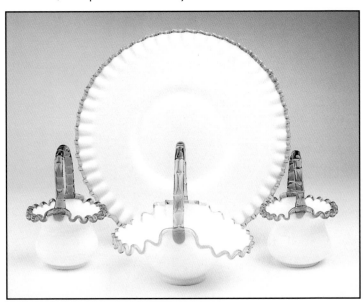

12" plate, 3 baskets. *Courtesy of Vic & Jean Laermans.*

Back: 8" plate; *front row:* 3.75" comport w/ 7" diameter, 5.5" bottle w/ stopper, 5.5" soup bowl, 3.75" tall comport. *Courtesy of Vic & Jean Laermans.*

EMERALD/GREEN CREST	White w/green rim	Qty
Basket, 5"	90	____
Basket, 6"	90	____
Basket, 7" w/smooth sides	110	____
Basket, 7" w/beaded sides	175	____
Bottle w/ stopper, 5.5"	140	____
Bowl, 4" low dessert	25	____
Bowl, 5" finger	25	____
Bowl, 5" crimped bonbon	30	____
Bowl, 5.5" soup	45	____
Bowl, 7" w/crimped rim	40	____
Bowl, 8.5" w/flared rim	50	____
Bowl, 9.5"	60	____
Bowl, 10.5" low salad	80	____
Cake plate, 13" w/foot	95	____
Candle holder, ea.	90	____
Comport, 3.75" w/5.5" dia.	45	____
Comport, 3.75" w/7" dia.	45	____
Comport, 6"	40	____
Creamer, 3.25" w/green twisted handle	50	____
Cup	40	____
Flower pot w/attached saucer, 4.5" tall	70	____
Mayonnaise, 3 pieces w/green ladle	100	____
Mayonnaise bowl	35	____
Ladle, crystal	10	____
Ladle, green	40	____
Under plate	25	____
Pitcher, 6" "beaded melon" w/twisted handle	70	____
Plate, 6.5" sherbet	20	____
Plate, 7"	25	____
Plate, 8"	35	____
Plate, 10.25" dinner	45	____
Plate, 11.5"	55	____
Plate, 12"	55	____
Plate, 13" cake w/foot	95	____
Plate, 16" torte	75	____
Relish, handled leaf	80	____
Saucer	15	____
Sherbet	30	____
Sugar, 3" w/twisted handles	50	____
Tidbit, 2-tier w/plates	60	____
Tidbit, 3-tier w/bowls	125	____
Tidbit, 3-tier w/plates	85	____
Top hat	45	____
Vase, 4" w/crimped rim	45	____
Vase, 4.5" fan	30	____
Vase, 5.5" w/1 turned up side	50	____
Vase, 6" w/crimped rim	45	____
Vase, 6" w/1 turned up rim	65	____
Vase, 6.5" fan	40	____
Vase, 8" w/crimped rim	60	____
Vase, bud w/ beaded sides	50	____

ENGLISH HOBNAIL

(1928-1950, Crystal & Amber until 1983
Westmoreland Glass Company)

Attention collectors of English Hobnail . . . it's all here even the 15.5" master candy! This expansive pattern is shown with pricing for all colors. English Hobnail has the longest list of items available compared to every other pattern.

The options for collecting this pattern are almost endless. There are many bowls, several candlesticks, and plenty of plates. The one thing to watch is that you are buying English Hobnail and not Miss America. To simplify this, the starburst in the center of English Hobnail is not circular, but uneven. The points on English Hobnail rims are rounded and not quite triangular, and on some pieces the points appear a bit stretched. If you are new to this pattern cross reference an item in question against the Miss America list. Many a dealer have inadvertently mislabeled one pattern for the other. This is a common error, especially if the seller is not used to handling Depression Glass.

3 oz. cocktail w/ round foot, cup & saucer, 5.5" plate,
sherbet w/ tall stem & round foot, pair of 9" candlesticks.

Back: sherbet w/ short stem & round foot; *front row:* creamer
w/ hexagonal foot, 4.5" finger bowl, 5 oz. claret w/ round foot.

2 oz. oil cruet w/ stopper.

ENGLISH HOBNAIL	Pink & green	Turquoise/ Ice blue	Amber & Crystal	Qty
Ash tray, 3"	20		5	____
Ash tray, 4.5" round or square		25	5	____
Basket, 5" w/handle			30	____
Basket, 6" w/ handle			40	____
Bon bon, 6.5" w/1handle	25	40	15	____
Bottle, 5 oz. toilet	35	60	25	____
Bowl, 3" cranberry	20			____
Bowl, 4" rose (curves inward)	50		15	____
Bowl, 4.5" finger	18		10	____
Bowl, 4.5" round nappy	15	30	10	____
Bowl, 4.5" square finger w/foot	18	35	10	____
Bowl, 5" round nappy	18	40	10	____
Bowl, cream soup			15	____
Bowl, 5.5" bell nappy			12	____
Bowl, 6" crimped dish, flat	20		14	____
Bowl, 6" rose (curves inward)			20	____
Bowl, 6" mayonnaise, flat w/flared rim	20		10	____
Bowl, 6" round nappy	17		10	____
Bowl, 6" square nappy	17		10	____
Bowl, 6.5" grapefruit w/ inner rim	25		12	____
Bowl, 6.5" round nappy	22		14	____
Bowl, 6.5" square nappy			14	____
Bowl, 7" w/6 points (pinched and crimped)			25	____
Bowl, 7" oblong spoon			20	____
Bowl, 7" preserve			15	____
Bowl, 7" round nappy	25		15	____

ENGLISH HOBNAIL (Cont.)	Pink & green	Turquoise/ Ice blue	Amber & Crystal	Qty
Bowl, 7.5" bell nappy			18	____
Bowl, 8" cupped nappy (curves inward)	30		25	____
Bowl, 8" w/foot	50		30	____
Bowl, 8" 2-handled hexagonal w/foot	75	125	50	____
Bowl, 8" pickle, flat	30		15	____
Bowl, 8" round nappy	35		25	____
Bowl, 8"w/6 points (pinched and crimped)			25	____
Bowl, 9" bell nappy			30	____
Bowl, 9" celery, flat	35		18	____
Bowl, 9.5" round, crimped			30	____
Bowl, 10" flared, flat	45		35	____
Bowl, 10" crimped oval			35	____
Bowl, 11" bell			35	____
Bowl, 11" rolled edge	50	100	30	____
Bowl, 12" celery, flat w/outward roll	35		20	____
Bowl, 12" flanged console	60		30	____
Bowl, 12" w/flare			35	____
Bowl, 12" crimped oval			40	____
Candelabra, each			20	____
Candlestick, each, 3.5"	15	20	10	____
Candlestick, each, 5.5"			10	____
Candlestick, each, 9"	25		10	____
Candy dish w/lid, 6" w/3 feet	60		30	____
Candy jar w/lid, ½ lb., diamond shaped	65	120	35	____
Candy jar w/lid, master	250		150	____
Chandelier, 17" shade w/prisms			500	____
Cheese and cover, 6"			40	____
Cheese and cover, 8.75"			60	____
Cigarette box w/cover, 4.5" x 2.5"	35	60	25	____
Cigarette Jar w/cover (round)	35	70	25	____
Coaster 3"			8	____
Compote, 5", round & square foot	25		15	____
Compote, 5.5" sweetmeat (ball at base of stem)			25	____
Compote, 5.5" bell, round & square foot			20	____
Compote, 6" honey, flat w/ round foot	30		18	____
Compote, 6" honey, flat w/square foot			18	____
Compote, 8" sweetmeat	60		40	____
Creamer, w/foot hexagonal	25	50	10	____
Creamer, low & flat			10	____
Creamer, square w/foot	50		10	____
Cup	20	30	10	____
Cup, demitasse	60		30	____
Cup, punch			8	____
Decanter w/stopper, 20 oz.			70	____
Egg cup			18	____
Hat dish, high			20	____
Hat dish, low			18	____
Ice tub, 4"	50	80	25	____
Ice tub, 5.5"	75	100	50	____
Icer, square base			50	____
Ladle for punch bowl			30	____
Lamp, candlestick (several styles)			40	____
Lamp, 6.25" (electric)	75		40	____
Lamp, 9.25" (electric)	150		50	____
Lampshade			200	____
Marmalade w/cover	50	75	30	____
Mustard w/cover, square			28	____
Nut, individual, w/foot	15		8	____

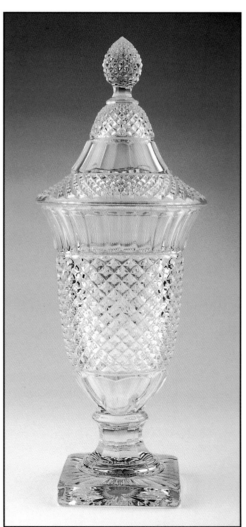

15.5" master candy. *Courtesy of Michael Rothenberger/ Mike's Collectables.*

ENGLISH HOBNAIL (Cont.)	Pink & green	Turquoise/ Ice blue	Amber & Crystal	Qty
Oil cruet w/stopper, 2 oz. (1 handle)			20	____
Oil cruet w/ stopper, 6 oz. (1 handle)			30	____
Oil-vinegar combination bottle, 6 oz. (no handles)			40	____
Parfait, round foot			15	____
Pitcher, 23 oz., round	150		60	____
Pitcher, 32 oz., straight sides	200		70	____
Pitcher, 38 oz., round	250		80	____
Pitcher, 60 oz., round	320		90	____
Pitcher, 64 oz., straight sides	350		100	____
Plate, 5.5"	10		5	____
Plate, liner for cream soup			8	____
Plate, 6" square liner for finger bowls	10		5	____
Plate, 6", square			5	____
Plate, 6.5"	10		7	____
Plate, 6.5" round liner for finger bowls	10		7	____
Plate, 6.5" w/ depressed center			7	____
Plate, 8"	14		8	____
Plate, 8.5"	14	30	15	____
Plate, 8.5", plain edge			10	____
Plate, 8.5" w/ 3 feet			10	____
Plate, 8.75"			10	____
Plate, 10"	40	70	15	____
Plate, 10" square			15	____
Plate, 10.5" grill			15	____
Plate, 12" square			25	____
Plate, 14" torte	65		30	____
Plate, 12" square			35	____
Plate, 20.5" torte			65	____
Puff box w/lid, 6" round	50	80	30	____
Punch bowl			225	____
Punch bowl stand			75	____
Relish, 8" w/3 sections			18	____
Salt & pepper, flat	150	225		____
Salt & pepper, round foot	85		30	____
Salt & pepper, square foot			30	____
Saucer	5	8	3	____
Saucer, square			3	____
Saucer, demitasse	15		10	____
Saucer, demitasse, square			10	____

ENGLISH HOBNAIL (Cont.)	Pink & green	Turquoise/ Ice blue	Amber & Crystal	Qty
Sherbet, low w/ 1 glass ball on stem			8	____
Sherbet, short stem, round foot		15	8	____
Sherbet, short stem, square foot	12		8	____
Sherbet, tall stem, round foot	18		10	____
Sherbet, tall stem, square foot	18	40	10	____
Sherbet, tall, 2 balls of glass on stem, round foot			10	____
Stem, 1 oz. cordial, round foot			15	____
Stem, 1 oz. cordial, glass ball on stem, round foot			15	____
Stem, 1 oz. cordial, square foot			15	____
Stem, 2 oz. wine, square foot	30	60	10	____
Stem, 2 oz. wine, round foot			10	____
Stem, 2.25 oz. wine, glass ball on stem, round foot			10	____
Stem, 3 oz. cocktail, round foot	20	40	10	____
Stem, 3 oz. cocktail, square foot			10	____
Stem, 3.5 oz. cocktail, glass ball on stem			8	____
Stem, 5 oz. claret, round foot			15	____
Stem, 5 oz. oyster cocktail, square foot	20		10	____
Stem, 8 oz. water, square foot	30	50	10	____
Stem, champagne, 2 glass balls on stem, round foot			10	____
Sugar, w/foot hexagonal	25	50	10	____
Sugar, low, flat			10	____
Sugar, square foot	50		10	____
Tid-bit, 2 tier	50	80	30	____
Tumbler, 1.5 oz. whiskey			15	____
Tumbler, 3 oz. whiskey			13	____
Tumbler, 5 oz. ginger ale, flat			10	____
Tumbler, 5 oz. old fashioned			10	____
Tumbler, 5 oz. ginger ale, round foot			10	____
Tumbler, 5 oz. ginger ale, square foot			10	____
Tumbler, 7 oz. juice, round foot			10	____
Tumbler, 7 oz. juice, square foot			10	____

Far left: Salt & pepper shakers. *Courtesy of Michael Rothenberger/ Mike's Collectables*.

Left: 6" candy jar w/ lid & 3 feet. *Courtesy of Bettye S. James.*

Below: Creamers & sugars w/ hexagonal feet. *Courtesy of Michael Rothenberger/Mike's Collectables.*

6" round puff box w/ lid.
*Courtesy of Marie Talone
& Paul Reichwein.*

9.25" lamp. *Courtesy of
Michael Rothenberger/
Mike's Collectibles.*

ENGLISH HOBNAIL (Cont.)	Pink & green	Turquoise/ Ice blue	Amber & Crystal	Qty
Tumbler, 8 oz. water, glass ball on short stem, round foot			10	____
Tumbler, 8 oz. water, flat	25		10	____
Tumbler, 9 oz. water, glass ball on short stem, round foot			10	____
Tumbler, 9 oz. water, round foot			10	____
Tumbler, 9 oz. water, square foot			10	____
Tumbler, 10 oz. iced tea, flat	30		15	____
Tumbler, 11 oz. iced tea, glass ball on short stem, round foot			10	____
Tumbler, 11 oz. iced tea, square foot			14	____
Tumbler, 12 oz. iced tea, flat	33		12	____
Tumbler, 12.5 oz. iced tea, round foot			10	____
Urn, 11" (w/lid 15")	400		50	____
Vase, 6.5" ivy bowl, square foot, crimped rim			35	____
Vase, 6.5" flower holder, square foot			25	____
Vase, 7.5" flip	100		30	____
Vase, 7.5", flip jar w/ cover	120		70	____
Vase, 8" w/square foot			35	____
Vase, 8.5", flared top	125	275	40	____
Vase, 10", Straw jar	110		75	____

Note: Cobalt and Black items 30% higher than Turquoise prices.
Milk glass cigarette lighter, $25.

Above: Cup & saucer, 9.5" dinner w/ blue trim.

Right: Cup & saucer, 9.5" dinner in jade-ite.

FIRE-KING ALICE

(1945-1949 Anchor Hocking Glass Corporation)

Every once in a while someone will ask about Alice bowls but there are no bowls. Alice was introduced in 1945 by packing cups and saucers in oatmeal, Jade-ite having been distributed in the greatest quantity. Dinner plates could be purchased at a five and dime store. As dinners didn't sell that well, Anchor Hocking added no other pieces to this line. Now the few Alice dinner plates that were made are in demand. Unscratched Jade-ite Alice dinners are easy to sell as there are many Jade-ite collectors. Fire-King collectors are interested in the other Alice colors.

FIRE-KING ALICE	Jade-ite	Blue trim	Red trim	Vitrock	Qty
Cup	10	15	35	7	____
Plate, 9.5" dinner	35	35	50	15	____
Saucer	2	5	15	3	____

FIRE-KING BREAKFAST SET
(1954-1956 Anchor Hocking Glass Corporation)

The pieces that make up this Fire-King line are not easy to find. Here is a breakdown of each item. The 5" cereal bowl is just a challenge to locate! The St. Denis cup is the easiest thing to find, even easier than the St. Denis saucer. Interesting to note, Anchor Hocking used the same St. Denis mold to create cups and saucers for Lake Como. Egg cups are available, but the $45 price is a far cry from the $7 price of 1994. The milk pitcher is very popular especially in variations not part of the Breakfast Set. Finally, the dinner plate is sometimes confused with a Restaurantware dinner plate. The rim of this plate is broader and turns up slightly. A Breakfast Set dinner plate is more valuable, so take care.

Any piece in this line is a worthwhile investment as availability continues to decrease and interest continues to grow.

FIRE-KING BREAKFAST SET	Jade-ite	Qty
Bowl, 5" cereal, 2.5" deep	55	____
Cup, 9 oz. St. Denis cup		
w/round handle	10	____
Egg cup, 4" tall	45	____
Pitcher, milk, 4.5" tall, 20 oz.	95	____
Plate, 9.25" dinner	30	____
Saucer, 6" St. Denis	5	____

Above: *Back:* egg cup, 9.25" dinner, 4.5" milk pitcher; *front:* St. Denis cup & saucer, 5" cereal bowl.

FIRE-KING CHARM
(1950-1956 Anchor Hocking Glass Corporation)

The distinctive square shape and clean lines of this pattern make it unique when compared to other Fire-King dinnerware lines. White and Ivory Charm are almost impossible to find. Jade-ite collectors are avid Charm fans and probably know how elusive the 11" x 8" platter, 9.25" dinner plate, 6" soup bowl, and 7.25" salad bowl are. Even cups and saucers will disappear when offered for sale.

Royal Ruby collectors often add Ruby Charm to their collections. Forest Green collectors tend to be loyal to one pattern such as Sandwich, Bubble, or Charm and seem less likely to mix and match patterns as often as Ruby collectors.

Azurite, a grayish-blue color used in this pattern and in Swirl, is becoming increasingly popular. Even Japanese collectors are now looking for this!

Forest green. *Back:* 9.25" dinner plate; *front row:* 6" soup bowl, creamer, sugar, cup & saucer.

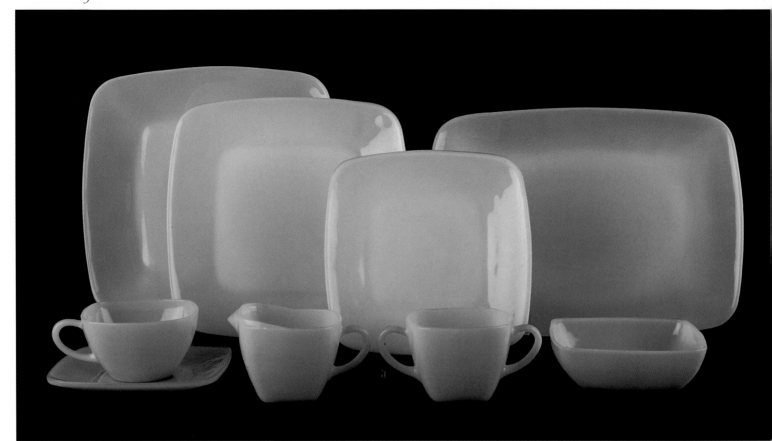

Above: Jade-ite. *Back row:* 9.25" dinner plate, 8.25" luncheon plate, 6.5" salad plate, platter; *front row:* cup & saucer, creamer, sugar, 4.75" dessert bowl.

Right & below: Azurite cup & saucer, 9.25" dinner plate, 8.5" luncheon plate, creamer, sugar.

FIRE-KING CHARM	Jade-ite White & Ivory	Azurite	Forest Green	Royal Ruby	Qty
Bowl, 4.75" dessert	20	8	5	8	____
Bowl, 6" soup	40	18	18		____
Bowl, 7.25" salad	40	20	15	25	____
Creamer	20	10	6		____
Cup	12	5	5	5	____
Plate, 6.5" salad	35	8	8		____
Plate, 8.25" luncheon	20	8	8	10	____
Plate, 9.25" dinner	60	20	30		____
Platter	65	25	24		____
Saucer	8	2	1	3	____
Sugar	20	12	6		____

Note: Pink saucer, $25

FIRE-KING JANE RAY
(1946-1965   Anchor Hocking Glass Corporation)

Jade-ite Fire-King Jane Ray is the most recognizable Fire-King dinnerware of all. The pieces are readily available and relatively affordable.

Here's an item we hope you find interesting. We sold dozens of platters to a catering company in Seattle, Washington, whose major client is a petroleum company. This company used to give away Jane Ray platters with the purchase of gasoline, and today the executives enjoy being served on these platters.

Ivory and Vitrock Jane Ray will be a challenge to locate. As with many elusive Fire-King pieces it tends to be the advanced Fire-King collectors who are chasing after these.

FIRE-KING JANE RAY	Jade-ite	Qty
Bowl, 4.75" dessert	12	____
Bowl, 5.75" oatmeal	25	____
Bowl, 7.5" soup	23	____
Bowl, 8.25" vegetable	30	____
Bowl, 9" soup plate	trtp*	____
Creamer	8	____
Cup	3	____
Cup, demitasse	85	____
Plate, 6.25"	trtp*	____
Plate, 7.75" salad	12	____
Plate, 9" dinner	10	____
Platter, 12"	30	____
Saucer	1	____
Saucer, demitasse	35	____
Sugar base	5	____
Sugar lid	15	____

*trtp = too rare to price

Note: Ivory & Vitrock items twice prices of Jade-ite.

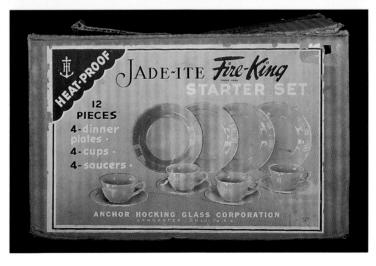

Above: *Back row:* 7.5" soup bowl, 12" platter, 9" dinner plate, 7.25" salad plate; *front row:* sugar w/ lid, creamer, cup & saucer, demitasse cup & saucer, 5.75" oatmeal bowl, 4.75" dessert bowl.

Left: Jane Ray Starter Set in original box.

11" serving plate, 4.75" dessert bowl, 9.25" dinner plate.

Above: 1954 advertisement featuring Gray Laurel, Peach Lustre Laurel, and Jane Ray.

Right: Cup & saucer, 9.25" dinner plate, 4.75" dessert bowl, sugar, creamer.

FIRE-KING LAUREL
(1951-1965 Anchor Hocking Glass Corporation)

Gray Laurel has recently become a more popular Fire-King pattern. Gray Laurel works perfectly with many color schemes from the 1950s, which is currently a popular decorating style. When making a selection look for a scratch-free shine and unfaded color.

Peach Lustre is a color you either love or hate. Here's an added bit of information pertaining to Peach Lustre. The Peach Lustre batter bowl is becoming scarce. The last one we saw was at a Pennsylvania auction in the middle of nowhere and sold for $125. Remember, at an auction there is an underbidder, so at least two people were willing to spent more than $100 for one.

The other Laurel colors are very hard to find, placing them in the category of what advanced Fire-King collectors are seeking. Generally there are few customers of these colors.

FIRE-KING LAUREL	Gray	Peach Lustre	Ivory, White, & Ivory white	Qty
Bowl, 4.75" dessert	10	4	12	
Bowl, 7.5" soup plate	20	10	25	____
Bowl, 8.25" vegetable	30	10	40	____
Creamer	10	4	10	____
Cup	8	4	8	____
Plate, 7.25" salad	15	8	15	____
Plate, 9.25" dinner	10	8	15	____
Plate, 11" serving	30	15	40	____
Saucer	5	1	5	____
Sugar	10	4	10	____

Note: Jade-ite cup, $50.

FIRE-KING RESTAURANTWARE
(1948-1967   Anchor Hocking Glass Corporation)

Of all the surprises in the recent surge of Fire-King popularity this has to be the biggest. Who would think that diner-ware that was thrown away for years would become one of the most popular lines of dinnerware of any variety? (Doesn't this sound like Depression glass not so long ago?) Being featured on television certainly has had a great deal of influence on the appreciation many collectors feel toward the Jade-ite color and its general utility. The sudden vast interest in Restaurantware created a volatile market with prices spiraling upward faster than a healthy stock market. At this point in time prices have settled. White Restaurantware is much harder to find than Jade-ite and is gaining a serious following of collectors, perhaps because it is still less expensive.

Back row: 9.25" flat soup bowl, 8 oz. cereal bowl w/ flanged rim; *front row:* 15 oz. beaded rim bowl (deep), 4.75" fruit bowl.

Above: *Back row:* 9.5" 3-compartment plate/grill, 9.5" 5-compartment plate, 9" dinner plate; *front row:* 5.5" bread & butter plate, 8" luncheon plate, 6.75" pie plate.

Left: *Back row:* 7 oz. extra heavy coffee mug slightly different from one in front row, 7 oz. extra heavy cup & saucer; *front row:* 6 oz. slim hot chocolate mug, 7 oz. extra heavy coffee mug, 6 oz. straight cup & saucer.

Back row: 9.75" oval "football" platter, 8.75" oval partitioned plate/indent platter, 11.5" oval platter; *front row:* 10 oz. bowl w/ beaded rim (sits on oval partitioned plate), 9.5" oval platter.

Demitasse cup & saucer.

Back row: two 9.5" 3-compartment grill plates, 11.5" platter; *middle row:* 7 oz. extra heavy coffee mug, 5" teardrop bowl ($20), 9.5" oval platter, 5.5" bread & butter plate; *front row:* 8 oz. cereal bowl w/ flanged rim, 4.75" fruit bowl, saucer, 6.75" pie plate. *Courtesy of Jesse Speicher.*

FIRE-KING REST. WARE	Jade-ite	White	Qty
Bowl, 4.75" fruit (G294)	12	8	____
Bowl, 5", handled	trtp*		____
Bowl, cereal w/flanged rim, 8 oz. (G305)	35	20	____
Bowl, 10oz. (G309) w/beaded rim	50	25	____
Bowl, deep, 15 oz. (G300) w/beaded rim	35	20	____
Bowl, 9.25" flat soup (G298)	125	80	____
Cup, 6 oz. straight (G215) (resembles a mug)	14	8	____
Cup, 7 oz. extra heavy (G299) (resembles a coffee cup)	10	8	____
Cup, 7 oz. narrow rim (G319)	20		____
Cup, 7 oz. tapered (G207)	20		____
Cup, demitasse	50		____
Gravy/sauce boat	trtp*	35	____
Mug, coffee, 7 oz. (G212) (extra heavy)	20	7	____
Mug, slim hot chocolate, 6 oz.	25		____
Pitcher, ball jug (G787)	500		____
Plate, 5.5" bread & butter (G315)	15		____
Plate, 6.75" pie (G297)	12	7	____
Plate, 8" luncheon (G316)	80	25	____
Plate, 8.75" oval partitioned/ indent platter (G211)	95		____
Plate, 8.75" oval, no indent (G310)	110		____
Plate, 9" dinner (G306)	25	12	____
Plate, 9.5" 3-compartment/ grill w/or w/out a tab for stacking (G292)	35	12	____
Plate, 9.5" 5-compartment (G311)	40		____
Platter, 9.5" oval (G307)	60	25	____
Platter, 9.75" oval "football"	80		____
Platter, 11.5" oval (G308)	50	30	____
Saucer, 6" (G295)	4	2	____
Saucer, demitasse	35		____

Note: Azurite G294 Fruit bowl, $40. Roseite G299 Cup, $50.
*trtp = too rare to price

FIRE-KING SAPPHIRE BLUE
(1941-1956 Anchor Hocking Glass Corporation)

FIRE-KING SAPPHIRE BLUE	Blue	Qty
Baker, 1 pt., 4.5" x 5"	10	____
Baker, 1 pt., 5.5" round	8	____
Baker, 1 qt., 7.25" round	10	____
Baker, 1.5" qt., 8.25" round	12	____
Baker, 2 qt., 8.75" round	14	____
Bowl, 4.25" individual pie	25	____
Bowl, 5.25" cereal	20	____
Bowl, 5.75", 2.75" deep	trtp*	____
Bowl, 16 oz., w/measures	25	____
Cake pan, 8.75"	35	____
Casserole, 4.75" individual w/lid	12	____
Casserole, 1 pt., 5.5" knob-handled lid	20	____
Casserole, 1 qt., 7.25" knob-handled lid	25	____
Casserole, 1 qt., pie plate lid	20	____
Casserole, 1.5 qt., 8.25" knob-handled lid	30	____
Casserole, 1.5 qt., pie plate lid	25	____
Casserole, 2 qt., 8.75" knob-handled lid	30	____
Casserole, 2 qt., pie plate lid	25	____
Cup, 1 spout 8 oz. liquid measure	25	____
Cup, no spout 8 oz. dry measure	trtp*	
Cup, 3 spouts, 8 oz. liquid measure	30	____
Custard cup, 5 oz.	4	____
Custard cup, 6 oz., 3 styles	4	____
Loaf pan	10	____
Mug, 2 styles	35	____
Nipple cover, "Binky's Nip-cap"	250	____
Nursing bottle, 4 oz.	20	____
Nursing bottle, 8 oz.	35	____
Nursing bottle, 8 oz., Fyrock	30	____
Nursing bottle, 8 oz., "Tuffy"	30	____
Percolator top, 2.25"	4	____
Pie plate, 8.25"	6	____
Pie plate, 9"	6	____
Pie plate, 9.5"	6	____
Pie plate, 10.25", juice saver	135	____
Popcorn popper	40	____
Refrigerator dish w/lid, 4.5" x 5"	22	____
Refrigerator dish w/lid, 5.25" x 9.25"	20	____
Roaster, 8.75"	75	____
Roaster, 10.25"	60	____
Skillet, 7" w/4.5" handle	trtp*	____
Silex 2-cup dripolator	45	____
Silex 6-cup dripolator	200	____
Trivet w/2 tab handles	20	____
Utility bowl, 1 qt., 6.75"	25	____
Utility bowl, 1.5 qt., 8.25"	20	____
Utility bowl, 2 qt., 10.25"	20	____
Utility pan, 8.25" x 12.5"	35	____
Utility pan, 10.5" x 2" deep	35	____

*trtp = too rare to price

Anchor Hocking created this wonderful line of ovenware that is extremely popular because it is usable! Here's a hint if you find a piece with baked-in dirt that fills the Philbe design: spray the glass with oven cleaner, let it stand for at least twenty minutes (or several weeks like someone we won't mention), and then scrub it with a stiff brush such as a discarded toothbrush. The dirt will break free from the glass and the item will be restored to its original beauty.

The 7.5" skillet is a treasure coveted by many Fire-King enthusiasts. From personal experience several lucky collectors recommend searching among shot glasses for the "Binky's Nip-cap." Finally, note that both halves of the two roasters are identical. You may be able to save money by purchasing these one part at a time.

Back: 10.25" juice saver pie plate; *front row:* 4.75" individual casserole w/ lid, 1.5 quart casserole w/ knob-handled lid on trivet w/ 2 tab handles, 1.5 quart casserole w/ pie plate lid. *Courtesy of Charlie Diefenderfer.*

8 oz. nursing bottle, mug, 9.5" pie plate, 5 oz. custard, 4.5" x 5" refrigerator dish w/ lid on 5.25" x 9.25" refrigerator dish w/ lid. *Courtesy of Charlie Diefenderfer.*

Back row: 9.25" dinner plate, 5.75" cereal bowl; *front row:*
Ransom cup, St. Denis saucer, St. Denis cup & saucer.

FIRE-KING 1700 LINE	Jade-ite	Ivory	Milk white	Qty
Bowl, 5.75" cereal	15	25	8	____
Bowl, 7.5" flat soup	25	35	12	____
Bowl, 8.5" vegetable	35			____
Cup, 8 oz. Coffee	10		6	____
Cup, 9 oz. St. Denis w/round handle	8	10	5	____
Cup, 9 oz. Ransom w/pointy handle	15	30	6	____
Plate, 7.75" salad			8	____
Plate, 9.25" dinner	30	7	5	____
Platter, 9" x 12" oval	30		15	____
Saucer, 7.5"	5	5	2	____

FIRE-KING 1700 LINE
(1946-1958   Anchor Hocking Glass Corporation)

Three items in the 1700 Line are also part of the Breakfast Set: the St. Denis cup, the St. Denis saucer, and the 9.25" dinner plate. These will be the easiest pieces to find. Everything else in any color will be difficult. Many general collectors aren't even familiar with the 1700 Line. Ask them what a "Ransom cup" is and they might not have any idea, but serious Fire-King collectors might be able to tell you where they found their first one! The 5.75" cereal bowl is a 5.75" Jane Ray oatmeal bowl without the ribs.

Back row: 9" x 12" platter, 9.25" dinner plate; *front row:* St. Denis cup & 5.75" cereal bowl.

FIRE-KING SHELL
(1965-1976   Anchor Hocking
Glass Corporation)

Shell has always been much harder to find than Jane Ray, and it has always commanded a higher price. The dinner plates are larger, but overall these two Anchor Hocking lines are similar. They have almost the same assortment of pieces, except for Shell having one more platter than Jane Ray. Jade-ite is the most popular color for both.

One of the phenomenal price increases worth noting is the Shell sugar lid. It is difficult to find and worth considerably more than the $15 Jane Ray lid.

Demitasse Shell cups and saucers are the most common of all Fire-King demitasse sets. For this reason they continue to be inexpensive. They are readily available in Peach Lustre and white.

The gold trim on white dinnerware is real gold so do not microwave these pieces.

Back row: 8.5" round vegetable bowl, 7.75" soup bowl;
front row: 6.25" cereal bowl, 4.75" dessert bowl.

Above: *Back row:* 7.25" salad plate, 10" dinner plate, 9.5" x 13" platter; *front row:* cup & saucer, sugar w/ lid, creamer.

Left: 7.25" salad plate, 7.75" soup bowl in Peach Lustre.

FIRE-KING SHELL	Jade-ite	"Mother of Pearl"	Other colors	Qty
Bowl, 4.75" dessert	18		4	___
Bowl, 6.25" cereal	28	15	10	___
Bowl, 7.75" soup	35	24	10	___
Bowl, 8.5" oval vegetable	125			___
Bowl, 8.5" round vegetable	30	25	10	___
Creamer	20		3	___
Cup	8	8	3	___
Cup, demitasse		15	10	___
Plate, 7.25" salad	22	10	4	___
Plate, 10" dinner	20	15	4	___
Platter, 9" oval		20		___
Platter, 9.5" x 13" oval	110		10	___
Platter, 11.5" x 15.5" oval			20	___
Saucer	5	5	1	___
Saucer, demitasse		15	10	___
Sugar base	25	10	4	___
Sugar lid	100	15	8	___

Two hand painted 7.25" salad plates.

FIRE-KING SWIRL-SUNRISE
(1949-1962 Anchor Hocking Glass Corporation)

Many of you who decorate kitchens in red and white have known about Sunrise for years. The recent interest in Fire-King has resulted in a broader group of people buying Sunrise. This really has worked in everyone's favor. Sunrise had been an obscure, little-known pattern. Now that additional dealers are selling Fire-King dinnerware, Sunrise is more available than at any time during the past ten years.

Condition of the trim is very important. The red rim is an applied color that will be negatively affected if cleaned in a dishwasher. It can fade, chip, or scratch. Most collectors want pieces with a true red tone that has maintained its integrity.

The three largest bowls are the hardest items to find. Platters are available but ones in excellent condition will take more time to locate.

Back row: platter, 9.25" dinner plate, 7.25" salad plate; *front row:* cup & saucer, creamer.

FIRE-KING SWIRL-SUNRISE	Ivory w/red rim	Qty
Bowl, 4.75" dessert	10	____
Bowl, 5.75" cereal	25	____
Bowl, 7.75" soup	25	____
Bowl, 8.25" vegetable	30	____
Creamer	12	____
Cup	8	____
Plate, 7.25" salad	10	____
Plate, 9.25" dinner	12	____
Platter	25	____
Saucer	4	____
Sugar base	10	____
Sugar lid	15	____

FIRE-KING TURQUOISE BLUE
(1956-1958   Anchor Hocking Glass Corporation)

For years many collectors have been building sets of Turquoise Blue Fire-King. In particular the Swedish Modern (Teardrop) and Splash Proof bowls have been very popular. As with other Fire-King lines, Turquoise Blue dinnerware has enjoyed a surge of popularity as more and more people discover Anchor Hocking's Fire-King. The dinnerware is still easy to find and relatively inexpensive, except for the 10" dinner plate.

The most difficult item to locate is the batter bowl. It is actually one of the most elusive Fire-King pieces of all. Many devoted Fire-King collectors are without this treasure. As abundant as it is in Jadeite, the batter bowl in Turquoise Blue is scarce.

As with Azurite, Turquoise Blue Fire-King has become very popular in Japan.

Back row: 10" dinner plate, 9" dinner plate, 7.25" salad plate; *front row:* mug, cup & saucer, cup trimmed in gold.

Back row: hard boiled egg plate, three-part relish, both w/ gold trim; *front:* creamer & sugar.

Original 12-piece "Starter Set" of Turquoise Blue Dinnerware.

FIRE-KING TURQUOISE BLUE	Turquoise blue	Qty
Ash tray, 3.5"	8	_____
Ash tray, 4.5"	8	_____
Ash tray, 5.75"	12	_____
Batter bowl, w/spout & 1 handle	300	_____
Bowl, 4.5" dessert	8	_____
Bowl, 5" cereal, 2" tall	10	_____
Bowl, 5" chili, 2.25" tall	12	_____
Bowl, 6.5" soup	25	_____
Bowl, 8" vegetable	20	_____
Bowl, Swedish Modern, 1 pt., 5"	40	_____
Bowl, Swedish Modern, 1 qt., 6"	40	_____
Bowl, Swedish Modern, 2 qt., 7.25"	40	_____
Bowl, Swedish Modern, 3 qt., 8.25"	45	_____
Bowl, Splash Proof, 1 qt., 6.75"	25	_____
Bowl, Splash Proof, 2 qt., 7.5"	20	_____
Bowl, Splash Proof, 3 qt., 8.5"	20	_____
Creamer	8	_____
Cup	3	_____
Mug	10	_____
Plate, 6.25" bread & butter	20	_____
Plate, 7.25" salad	18	_____
Plate, 9" dinner	10	_____
Plate, 9"w/ indent for cup	6	_____
Plate, 10" dinner	40	_____
Plate, hard boiled egg w/ gold rim	25	_____
Relish, 3-part w/gold rim	15	_____
Saucer	1	_____
Sugar	8	_____

Three Splash Proof bowls.

Four Swedish Modern (Teardrop) bowls.

Back row: 13.5" tray w/ center indent, 13.5" tray; *front row:* butter, shaker, sherbet, candy dish w/ 1 handle. *Courtesy of Marie Talone.*

Sugar w/ lid, 10 oz. tumbler, cup & saucer, creamer, 4.5" square berry bowl. *Courtesy of Marie Talone.*

FLORAGOLD
(1950s   Jeannette Glass Company)

Iridescent Floragold is sometimes mistaken as Carnival Glass. This error is often made with a number of iridescent Depression Glass patterns when first discovered. The years of production make it much newer than Carnival Glass and among one of the newest patterns featured in this book.

There are many Floragold pieces from which to choose with a broad range of prices. The 5.5" ruffled fruit bowl and 5.25" oval candy are extremely common and can often be found on tray lots at auctions. On the other end of the spectrum is the vase/celery. This item is quite rare and we are pleased to have one pictured. We would love to have comports in the next book. Let us know if you can help!

The white plastic tops on the salt and pepper shakers are authentic. In fact half of the value of the shakers is in these tops. They must be in excellent condition so take note as they do crack.

Vase/celery. *Courtesy of Paul Reichwein.*

Back row: 8.25" square dinner, 11.25" platter; *front row:* 9.5" deep salad bowl, 5.5" cereal bowl, 4" ashtray/coaster, crystal ashtray/coaster w/ only 1 indent for cigarette. *Courtesy of Marie Talone.*

FLORAGOLD	Iridescent	Qty
Ash tray/coaster, 4"	7	____
Bowl, 4.5" square berry	6	____
Bowl, 5.5" cereal	50	____
Bowl, 5.5" ruffled fruit	8	____
Bowl, 8.5" square	18	____
Bowl, 9.5" deep salad	50	____
Bowl, 9.5" ruffled	8	____
Bowl, 12" ruffled fruit	8	____
Butter dish base (1/4 lb.)	35	____
Butter dish lid (1/4 lb.)	15	____
Butter complete (1/4 lb.)	50	____
Butter dish base (6.25" square base)	20	____
Butter dish lid (round to fit 6.25" base)	40	____
Butter dish complete (square base, round lid)	60	____
Butter dish, 5.5" complete (square base, rd. lid)	trtp*	____
Candlestick, ea.	30	____
Candy dish, 1 handle	12	____
Candy/Cheese dish w/lid	60	____
Candy, 5.25" oval scalloped w/4 feet	6	____
Comport, 5.25" smooth rim	trtp*	____
Comport, 5.25" ruffled rim	trtp*	____
Creamer	12	____
Cup	5	____
Pitcher	45	____
Plate, 5.25" sherbet/saucer	10	____
Plate, 8.25" square dinner	45	____
Platter, 11.25"	25	____
Salt & pepper	60	____
Sherbet	14	____
Sugar base	10	____
Sugar lid	14	____
Tid-bit, 2-tier, 9.5" ruffled bowl above 12" ruffled bowl	40	____
Tray, 13.5"	25	____
Tray, 13.5" w/center indent	65	____
Tumbler, 10 or 11 oz., 5" tall	20	____
Tumbler, 15 oz.	125	____
Vase/celery	500	____

Note: Shell Pink 5.25" scalloped candy, $25. Crystal ashtray/coaster with indent for only one cigarette, $15

*trtp = too rare to price

Above: *Back:* candy/cheese dish w/ lid; *front row:* candlestick, 1/4 lb. butter, 5.25" scalloped oval candy w/ 4 feet. *Courtesy of Diefenderfer's Collectibles & Antiques.*

Right: Salt & pepper. *Courtesy of Michael Rothenberger/Mike's Collectables.*

12" ruffled fruit bowl, 9.5" ruffled bowl, 5.5" ruffled fruit bowl. *Courtesy of Marie Talone.*

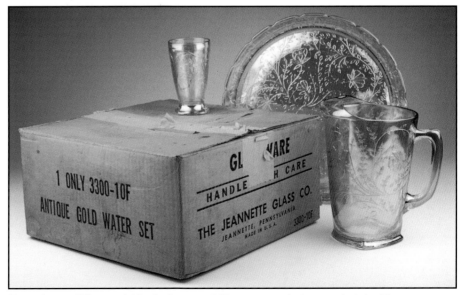

Boxed set of Floragold includes one 13" tray, one pitcher, and eight 10 oz. tumblers. *Courtesy of Michael Rothenberger/Mike's Collectables.*

10.25" footed lemonade pitcher, 5.25" lemonade tumbler, 8" footed pitcher. *Courtesy of Donna L. Cehlarik.*

Right: 11" faceted rim platter. *Courtesy of Mike Rothenberger/ Mike's Collectables.*

Below: *Back row:* 8" salad plate, 10.75" platter, 9" dinner; *front row:* cup & saucer, 8" vegetable bowl w/ cover. *Courtesy of Diefenderfer's Collectibles & Antiques.*

FLORAL
Reproduced
(1931-1935 Jeannette Glass Company)

Back in the early 1930s, the employees at Jeannette Glass Company must have loved Floral. There are many variations and experimental pieces in Floral, so someone or some group at the factory had fun with these molds. Several excellent examples of unique Floral delights are pictured here.

Green Floral is a very complete line with many items to collect. Fortunately there are almost as many pieces in pink as more people collect pink than green. But make no mistake, this is a very popular pattern in both colors. Only a few pieces were made in Delphite, and usually only serious Depression Glass collectors who are willing to invest larger sums of money in unique treasures buy these. Delphite Floral is not easy to find.

The prices of Jade-ite canisters with the Floral motif inside the lid have risen sharply as Jade-ite in general has become tremendously popular.

Interesting and newly found Floral items have been discovered in England. Fortunately for collectors, dealers and auctioneers in the States have networked with sources abroad to have Depression Glass sent to America. Apparently higher prices can be obtained in the American market than in Europe and England, but we benefit by having the opportunity to add wonderful new discoveries to our collections. Several of these British additions are shown, including a 4" flat tumbler, the 9" dinner plate with a rim, and the butter dish in a slightly bluer tint.

Back row: 4" footed salt & pepper, 2-part relish, candy jar w/ lid, sugar w/ lid;
front row: butter, creamer, 4" candlesticks. *Courtesy of Donna L. Cehlarik.*

Lamp. *Courtesy of Michael
Rothenberger/Mike's Collectables.*

Left: 6" flat salt &
pepper. *Courtesy
of Maria
McDaniel*.

Below: 4" footed
salt & pepper
shakers in 2
colors. *Courtesy
of Michael
Rothenberger/
Mike's
Collectables*.

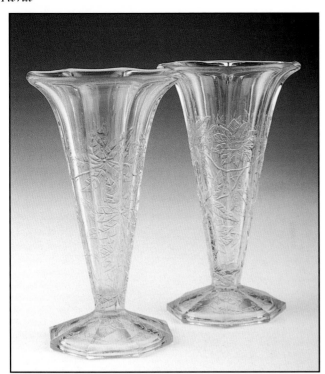

6.75" 8-sided vases. *Courtesy of Diefenderfer's Collectibles & Antiques.*

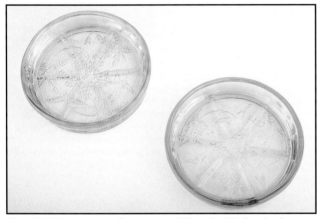

Two 3.25" coasters. *Courtesy of Charlie Diefenderfer.*

FLORAL	Pink	Green	Delphite	Qty
Bowl, 4" berry, smooth rim	25	30	100	____
Bowl, 4" berry, ruffled rim	175	175		____
Bowl, 5.5" cream soup	850	850		____
Bowl, 7.5" salad, smooth rim	30	30	75	____
Bowl, 7.5" salad, ruffled rim	400	400		____
Bowl, 8" vegetable	30	40	85	____
Bowl, 9" oval vegetable	30	30		____
Butter dish base	40	30		____
Butter dish lid	80	70		____
Butter complete	120	100		____
Candlestick, 4" each	40	45		____
Candy jar w/lid	50	50		____
Coaster, 3.25"	18	14		____
Comport, 9"	1000	1200		____
Cover for 8" vegetable bowl	30	30		____
Creamer	18	18	100	____
Cup	15	15		____
Dresser set powder jar w/lid, ea.		1800		____
(set has 2 powder jars)		400		____
rouge box w/lid (1 per set)		600		____
tray		400		____
Frog, for vase		800		____
Ice tub, 3.5" tall, oval	1000	1000		____
Lamp	325	325		____
Pitcher, 5.5" flat		550		____
Pitcher, 8" with foot	45	45		____
Pitcher, 10.25" with foot				
(lemonade pitcher)	375	375		____
Plate, 6" sherbet	8	8		____
Plate, 8" salad	15	15		____
Plate, 9" dinner	20	20	300	____
Plate, 9" grill		300		____
Platter, 10.75"	25	25	250	____
Platter, 11", facetted rim	150	trtp*	trtp*	____
Refrigerator dish w/lid (inside of lid embossed w/Floral motif)		65	65	____
Relish, 2-part	25	25	200	____
Salt & pepper, 4" footed *R*	60	60		____
Salt & pepper, 6" flat	65			____
Saucer	12	12		____
Sherbet	20	22	100	____
Sugar base	18	18	100	____
Sugar lid (same lid on candy jar)	30	30		____

Back: 9" oval vegetable bowl; *front row:* 2-part relish, 4.5" flat water tumbler, cup & saucer. *Courtesy of Diefenderfer's Collectibles & Antiques.*

FLORAL (Cont.)

	Pink	Green	Delphite	Qty
Tray, 6" square w/ tab handles	22	25		____
Tray, 9.25" oval for dresser set		400		____
Tumbler, 3.5" w/foot		225		____
Tumbler, 4" juice w/foot	20	25		____
Tumbler, 4.5" flat		200		____
Tumbler, 4.75" water w/foot	20	25	250	____
Tumbler, 5.25" lemonade w/foot	60	65		____
Vase, rose bowl w/3 feet		850		____
with frog		1650		____
Vase, flared w/3 feet		700		____
Vase, 7" w/8 sides		600		____

Reproduction information: Shakers: red, cobalt, & dark green were never originally produced. Pink shakers: the color is wrong & the threads to screw on the lid **should have** two parallel threads; new shakers have one continuous thread winding around the top. New shakers missing Floral pattern on feet.

Note: Jade-ite: Canisters (cereal, coffee, sugar, tea), 5.25" tall, square with Floral motif inside lid, $150 each. Jade-ite refrigerator dish, 5" square with Floral design inside lid, $65. Transparent green refrigerator dish, $50. Cremax 7.5" bowl, creamer, & sugar, $200 each. Crystal: 3-footed flared vase, $500; with frog, $950; 6.75" 8-sided vase, $450.

*trtp = too rare to price

4" berry bowl in Delphite. *Courtesy of Helen & Edward Betlow*.

Above: Butter dish from England. *Courtesy of Charlie Diefenderfer.*

Above: Two 4.5" flat water tumblers; the one on the right is from England and only has the pattern at the top. *Courtesy of Charlie Diefenderfer.*

Left: Close-up of the English 9" dinner plate w/ a rim. *Courtesy of Charlie Diefenderfer.*

11" faceted rim platter in Delphite. *Courtesy of Charlie Diefenderfer.*

Very rare plate, too rare to price, in tortoise shell or ruby. *Courtesy of Charlie Diefenderfer.*

Very rare bowl and plate, too rare to price, in pumpkin orange. *Courtesy of Charlie Diefenderfer.*

Very rare creamer & sugar, too rare to price, in Cremax. *Courtesy of Vic & Jean Laermans.*

FLORAL AND DIAMOND BAND
(1927-1931 U.S. Glass Company)

Green Floral and Diamond Band sherbets seem to be in almost *every* antique shop in the Midwest. Beyond that, Floral and Diamond Band is not an easy pattern to find.

The butter dish base is the same, plain base used in other U.S. Glass Company patterns like Aunt Polly, Cherryberry, and Strawberry. The only detail in this base is a starburst centered in the bottom.

Floral and Diamond Band pieces are heavier than many other Depression Glass patterns. This pattern has an older look and feel to it as if mimicking earlier pressed glass patterns, and its production dates show that it is one of the first Depression Glass patterns made.

Above: 8" luncheon plate & butter. *Courtesy of Diefenderfer's Collectibles & Antiques.*

Left: *Back row:* 5.25" sugar w/ lid & 4.75" creamer; *front row:* 2.5" sugar & 2.5" creamer. *Courtesy of Vic & Jean Laermans.*

Below: 8" pitcher, sherbet, 5.5" compote.

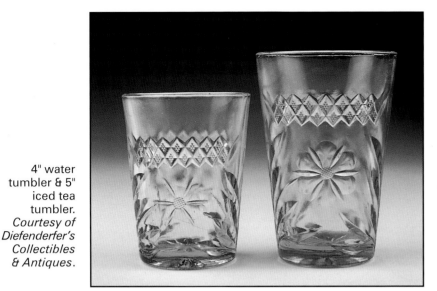

4" water tumbler & 5" iced tea tumbler. *Courtesy of Diefenderfer's Collectibles & Antiques.*

FLORAL AND DIAMOND BAND	Pink & green	Qty
Bowl, 5.75" w/handles	14	____
Bowl, 8" berry	18	____
Butter dish base (no design of any kind)	75	____
Butter dish lid	50	____
Butter complete	125	____
Compote, 5.5"	25	____
Creamer, small, 2.5"	12	____
Creamer, 4.75"	20	____
Pitcher, 8"	120	____
Plate, 8" luncheon	50	____
Sherbet	10	____
Sugar, small, 2.5"	12	____
Sugar base, 5.25"	20	____
Sugar lid	70	____
Tumbler, 4" water	30	____
Tumbler, 5" iced tea	65	____

Note: Iridescent butter & pitcher, $300 each. Crystal items ½ of pink & green.

6.5" footed pitcher, 10" dinner plate, 8.5" salad plate. *Courtesy of Diefenderfer's Collectibles & Antiques.*

FLORENTINE NO. 1
Reproduced
(1932-1934 Hazel-Atlas Glass Company)

Florentine No. 1 has a decorative edge or rim on most of its pieces. This is the easiest way to discern the difference between Florentine No. 1 and Florentine No. 2, which has a smooth edge or rim. These little protrusions of glass on No. 1 are highly susceptible to damage making perfect pieces sometimes difficult to find. Great care must be taken to examine each point as chipping can be camouflaged just by the nature of this pattern's design.

Plates are becoming more and more difficult to find, particularly dinner plates. This pattern is collected in green, yellow, and pink, and locating dinners in any of these colors has gotten to be a bit of a challenge.

The lovely cobalt blue Florentine No. 1 pieces are very popular with collectors of cobalt glass. There are only a few pieces made, and they are all good sellers.

There are no lids for sugar bowls with a ruffled rim. Two lids, a metal one and an all-glass one, fit the sugar bases having smooth rims.

Back row: 3.25" footed juice tumbler, 10" dinner plate, sugar w/ lid; *front row:* sugar w/ ruffled rim, creamer on saucer, shakers in 2 different colors, creamer. *Courtesy of Marie Talone and Paul Reichwein.*

FLORENTINE NO. 1	Green	Yellow	Pink	Cobalt	Qty
Ash tray, 5.5"	25	30	30		____
Bowl, 5" berry	20	20	20	35	____
Bowl, 5" ruffled nut/ cream soup	25		25	65	____
Bowl, 6" cereal	40	40	50		____
Bowl, 8.5" berry	45	45	45		____
Bowl, 9.5" oval vegetable	50	60	65		____
Butter dish base	40	60	60		____
Butter dish lid	100	120	120		____
Butter complete	140	180	180		____
Coaster/ash tray. 3.75"	20	20	25		____
Comport, 3.5" w/ruffled rim	50		25	75	____
Cover for 9.5" oval vegetable	40	45	45		____
Creamer, 3"	10	20	20		____
Creamer w/ruffled rim	50		40	75	____
Cup	10	10	10	100	____
Pitcher, 6.5" w/foot	50	50	50	trtp*	____
Pitcher, 7.5" flat with or without ice lip	85	200	150		____
Plate, 6" sherbet	10	10	10		____
Plate, 8.5" salad	15	15	15		____
Plate, 10" dinner	25	28	30		____
Plate, 10" grill	20	22	25		____
Platter, 11.5"	30	35	35		____
Salt & pepper *R*	50	60	65		____
Saucer	10	10	10	25	____
Sherbet	15	15	15		____
Sugar base	10	20	20		____
Sugar lid, glass	25	35	35		____
Sugar lid, metal	15				____
Sugar w/ruffled rim	50		40	75	____
Tumbler, 3.25" juice w/foot	20				____
Tumbler, 4" juice w/foot	20	25	30		____
Tumbler, 4" w/ribs	25		30		____
Tumbler, 4.75" water w/foot	25	30	30		____
Tumbler, 5.25", 9 oz. lemonade			150		____
Tumbler, 5.25", 12 oz. iced tea w/foot	35	40	40		____

Reproduction information: Shakers: Cobalt & red never originally produced. Pink: new poppy resembles a cauliflower, missing 7 distinct circles around blossom.

*trtp = too rare to price   Note: Crystal comport, $10.

Above: 3.5" comport w/ ruffled rim & creamer w/ ruffled rim. *Courtesy of Don & Terry Yusko.*

Left: 5" berry bowl. *Courtesy of Charlie Diefenderfer.*

Below: Assortment of creamers & sugars. *Courtesy of Charlie Diefenderfer.*

4" footed juice tumbler, 4.75" footed water tumbler, 6.5" footed pitcher, creamer, sugar w/ lid. *Courtesy of Vic & Jean Laermans.*

Back row: 8" berry bowl, 10" dinner plate, 6.25" footed pitcher; *middle row:* butter, sherbet, gravy boat on 11.5" platter, sugar w/ lid, creamer; *front row:* 3.75" coaster/ash tray, 5" ruffled nut/cream soup bowl, 3.75" coaster/ash tray. *Courtesy of Marie Talone and Paul Reichwein.*

FLORENTINE NO. 2
Reproduced
(1932-1935 Hazel-Atlas Glass Company)

The smooth rims and edges on Florentine No. 2 items help to distinguish them from Florentine No. 1. This is one of the most popular patterns of Depression Glass manufactured in yellow as this is a true yellow. People react positively to the cheerful, bright color and perky design. There are many items available to build a collection including several unique pieces such as a gravy boat with a platter and an indented tray for the salt, pepper, creamer, and sugar.

Pink Florentine No. 2 is not as popular as yellow and green. There are no dinner plates in pink, so this creates difficulty in setting a table. The cream soup bowl is plentiful while other pink items are less available in varying degrees.

A sign of popularity is when an item has been reproduced. Be sure to read the reproduction information on this pattern. Reproduction pitchers and tumblers are appearing in greater numbers in antique malls.

Back row: 10" dinner plate, 9" bowl, 10" 3-part relish; *middle row:* 6" vase/parfait, shakers in 2 different colors, candy jar base, 4.5" berry bowl, candlesticks, 3.25" footed juice tumbler. *Courtesy of Marie Talone and Paul Reichwein.*

Back: indented 8.75" tray for salt, pepper, creamer & sugar; *front row:* creamer, salt & pepper, sugar w/ lid. *Courtesy of Donna L. Cehlarik.*

FLORENTINE NO. 2	Green	Yellow	Pink	Qty
Bowl, 4.5" berry	20	25	20	____
Bowl, cream soup	18	25	18	____
Bowl, 5", ruffled nut/cream soup	25		25	____
Bowl, 5.5"	40	45		____
Bowl, 6" cereal	40	50		____
Bowl, 7.5"		100		____
Bowl, 8" berry	30	40	40	____
Bowl, 9" oval vegetable	40	50		____
Bowl, 9" round	35			____
Butter dish base	40	60		____
Butter dish lid	100	120		____
Butter complete	140	180		____
Candlestick, ea.	30	40		____
Candy jar w/lid	150	200	165	____
Coaster/ash tray, 3.75"	18	25	18	____
Coaster/ash tray, 5.5"	20	35		____
Comport, 3.5" w/ruffled rim	50		25	____
Cover for 9" oval vegetable	40	45		____
Creamer	10	10	12	____
Cup	10		10	____
Custard/jello	75	100		____
Gravy boat		75		____
Pitcher, 6.25" w/foot		200		____
Pitcher, 7.5", 28 oz. w/foot	40	40		____
Pitcher, 7.5", 48 oz.	85	225	150	____
Pitcher, 8.25"	120	500	250	____
Plate, 6" sherbet	8	8		____
Plate, 6.25" w/indent	25	40		____
Plate, 8.5" salad	10	10	10	____
Plate, 10" dinner	20	20		____
Plate, 10.25" grill	15	15		____
Plate, 10.25" grill w/cream soup ring	45			____
Platter, 11"	25	25	30	____
Platter, 11.5" to elevate gravy boat		60		____
Relish, 10", 3 part	25	35	35	____
Salt & pepper	50	60		____
Saucer	8	8		____
Sherbet	12	12		____
Sugar base	12	12		____
Sugar lid	25	25		____
Tray, 8.75", round with indents for salt, pepper, cream, sugar		100		____
Tumbler, 3.25" flat juice	15	22	15	____
Tumbler, 3.25" footed juice	15		20	____
Tumbler, 3.5" flat (blown)	22			____
Tumbler, 4" footed juice	15	18		____
Tumbler, 4" flat water	15	22	18	____
Tumbler, 4.5" footed water	30	40		____
Tumbler, 5" flat (blown)	25			____
Tumbler, 5" flat iced tea	45	60		____
Vase/parfait 6" footed	40	70		____

Note: Crystal items 1/2 of Yellow EXCEPT for the crystal covered candy, $150. Cobalt comport & tumbler, $75 each. Ice blue pitcher, $750. Amber: tumbler & cup, $75 each; saucer, $20; sherbet, $50.

Reproduction information: Tumblers and pitchers are being made in colors not originally produced. Measurements for these items are a "tad" smaller than the old ones. Old tumblers measure 4" tall with a base of almost 4". New tumblers are about 1/8 inch smaller in both of these measurements. New pitchers are 1/4" shorter with handles 1/8" wider than the 3/4" width of the old pitchers' handles. New pitchers and tumblers are heavier.

3.25" flat juice tumbler, 4" footed juice tumbler, 4" flat water tumbler, 4.5" footed water tumbler. *Courtesy of Diefenderfer's Collectibles & Antiques.*

Back row: 10" dinner plate, 8.5" salad plate; *front row:* 9" bowl, 5.5" bowl. *Courtesy of Diefenderfer's Collectibles & Antiques.*

Candy jar w/ lid. *Courtesy of Charlie Diefenderfer.*

9" oval vegetable bowl w/ cover. *Courtesy of Charlie Diefenderfer.*

FLOWER GARDEN WITH BUTTERFLIES
(Late 1920s   U.S. Glass Company)

This pattern is a tribute to wonderful design. Look carefully at the close-up of the pattern, you should be able to see a butterfly fluttering among the flowers, hence this name.

Finding absolutely anything in Flower Garden with Butterflies is difficult. This is a high quality pattern with relatively expensive pieces. One's best bet for finding this pattern is attending Depression Glass shows where dealers often display their very best.

Most collectors of Flower Garden with Butterflies buy any color they find. There are some who specialize in one color, as is the norm for the majority of collectors of other patterns, but individuals hunting for this pattern are usually delighted to find and purchase anything they don't own, regardless of color.

Above: Close-up of pattern.

Right: Two 8.25" plates. *Courtesy of Charlie Diefenderfer.*

Below: *Back row:* 4.75" tall/10.25" wide comport, 7.25" plate; *front row:* 8.25" plate, candy jar base. *Courtesy of Neil McCurdy - Hoosier Kubboard Glass.*

FLOWER GARDEN WITH BUTTERFLIES	Black	Blue & Blue-Canary yellow	Pink & green, & Green	Amber & Crystal	Qty
Ashtray		200	200	175	___
Bon bon w/cover, 6.5" across	300				___
Bottle, cologne w/stopper, 7.5"		250	350		___
Bowl, 7.25" w/lid	400				___
Bowl, 8.5" console w/base	200				___
Bowl, 9" rolled edge w/base	250				___
Bowl, 11" orange w/foot	300				___
Bowl, 12" console w/rolled edge	250				___
Candlestick, 4" each	50	75	75	45	___
Candlestick, 6" each	250				___
Candlestick, 8" each	200	85	85	45	___
Candlestick, w/candle, 12" (candle is 6.5" tall and .75" square)	500				___
Candy w/lid, 6", no foot			175	150	___
Candy w/lid, 7.5"		150	200	100	___
Candy w/lid, heart-shaped		trtp*	trtp*		___
Cheese & cracker, 10" base, 5.25" tall	400				___
Cigarette box w/lid, 4.25" long	200				___
Comport w/lid, 2.75" tall for 10" indented plate	250				___
Comport, 2.75" tall		50	50		___
Comport, 4.25" tall, 4.75" wide			50		___
Comport, 4.25" tall, 10" wide; tureen	300				___
Comport, 4.75" tall, 10.25" wide		80	100	65	___
Comport w/foot, 5.5" tall, 10" wide	250				___
Comport, 5.75" tall, 11" wide			120	75	___
Comport w/foot, 7" tall	200				___
Comport, 7.25" tall, 8.25" wide		100		85	___
Creamer		100			___
Cup		70			___
Mayonnaise, 3-piece set		150	175	100	___
Mayo. comport		75	85	50	___
Mayo. ladle		20	25	20	___
Mayo. under plate		55	65	30	___
Plate, 7.25"		35	50	25	___
Plate, 8.25", 2 styles		35	45		___
Plate, 10"		65	75		___
Plate, 10" w/indent for 3" comport	150	65	70	45	___
Powder jar, 3.5", no foot		120			___
Powder jar, 6.25" w/foot		150	225	100	___
Powder jar, 7.5" w/foot		150	120	100	___
Sandwich server w/center handle	150	70	100	55	___
Saucer		35			___
Sugar		100			___
Tray, 5.5" x 10" oval		65		65	___
Tray, 7.75" x 11.75" rectangular		75		65	___
Tumbler, 7.5 oz.				200	___
Vase, 6.25" Dahlia, cupped	150	120	175	80	___
Vase, 8" Dahlia, cupped	200				___
Vase, 9", wall	350				___
Vase, 10" w/2 handles	250				___
Vase, 10.5" Dahlia, cupped	300	150	250		___

*trtp = too rare to price

Left: Candlestick w/ 6.5" candle. *Courtesy of Neil McCurdy - Hoosier Kubboard Glass.*

Below: 7.75" x 11.75" rectangular tray. *Courtesy of Marie Talone and Paul Reichwein.*

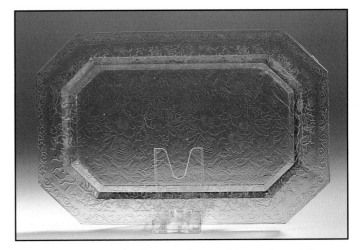

Cup & saucer.

FORTUNE
(1936-1937 Hocking Glass Company)

This abbreviated set of Depression Glass offering no dinner plate is still very popular in pink. There are many little items: a 4" berry bowl, a 4.5" dessert bowl, a 5" bowl with a handle, and so on. When looking for a small bowl for this or that, Fortune is often selected. Many a piece of Fortune has been purchased by someone looking for "a pink piece of glass for my friend who collects that stuff." You don't have to pay a fortune to own some Fortune.

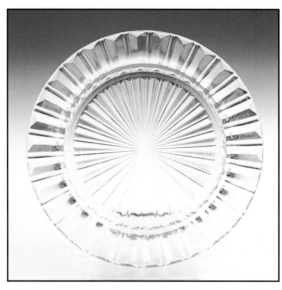

FORTUNE	Pink	Qty
Bowl, 4" berry	10	____
Bowl, 4.5" dessert	10	____
Bowl, 4.5" w/tab handles	10	____
Bowl, 5" w/ one handle	10	____
Bowl, 5.25" w/flared top	18	____
Bowl, 7.75" salad	25	____
Candy dish w/lid	35	____
Candy dish w/ Ruby lid	50	____
Cup	10	____
Plate, 6" sherbet	8	____
Plate, 8" luncheon	25	____
Saucer	5	____
Tumbler, 3.5" juice	15	____
Tumbler, 4.25" water	18	____

Note: Crystal items 1/2 of pink

Top: *Back row:* 4.5" bowl w/ 2 tab handles, saucer, 4.25" water tumbler, 3.5" juice tumbler; *front row:* 5" bowl w/ 1 handle, 4.5" dessert bowl, 4" berry bowl. *Courtesy of Neil McCurdy - Hoosier Kubboard Glass and Staci & Jeff Shuck/Gray Goose Antiques.*

Left: 6" sherbet plate. *Courtesy of Joan Kauffman.*

FRUITS
(1931-1953 Hazel-Atlas Glass Company & others)

Fruits is primarily found and collected in green. The prices clearly reflect the availability of the individual pieces. One would think that if a pattern had been produced for over twenty years more bowls, 5" tumblers, and pitchers would be seen, but this is not the case.

There are several fruit motifs, and most collectors pick only one. Look carefully at the photographs to see the differences.

Above: Close-up of a pattern variations on 4" tumblers. *Courtesy of Neil McCurdy - Hoosier Kubboard Glass and Staci & Jeff Shuck/Gray Goose Antiques.*

Right: Cup, saucer, sherbet.

FRUITS	Green	Pink	Qty
Bowl, 5" cereal	40	30	____
Bowl, 8" berry	90	60	____
Cup	10	12	____
Pitcher	120		____
Plate, 8" luncheon	10	12	____
Saucer	6	8	____
Sherbet	10	10	____
Tumbler, 3.5" juice	60	50	____
Tumbler, 4" multiple fruits	25	25	____
Tumbler, 4.25" single fruit shown	20	18	____
Tumbler, 5"	150		____

Note: Crystal & iridescent 1/2 of green items.

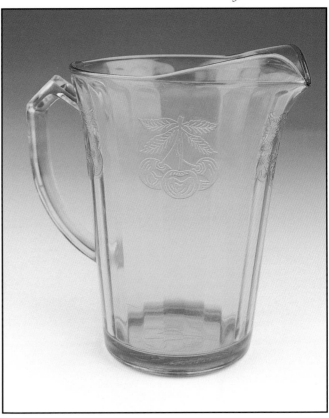

Pitcher.

8" luncheon plates, two 4" tumblers. *Courtesy of Neil McCurdy - Hoosier Kubboard Glass and Staci & Jeff Shuck/Gray Goose Antiques.*

GEORGIAN LOVEBIRDS
(1931-1935 Federal Glass Company)

Here is one of the most popular green patterns in Depression Glass. Federal Glass Company created a line of dinnerware just complete enough to set a table with all the necessary pieces with a few delightful extras.

Georgian is fairly easy to track down, so building a collection won't require the stamina needed for amassing some sets. The cold cut server and sugar lid for the 4" sugar base are the most difficult items to find. Neither tumbler is easy, and the 5.25" tumbler seems to be disappearing. Likewise, luncheon plates are easy to find, but dinner plates in good condition are getting difficult to locate. 4.5" berry bowls, creamers, and sugar bases are the easiest items to find. There are two sizes of creamers and sugars so make sure to note this.

Back row: 7.5" berry bowl, 9.25" dinner plate; *front row:* 4.5" berry bowl, 5.75" cereal bowl, 6.5" deep bowl. *Courtesy of Ardell & George Conn.*

Top: Butter, 11.25" platter w/ tab handles, 3" creamer, 3" sugar w/ lid. *Courtesy of Ardell & George Conn.*

Center: 4" tumbler, 5.25" tumbler, 9.25" dinner plate, cup & saucer, sherbet. *Courtesy of Ardell & George Conn.*

Bottom: *Back row:* 9" oval vegetable bowl, 8" luncheon plate, 5" hot plate dish; *front:* 6" sherbet plate. *Courtesy of Ardell & George Conn.*

GEORGIAN LOVEBIRDS	Green	Qty
Bowl, 4.5" berry	12	____
Bowl, 5.75" cereal	25	____
Bowl, 6.5", deep	70	____
Bowl, 7.5" berry	70	____
Bowl, 9" oval vegetable	60	____
Butter dish base	30	____
Butter dish lid	50	____
Butter complete	80	____
Cold Cut Server (18.5" wooden lazy Susan w/7 indentations for 5" hot plate dishes)	trtp*	____
Creamer, 3"	14	____
Creamer, 4"	18	____
Cup	12	____
Hot plate dish, 5"	100	____
Plate, 6" sherbet	10	____
Plate, 8" luncheon	12	____
Plate, 9.25" dinner	40	____
Plate, 9.25" dinner, center design only	25	____
Platter, 11.25" w/tab handles	70	____
Saucer	8	____
Sherbet	15	____
Sugar base, 3"	14	____
Sugar lid for 3" base	50	____
Sugar base, 4"	18	____
Sugar lid for 4" base	300	____
Tumbler, 4"	75	____
Tumbler, 5.25"	150	____

Note: Crystal hot plate, $35. Amber sherbet, $40.

*trtp = too rare to price

HARP

(1954-1957   Jeannette Glass Company)

Dating from the 1950s, Harp is one of the more recent patterns in this book, but it is collected by many so it is included. The current interest in pedestal cake stands has led to a greater number of Harp collectors. There are several different colors and styles of Harp cake stands, and after buying one some people will occasionally go on to buy additional pieces of Harp.

Collecting a set of Harp provides the necessities for a luncheon, bridge party, or dessert. There are cups and saucers for coffee and tea, and coasters for those partaking in cold beverages. The cake stand holds the dessert, and other edible offerings can be served on the tray. A vase is available to grace the table while all dine on 7" plates, allowing one to create a symphony of proper hostessing using Harp.

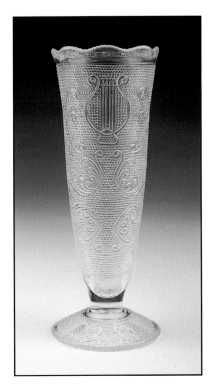

Left: 7.5" vase.

Below: *Back:* tray w/ open handles; *front:* 9" cake stand, cup & saucer, ashtray/coaster, 7" plate. *Courtesy of Bettye S. James.*

HARP	Crystal	Qty
Ashtray/coaster	7	____
Coaster	5	____
Cup	35	____
Cake stand, 9"	25	____
Plate, 7"	25	____
Saucer	15	____
Tray w/2 open handles	35	____
Vase, 7.5"	35	____

Note: Colored cake stands, $50 each.
Shell Pink tray, $70.

9" cake stands in ice blue and white. *Courtesy of Bettye S. James.*

HERITAGE
Reproduced
(1940-1955 Federal Glass Company)

Above: Sugar & creamer. *Courtesy of Vic & Jean Laermans.*

Below: *Back row:* 9.25" dinner plate, 8" luncheon plate; *front row:* 10.5" fruit bowl, 5" berry bowl, cup & saucer.

When Heritage was introduced in 1940 pink was no longer the fashionable color that it had been in previous years. Thus, Federal Glass Company issued this pattern primarily in crystal (clear). There are only ten items in this pattern with the 8.5" berry bowl and 10.5" fruit bowl being the most difficult to find. There are not many collectors of this pattern, so the competition among potential owners to have these bowls is not as great as the demand for many other Depression Glass patterns and pieces.

Take note of the reproduction information prior to making a purchase. The reproduction green color is more like the avocado seen in the 1960s and 1970s. Indiana Glass Company used this shade of green in newer releases of Daisy. The older green bowls are produced in the transparent green color seen in other Depression Glass patterns.

HERITAGE	Crystal	Pink	Blue & Green	Qty
Bowl, 5" berry	8	50	60	____
Bowl, 8.5" berry	45	125	200	____
Bowl, 10.5" fruit	15			____
Creamer, 3"	30			____
Cup	8			____
Plate, 8" luncheon	10			____
Plate, 9.25" dinner	14			____
Plate, 12" sandwich	15			____
Saucer	5			____
Sugar, 3"	28			____

Reproduction information: All berry bowls marked "MC" are new. All amber pieces are new. Green pieces that are too dark are new.

HEX OPTIC
(1928-1932 Jeannette Glass Company)

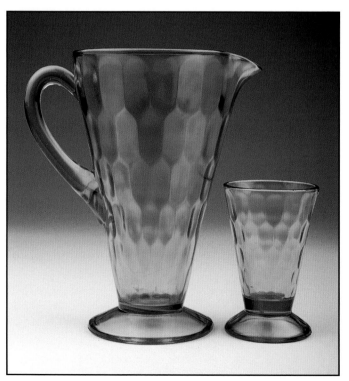

Hex Optic has confused some collectors. You may want to refer to Raindrops and Thumbprint if you are uncertain of an item. If the piece isn't pictured, check the list for each pattern to determine what you might have.

The ruffled edge mixing bowls are usually nicked. It is fair to say that one could expect to pay even more for these bowls if they are really and truly in mint condition. The nature of the design makes them prone to damage even if they received minimal use. Refrigerator dishes are also found with nicks and dings from lids bumping into the bases. Too bad all of our grandmothers didn't just save these pieces for us to enjoy in pristine condition.

The triangular handle of the creamer and cup was also used by Jeannette Glass on several measuring cups. It is nice to recognize "signature" characteristics that can aid in identification while on the hunt.

9" footed pitcher, 5.75" footed tumbler. *Courtesy of Michael Rothenberger/Mike's Collectables.*

HEX OPTIC	Pink & green	Qty
Bowl, 4.25" berry, ruffled edge	10	____
Bowl, 7.5" berry	15	____
Bowl, 7.25" mixing, ruffled edge	20	____
Bowl, 8.25" mixing, ruffled edge	22	____
Bowl, 9" mixing, ruffled edge	25	____
Bowl, 10" mixing, ruffled edge	28	____
Bucket reamer	65	____
Butter dish base (rectangular)	50	____
Butter dish lid (rectangular)	50	____
Butter complete (rectangular to hold 1 lb. of butter)	100	____
Creamer, 2 handle designs	10	____
Cup, 2 handle designs	10	____
Ice bucket w/ metal handle	40	____
Pitcher, 5" w/ sunflower base	25	____
Pitcher, 8" flat	225	____
Pitcher, 9" w/foot	65	____
Plate, 6" sherbet	8	____
Plate, 8" luncheon	10	____
Platter, 11" round	25	____
Refrigerator dish, 4" x 4"	25	____
Refrigerator dishes, 3 round containers stacked w/ 1 lid	100	____
Salt & pepper	50	____
Saucer	8	____
Sherbet	12	____
Sugar, 2 handle designs	10	____
Tumbler, 2" whiskey	12	____
Tumbler, 3.75" flat	8	____
Tumbler, 4.75" w/foot	10	____
Tumbler, 5" flat	8	____
Tumbler, 5.75" w/foot	12	____
Tumbler, 7" w/foot	15	____

Note: Iridescent items worth 1/2 of those in pink & green. Tumblers may be found in thick & thin styles.

Ice bucket w/ metal handle, 5" pitcher w/ sunflower base.

Salt & pepper shakers in 2 colors. *Courtesy of Michael Rothenberger/Mike's Collectables.*

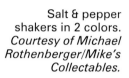

Above: Creamer. *Courtesy of Charlie Diefenderfer.*

Right: Cup & saucer.

7.25" ruffled edge mixing bowl, 5.75" footed tumbler, 5" flat tumbler.

HOBNAIL

(1934-1936 Hocking Glass Company)

The pink luncheon plate with the advertisement was issued in 1934 as a centennial celebration for Liberty Flour, George Urban Milling Co. in Buffalo, New York. This was the first year of Hobnail production.

There are a number of Hobnail variations: pink, crystal (clear), stripes of colors, colored feet on tumblers, etc. Most collectors are looking for pink, and few want more than one specific design. In other words, this is not a pattern commonly mixed and matched.

Don't confuse this pattern with Moonstone. Occasionally Hobnail and Moonstone are mistakenly identified by sellers unfamiliar with Depression Glass.

HOBNAIL	Pink & crystal	Qty
Bowl, 5.5" cereal	10	____
Bowl, 7" salad	10	____
Creamer	10	____
Cup	8	____
Decanter w/stopper	40	____
Goblet, 10 oz. water	10	____
Goblet, 13 oz. iced tea	10	____
Pitcher, 18 oz. milk	35	____
Pitcher, 67 oz.	45	____
Plate, 6" sherbet	8	____
Plate, 8.5" luncheon	10	____
Saucer, same as 6" sherbet plate	8	____
Sherbet	10	____
Sugar	10	____
Tumbler, 1.5 oz. flat whiskey	10	____
Tumbler, 3 oz. ftd. juice	10	____
Tumbler, 5 oz. flat juice	10	____
Tumbler, 5 oz. ftd. cordial	10	____
Tumbler, 9 or 10 oz. flat water	10	____
Tumbler, 15 oz. flat iced tea	12	____

Note: Items with red trim worth 50% more.

Top: 8.5" luncheon plate w/ advertisement ($35).

Center: 8.5" luncheon plate, 3 oz. footed tumbler w/ red trim, sherbet.

Bottom: Sherbet. *Courtesy Of Neil McCurdy-Hoosier Kubboard Glass.*

HOLIDAY

(1947-1949   Jeannette Glass Company)

Jeannette Glass used the Windsor molds from 1932 to create Holiday. Chances are good that if you like either one of these patterns you will like the other. Collectors often fall into three categories: those looking for relatively plain designs, those favoring floral motifs, and those who appreciate a geometric look. Those who prefer geometric designs can be most enthusiastic about Holiday. It is reminiscent of Escher artwork, causing one to stop and ponder "How did they do that?"

Pink is truly the primary color being sought by collectors. The 10.75" console bowl, 10.25" cake plate, 13.75" chop plate, and 6" footed tumbler are the most difficult pieces to find. Most everything else should pose little problem. Some patterns require the patience of Job to collect, but this is not the case with Holiday.

10.5" sandwich tray, 10.25" cake plate, 13.75" chop plate, 9" dinner plate. *Courtesy of Donna L. Cehlarik.*

Back row: 11.25" platter, 6.75" pitcher; *front row:* sugar w/ lid, 4.75" milk pitcher, creamer. *Courtesy of Donna L. Cehlarik.*

HOLIDAY	Pink	Qty
Bowl, 5.25" berry	15	____
Bowl, 7.75" soup	60	____
Bowl, 8.5" berry	40	____
Bowl, 9.5" oval vegetable	30	____
Bowl, 10.75" console	150	____
Butter dish base	25	____
Butter dish lid	50	____
Butter complete	75	____
Candlestick, ea.	75	____
Creamer	12	____
Cup, 2 styles	10	____
Pitcher, 4.75" milk	75	____
Pitcher, 6.75"	50	____
Plate, 6" sherbet	10	____
Plate, 9" dinner	20	____
Plate, 10.25" cake w/3 feet	125	____
Plate, 13.75" chop	125	____
Platter, 11.25"	35	____
Saucer	8	____
Sherbet	10	____
Sugar base	12	____
Sugar lid	38	____
Tray, 10.5" sandwich	25	____
Tumbler, 4" flat	25	____
Tumbler, 4" footed	50	____
Tumbler, 6" footed	175	____

Note: Iridescent pieces 1/2 the value of pink.

Top: *Back row:* butter, 9.5" oval vegetable bowl, sherbet on 6" sherbet plate; *front row:* 5.25" berry bowl, candlesticks, cup & saucer. *Courtesy of Donna L. Cehlarik.*

Center: *Back:* 7.75" soup bowl; *front row:* 8.5" berry bowl, 10.75" console bowl. *Courtesy of Donna L. Cehlarik.*

Bottom: 6" footed tumbler, 4" flat tumbler, 4" footed tumbler. *Courtesy of Donna L. Cehlarik.*

HOMESPUN

(1938-1940 Jeannette Glass Company)

As Homespun was only produced for two years, you may experience some frustration during your hunt. The 4" footed juice tumbler and 6" sherbet plate are quite common. Beyond these two items, the search gets increasingly difficult, culminating with the butter dish and child's tea set. Actually the single most prized piece in this pattern is the cover for the child's tea pot.

Hazel-Atlas manufactured several finely ribbed items that blend nicely with Homespun, but these are not Jeannette pieces. If you enjoy enhancing a collection with additional treasures, you may appreciate knowing about them. The tumblers pose the greatest concern, so if you are a purist, consult the Homespun listing for measurements prior to making a purchase. Both 9 ounce Hazel-Atlas water tumblers are not straight-sided; rather they curve outwardly in the middle and are rimmed at the top with a smooth band of glass. One style is completely ribbed while the other has bands of ribs separated by panels of plain glass. Smaller juice glasses in both of these designs are also available. Hazel-Atlas pitchers that resemble Homespun include an 80 ounce tilt pitcher that is fairly common and a 70 ounce water pitcher whose ribs are in an inverted "U" design. This second pitcher is not easily found. Two additional pitchers include an 80 ounce blown pitcher with an ice lip with clusters of fine ribs in between panels of smooth glass and a ribbed diminutive 20 ounce milk pitcher.

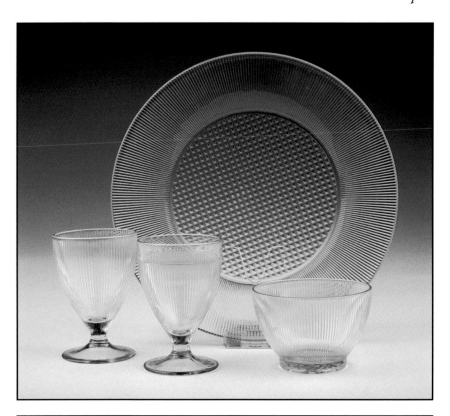

Top: *Back:* 9.25" dinner plate; *front row:* 4" footed juice tumbler w/ ribs extending to the top rim, 4" footed juice tumbler w/ smooth glass at rim, sherbet. *Courtesy of Diefenderfer's Collectibles & Antiques.*

Center: Sugar w/ Jeannette Glass Company lid (there is no Homespun sugar lid), butter, creamer. *Courtesy of Vic & Jean Laermans.*

Bottom: 13" platter/tray w/ tab handles. *Courtesy of Charlie Diefenderfer.*

Right: 5.25" flat iced tea tumbler. *Courtesy of Charlie Diefenderfer.*

Below: 6.5" footed tumbler & 5.75" flat iced tea tumbler, Hazel-Atlas tumbler. *Courtesy of Vic & Jean Laermans.*

HOMESPUN	Pink	Qty
Bowl, 4.5" berry w/tab handles	20	____
Bowl, 5" cereal w/tab handles	35	____
Bowl, 8.25" berry	40	____
Butter dish base	40	____
Butter dish lid	80	____
Butter complete	120	____
Coaster	12	____
Creamer	15	____
Cup	20	____
Plate, 6" sherbet	10	____
Plate, 9.25" dinner	20	____
Platter/tray, 13" w/tab handles	20	____
Saucer	10	____
Sherbet	25	____
Sugar	15	____
Tumbler, 3.75", 7 oz.	25	____
Tumbler, 4" 5 oz. ftd. juice	10	____
Tumbler, 4", 8 oz. flat water w/flare	25	____
Tumbler, 4.25", 9 oz. flat	25	____
Tumbler, 4.75", 9 oz. flat	25	____
Tumbler, 5.25", 12.5 oz. flat iced tea	35	____
Tumbler, 5.75", 13.5 oz. flat iced tea	35	____
Tumbler, 6.25", 15 oz. w/foot	40	____
Tumbler, 6.5" 15 oz. w/foot	40	____

Note: Crystal items worth 1/2 value of pink.

HOMESPUN CHILD'S TEA SET	Pink	Crystal	Qty
Cup	40	20	____
Plate	20	10	____
Saucer	25	10	____
Tea pot	60		____
Tea pot cover	150		____
Complete set			
Pink 14 items	550		____
Crystal 12 items		160	____

Homespun child's tea set: tea pot w/ cover, plate, cup & saucer.

HORSESHOE
(1930-1933 Indiana Glass Company)

The majority of collectors ask for this pattern by name rather than number, so to simplify matters we have elected to list this pattern by its nickname rather than by the accurate name of "Number 612."

Seekers of green Horseshoe far outnumber yellow. Yellow is more difficult to find than green, and there were slightly fewer yellow items produced. The pure, bright yellow color is so attractive that it is featured on the cover of *Mauzy's Comprehensive Handbook of Depression Glass Prices*.

Horseshoe is particularly susceptible to two types of damage. The first of these is scratching. It is difficult to find any plate that has not suffered knife damage. It behooves you to hold up to the light any Horseshoe plate that you may be considering for purchase. Finding a perfectly unscathed piece will be next to impossible, but you may want to pass on a plate that has a myriad of criss-crossed scratches. The second damage to consider involves the actual manufacture of these pieces. Horseshoe was molded with a minute rim of extra glass along the outer edge of many pieces. When running a fingernail along this rim, one should expect to find some nicking here as it was unavoidable. The dings to this extra glass do not represent the same kind of damage and chipping that would negatively impact the value of other Depression Glass patterns.

Back row: 9.5" luncheon plate, 10.5" grill plate, 9.5" bowl; *front row:* 9 oz. footed tumbler, cup & saucer, sugar, creamer. *Courtesy of Diefenderfer's Collectibles & Antiques*.

Back: 3-part relish; *middle row:* 8.5" vegetable bowl, cup & saucer, 7.5" salad bowl; *front row:* 6.5" cereal bowl, 4.5" berry bowl. *Courtesy of Vic & Jean Laermans.*

HORSESHOE	Green	Yellow	Qty
Bowl, 4.5" berry	30	30	____
Bowl, 6.5" cereal	35	35	____
Bowl, 7.5" salad	30	30	____
Bowl, 8.5" vegetable	40	40	____
Bowl, 9.5"	50	50	____
Bowl, 10.5" oval vegetable	40	40	____
Butter dish base	trtp*		____
Butter dish lid	trtp*		____
Butter complete	trtp*		____
Candy dish, lid has design, 3-part base is plain (may be in metal holder)	300		____
Creamer	20	25	____
Cup	12	15	____
Pitcher	400	500	____
Plate, 6" sherbet	10	10	____
Plate, 8.25" salad	15	15	____
Plate, 9.5" luncheon	15	15	____
Plate, 10.5" grill	125	175	____
Plate, 11.5" sandwich	25	35	____
Platter, 10.75"	30	40	____
Relish, 3-part	30	45	____
Saucer	10	10	____
Sherbet	18	18	____
Sugar	20	25	____
Tumbler, 4.25" flat	200		____
Tumbler, 4.75" flat	200		____
Tumbler, 9 oz. w/foot	30	40	____
Tumbler, 12 oz. w/foot	200	200	____

Note: Pink candy dish, $200
*trtp = too rare to price

9 oz. footed tumbler, 12 oz. footed tumbler, pitcher. *Courtesy of Vic & Jean Laermans.*

Butter. *Courtesy of Debora & Paul Torsiello, Debzie's Glass.*

INDIANA CUSTARD
(1933-1935 Indiana Glass company)

Herbert Moller submitted the patent for Indiana Custard in 1933. It was manufactured only in ivory, a color that is presently enjoying a resurgence of popularity. Because this pattern is becoming more popular and is already not easily found, one could realistically expect the prices to increase.

In 1957, Indiana Glass Company slightly altered Moller's design and manufactured a line of milk glass named Orange Blossom.

Creamer & sugar w/ lid. *Courtesy of Vic & Jean Laermans.*

INDIANA CUSTARD	Ivory	Qty
Bowl, 5.5" berry	20	____
Bowl, 6.5" cereal	30	____
Bowl, 7.5" soup	40	____
Bowl, 9" berry	50	____
Bowl, 9.5" oval vegetable	40	____
Butter dish base	20	____
Butter dish lid	40	____
Butter complete	60	____
Creamer, 3.5"	20	____
Cup	40	____
Plate, 6" sherbet	12	____
Plate, 7.5" salad	25	____
Plate, 8.75" luncheon	25	____
Plate, 9.75" dinner	45	____
Platter, 12" x 9"	60	____
Saucer	10	____
Sherbet	125	____
Sugar base, 3.5"	20	____
Sugar lid	30	____

12" x 9" platter, 9.5" oval vegetable bowl. *Courtesy of Staci & Jeff Shuck/Gray Goose Antiques.*

IRIS

(1928-1932, iridescent in 1950 & 1969, white in 1970   Jeannette Glass Company)

Iris is the official flower of several southern states enhancing its collectibility, and crystal (clear) and iridescent Iris are equally popular and very much in demand, especially in the South.

Beaded rim bowls pose a great deal of problems. Not only do the tiny beads of glass suffer damage, but the rim next to the beads also has a tendency to chip. One needs to be extremely thorough when examining a beaded rim bowl.

Identifying Iris goblets has been a frustrating experience for many collectors, so we hope this presentation brings clarity to the subject. Providing diameter measurements should simplify determining which goblet is which.

Two items worth noting are the pitcher and 6.5" tumbler which may have irises on the feet. It took countless attempts for our photographer to capture the subtle raised design of an iris on the foot of these tumblers. It was confirmed for us that several pitchers were also made the same way.

Production of Iris continued into the 1970s, so not every piece found will be from 1928. Occasionally the question may arise as to the age of a particular item. There really is no way of knowing on most pieces. However, here is some pertinent information regarding the candy jar base: the newer feet are missing lines or rays that are present on the feet of older candy jars. Keep in mind these newer bottoms are almost thirty years old now.

Variations in vase colors are not rare and not particularly popular with today's collectors. Likewise, the red and gold Iris from 1946 is not in demand. Collectors primarily are looking for either crystal or iridescent glassware to complete a collection.

Left: Detail of pattern. *Courtesy of Carol L. Ellis.*

Below: *Back row:* pitcher, candlesticks; *front row:* 4.25" wine goblet, sherbet on 5.5" sherbet plate, 6" tumbler w/ foot. *Courtesy of Carol L. Ellis.*

9" dinner plate, 8" luncheon plate, 5.5" sherbet plate, 11.75" sandwich plate. *Courtesy of Lucille & Joseph Palmieri.*

Back row: 7.5" coupe soup, 9" vase; front: candlestick, cup & saucer, 4" flat tumbler, demitasse cup & saucer. *Courtesy of Lucille & Joseph Palmieri.*

Back row: butter, sherbet, 9.5" pitcher; front row: sugar w/ lid, creamer, candy jar w/ lid, coaster. *Courtesy of Lucille & Joseph Palmieri.*

Back row: 5" sauce bowl w/ ruffled rim, 9.5" salad bowl w/ ruffled rim; front: 11" fruit bowl w/ flat rim, 11.5" fruit bowl w/ ruffled rim. *Courtesy of Lucille & Joseph Palmieri.*

IRIS	Crystal	Iridescent	Qty
Bowl, 4.5" berry w/beaded rim	60	30	____
Bowl, 5" sauce w/ruffled edge	15	30	____
Bowl, 5" cereal w/straight side	145		____
Bowl, 7.5" coupe soup	175	75	____
Bowl, 8" berry w/ beaded rim	100	40	____
Bowl, 9.5" salad w/ ruffled edge	15	10	____
Bowl, 11" fruit w/ flat rim	75		____
Bowl, 11.5" fruit w/ruffled edge	15	10	____
Butter dish base	15	15	____
Butter dish lid	35	35	____
Butter complete	50	50	____
Candlesticks, ea.	25	25	____
Candy jar w/lid	225		____
Coaster	140		____
Creamer	15	15	____
Cup, coffee	20	18	____
Cup, demitasse	50	200	____
Goblet, 4" wine		35	____
Goblet, 4.25" wine, 3 oz. 2" diameter	20		____
Goblet, 4.25" cocktail, 4 oz. 2.75" diameter	30		____
Goblet, 5.75" 4 oz. wine 2.25" diameter	30	225	____
Goblet, 5.75" 8 oz. water 3" diameter	30	225	____
Lamp shade, 11.5"	75		____
Pitcher, 9.5"	40	50	____
Pitcher, 9.5" w/iris on foot	trtp*		____
Plate, 5.5" sherbet	20	15	____
Plate, 8" luncheon	130		____
Plate, 9" dinner	65	50	____
Plate, 11.75" sandwich	35	35	____
Saucer, coffee	12	12	____
Saucer, demitasse	150	250	____
Sherbet, 2.5" w/foot	30	18	____
Sherbet, 4" w/stem 3.5" diameter	30	250	____
Sugar base	15	15	____
Sugar lid	20	25	____
Tumbler, 4" flat	160		____
Tumbler, 6" w/foot	20	20	____
Tumbler, 6.5" w/foot	40		____
Tumbler, 6.5" w/iris on foot	200		____
Vase, 9"	30	20	____

Note: Items in green/pink, $125 each. Lamp shade frosted in pink, blue, or white, $65. Demitasse cups & saucers in other colors too rare to price.
*trtp = too rare to price

Back: 11.5" nut bowl; front: 9.5" nut bowl, 11.5" fruit bowl. (Note: fruit bowls have 4 slots for knives; nut bowls have holes for a nut cracker and 6 picks.) *Courtesy of Lucille & Joseph Palmieri.*

8" berry bowl w/ beaded rim, 4.5" berry bowl w/ beaded rim, 5" cereal bowl. *Courtesy of Lucille & Joseph Palmieri.*

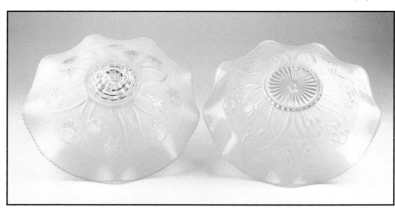

11.5" lamp shade w/ scalloped edge & 11.5" lampshade w/ smooth edge. *Courtesy of Lucille & Joseph Palmieri.*

Water goblet with diameter of 3"/height of 5.75", wine goblet with diameter of 2.25"/ height of 5.75", wine goblet with diameter of 2"/height of 4.25", cocktail goblet with diameter of 2.75"/height of 4.25", sherbet with diameter of 3.5"/height of 4". *Courtesy of Lucille & Joseph Palmieri.*

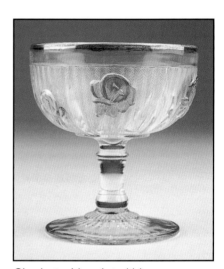

Sherbet with painted blossoms.

Detail of iris on foot of 6.5" tumbler. (Note: rare, similar design on foot of 9.5" pitcher.) *Courtesy of Lucille & Joseph Palmieri.*

6" tumbler w/ foot, 6.5" tumbler w/ iris on foot, 6.5" tumbler w/ foot. *Courtesy of Lucille & Joseph Palmieri.*

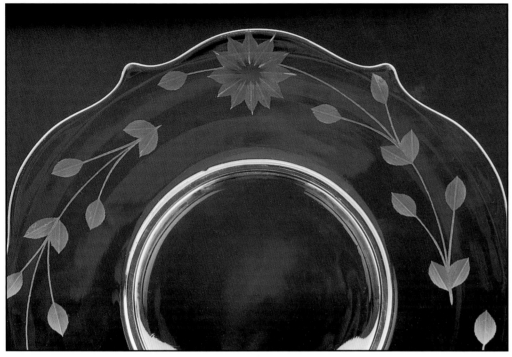

Detail of pattern. *Courtesy of Connie & Bill Hartzell.*

JUBILEE
(1930 Lancaster Glass Company)

Attention Jubilee collectors, we need your help! If you have a complete collection in pink or yellow we would love to take some pictures. In the meantime this is what we have!

There are many etched patterns of Depression glass. Jubilee is easy to identify because the flowers have twelve petals. The only exceptions are the candy jar and sherbet: both have eleven petals.

We spoke to a collector of pink Jubilee who stated she had the following pieces: a pitcher, a center-handled tray for the creamer and sugar, and a salt and pepper on a center-handled tray. We have not seen these and were unable to get any photographs, so all we can do is pass this along and see what information or items others can share.

6" footed water tumbler. *Courtesy of Deborah D. Albright.*

Back row: 11" sandwich plate, 8.75" luncheon plate; *front:* cup & saucer. *Courtesy of Deborah D. Albright.*

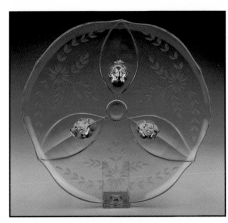

Left: 13.5" salad tray w/ 3 feet. *Courtesy of Diefenderfer's Collectibles & Antiques.*

Below: 11" sandwich tray w/ center handle. *Courtesy of Diefenderfer's Collectibles & Antiques.*

JUBILEE	Yellow	Pink	Qty
Bowl, 8" w/3 feet	250	350	____
Bowl, 9" fruit w/handles	150		____
Bowl, 11.5" fruit (flat)	175	225	____
Bowl, 11.5" w/3 feet	300	300	____
Bowl, 11.5" w/3 feet (curves inward)	250		____
Bowl, 13" w/3 feet	250	300	____
Candlestick, ea.	100	120	____
Candy jar w/lid (only 11 petals on this piece)	400	500	____
Cheese & cracker set	300	350	____
Creamer, 3.25"	25	35	____
Cup	15	45	____
Goblet, 4", 1 oz. cordial	300		____
Goblet, 4.75" 4 oz. oyster cocktail	100		____
Goblet, 4.75" 3 oz. cocktail	200		____
Goblet, 5.5" 7 oz. champagne or sherbet	125		____
Goblet, 7.5" 11 oz. water	200		____
Mayonnaise, under plate & spoon	300	400	____
Plate, 7" salad	15	30	____
Plate, 8.75" luncheon	15	40	____
Plate, 11" sandwich w/2 handles	50	70	____
Saucer, 2 styles	5	15	____
Sherbet (only 11 petals on this piece)	100		____
Sugar, 3.25"	25	35	____
Tumbler, 5" ftd. juice	120		____
Tumbler, 6" ftd. water	40	80	____
Tumbler, 6.25" ftd. iced tea	175		____
Tray, 11" sandwich w/center handle	225	225	____
Tray, 13.5" salad w/3 feet	250	250	____
Vase, 12"	450	650	____

Note: Crystal items worth 1/2 yellow prices.

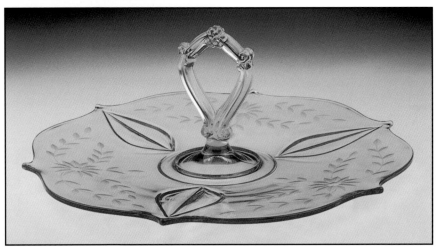

Left: Creamer & sugar on go-along tray. *Courtesy of Vic & Jean Laermans.*

Below: Mayonnaise w/ under plate & spoon, sugar, 11" sandwich tray w/ center handle. *Courtesy of Debora & Paul Torsiello, Debzie's Glass.*

Back: 9" vegetable bowl; *front:* candlesticks, cup, 4.5" sauce bowl, 4" tumbler.

Above: *Back:* 8.5" salad plate; *front row:* 3.5" mayonnaise compote, 5" cereal bowl, sugar, creamer. *Courtesy of Vic & Jean Laermans.*

Right: Sugar, cup & saucer, creamer. *Courtesy of Vic & Jean Laermans.*

KATY
(1930s Imperial Glass Company)

Imperial Glass Company created a number of pieces that resemble Katy. Similar geometric textured, lacy-edged opalescent glass was produced as "Sugar Cane Line" and "Tradition Pattern." There were also numerous Imperial console sets with the same general look as Katy. Many Katy collectors are content to add these to their displays.

Although this is a relatively short pattern, everything is available to set a table and serve a meal. This is one pattern that seems to look even better with every piece added, and a table full of Katy is magnificent!

Katy collectors know that this is a pattern rarely seen in any quantity. One can find a piece here and a piece there, but it is unlikely one will stumble upon a stack of plates or a selection of bowls. The Internet has been an excellent resource when searching for this pattern, so if you are at all technically inclined just click and go!

KATY	All opalescent colors	Qty
Bowl, basket	250	____
Bowl, +/- 4.5" sauce	40	____
Bowl, 5" cereal	40	____
Bowl, 5.5"	40	____
Bowl, 5.75"	40	____
Bowl, 7" soup	100	____
Bowl, 9" vegetable	120	____
Bowl, 11" 2-part oval	120	____
Bowl, 11" oval	165	____
Candlestick, ea.	100	____
Creamer	40	____
Cup	50	____
Mayonnaise complete w/under plate & spoon	160	____
Plate, 6.5" bread & butter	20	____
Plate, 8.5" salad	35	____
Plate, 10" dinner	100	____
Plate, 12" cake plate	80	____
Platter, 13"	200	____
Saucer	20	____
Sugar	50	____
Tidbit, 8" & 10" plates	150	____
Tumbler, 4"	75	____

LA FURISTE

(1920s-1930s Lotus Glass Company)

Consider the inclusion of La Furiste much like our fishing expedition. We were only able to locate limited information on this pattern, so we have cast out a line. While working on this book one of the contributors had this grouping in their collection. If you have more pieces or insight, please get in touch with us.

Ohio based Lotus Glass Company produced La Furiste in the 1920s and 1930s. Lotus made no glass, instead they embellished it. Overlays, etchings, and colors were added to blanks received from glass manufacturers. The gold was often 24 Karat and the silver was Sterling.

La Furiste, etching No. 0907, was available in amber, crystal (clear), green, and rose (pink). The border may have included a 22 Karat embellishment. Items listed come from Lotus catalog pages, and prices are imperfect as this is a first attempt at this pattern. Input is welcome and invited!

Back: 12.5" x 10" platter w/ 2 open handles; *front row:* 5.5" candlesticks, sugar, creamer, 10.5" muffin plate w/ 2 handles that turn up. *Courtesy of Bob & Cindy Bentley.*

LA FURISTE	Rose, Green, Amber, Crystal	Qty	LA FURISTE (Cont.)	Rose, Green, Amber, Crystal	Qty
Bowl, 7.75" x 5.5" rose bowl w/3 feet	65	____	Plate, 6" bread & butter	20	____
Bowl, 8.5" x 11" oval	75	____	Plate, 7.5" salad	25	____
Bowl, 8.75" x 5.5" rose bowl	65	____	Plate, 8" salad	25	____
Bowl, 9" bell w/ handles (8-sided)	75	____	Plate, 9" dinner	25	____
Bowl, 10" nut w/center handle (8-sided)	85	____	Plate, 10" cake w/center handle	35	____
Bowl, 10" w/rolled edge	75	____	Plate, 10.5" muffin w/2 handles that turn up	35	____
Bowl, 10.5" x 4.5" celery (boat shaped)	80	____	Plate, 11" sandwich w/2 open handles	35	____
Bowl, 11.25" w/rolled edge w/3 feet	85	____	Plate, 12" service (8-sided)	50	____
Bowl, 12" crimped w/3 feet	75	____	Plate, 12" pastry w/2 handles	45	____
Bowl, 12" flared rim w/3 feet	75	____	Platter, 12.5" x 10" w/2 open handles (8-sided)	50	____
Bowl, 12" x 3.5" w/rolled edge	85	____	Relish, 6" w/3 sections & lid	45	____
Bowl, 12.25" x 4.5" celery w/2 handles	75	____	Saucer	15	____
Bowl, 12.5" x 3" w/flared rim	75	____	Sherbet, 6.5 oz. high (tall stem)	40	____
Bowl, 13" w/flared rim	80	____	Sherbet, 6.5 oz. low (short stem)	40	____
Candlestick, ea. 3.5"	50	____	Stem, 1.5 oz. cordial	45	____
Candlestick, ea. 5.5"	55	____	Stem, 2.75 oz. wine	45	____
Cheese & Cracker	85	____	Stem, 3.5 oz. cocktail	45	____
Comport, 7"	60	____	Sugar	40	____
Creamer	40	____	Tumbler, 2.5 oz. whiskey w/foot	40	____
Cup	30	____	Tumbler, 6 oz. w/foot	40	____
Decanter w/stopper	175	____	Tumbler, 10 oz. w/foot	40	____
Fruit Salad w/foot (similar to a sherbet in other patterns)	40	____	Tumbler, 12 oz. iced tea w/foot	45	____
Goblet, 9 oz.	45	____	Whipped cream, 3 pieces, (comportunder plate, & spoon)	85	____
Ice tub, 4" w/2 handles	65	____			
Pitcher	150	____			

Salt & pepper. *Courtesy of Michael Rothenberger/Mike's Collectables.*

LAKE COMO
(1935-1937   Anchor Hocking Glass Company)

There aren't a great number of people looking for Lake Como. However, a current interest in Fire-King has led to an increased appreciation for all Anchor Hocking glass. One could deduce that eventually some Fire-King enthusiasts will move into collecting Lake Como. Like Fire-King dinnerware, with Lake Como there are only a few options: just enough to set a table and barely serve the meal. Lake Como does have two cups and two saucers. The St. Denis cup and saucer is the same mold used in the Fire-King Breakfast Set and the Fire-King 1700 Line.

Glassware used for Lake Como is plain white Vitrock with blue embellishments. For more information, see the Vitrock pattern.

Back: 7.25" salad plate; *front row:* St. Denis cup & saucer, sugar.

11" platter. *Courtesy of Charlie Diefenderfer.*

LAKE COMO	White w/ decorations	Qty
Bowl, 6" cereal	35	____
Bowl, 9.75" vegetable	80	____
Bowl, flat soup	120	____
Creamer	35	____
Cup	35	____
Cup, St. Denis	35	____
Plate, 7.25" salad	25	____
Plate, 9.25" dinner	40	____
Platter, 11"	85	____
Salt & pepper	55	____
Saucer	15	____
Saucer, St. Denis	15	____
Sugar	35	____

LAUREL
(1930s McKee Glass Company)

The recent hunger for Jade-ite has not be limited to Anchor Hocking Fire-King. Jeannette's Jade-ite is desirable, as is McKee's. Jade-ite Laurel prices have really increased as the demand for Jade-ite has escalated. If you already own Jade-ite Laurel, congratulations in your forethought; your Depression Glass has become a most profitable investment.

McKee has provided some interesting pieces in this pattern such as 6" and 10.5" three-footed bowls, a cheese dish with a lid, and a 3.75" wine goblet. These items are not available in any Fire-King lines.

Jade-ite is currently the favorite color of Laurel, but white opal and French ivory are also popular. Poudre blue is extremely rare and very much in demand by collectors looking for unique and wonderful examples of Depression Glass. It will be very difficult to assemble any quantities in blue.

6" bowl showing 3 feet on bottom, shaker, 6" sherbet plate, creamer, sugar. *Courtesy of Connie & Bill Hartzell.*

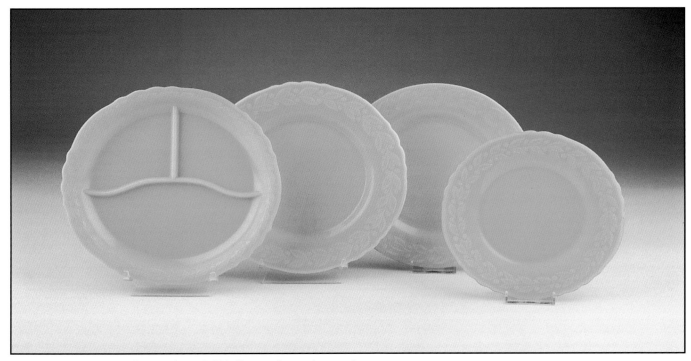

Back: 10.75" platter; *front row:* cheese dish w/ lid, candlestick, cup & saucer. *Courtesy of Connie & Bill Hartzell.*

9.25" grill plate, 9.25" dinner plate, 9.25" dinner plate w/ smooth rim, 7.5" salad plate. *Courtesy of Connie & Bill Hartzell.*

Right: 3.75" wine. *Courtesy of Staci & Jeff Shuck/Gray Goose Antiques.*

Far right: *Back row:* 11" bowl, 9.75" oval vegetable bowl; *front row:* 6" cereal bowl, 4.75" berry bowl. *Courtesy of Connie & Bill Hartzell.*

Back row: 10.75" platter, 9.25" dinner plate; *front row:* cup & saucer, creamer. *Courtesy of Vic & Jean Laermans.*

LAUREL	Jade & Poudre blue	Other colors	Qty
Bowl, 4.75" berry	15	8	____
Bowl, 6" cereal	25	12	____
Bowl, 6" w/3 feet	20	20	____
Bowl, 7.75" soup	75	40	____
Bowl, 9" berry	45	25	____
Bowl, 9.75" oval vegetable	50	25	____
Bowl, 10.5" w/3 feet	65	40	____
Bowl, 11"	70	35	____
Candlestick, ea.	30	20	____
Cheese dish w/lid	60	45	____
Creamer, 3" & 4"	35	15	____
Cup	20	10	____
Plate, 6" sherbet	10	8	____
Plate, 7.5" salad	18	12	____
Plate, 9.25" dinner	25	15	____
Plate, 9.25" grill	25	15	____
Platter, 10.75"	45	30	____
Salt & pepper	150	75	____
Saucer	8	5	____
Sherbet	20	12	____
Sugar, 3" & 4"	35	15	____
Tumbler, 4.5", 9 oz.	65	40	____
Tumbler, 5", 12 oz.		80	____
Wine, 3.75"	60	40	____

Back row: 9.25" dinner plate, creamer; *front row:* candlesticks, 4.75" berry bowl, cup & saucer, shaker.

LAUREL CHILD'S TEA SET	Ivory	Decorated rim	Scotty on Jade	Scotty on Ivory	Qty
Creamer	35	50	150	120	___
Cup	30	40	100	75	___
Plate	20	25	100	75	___
Saucer	12	15	75	50	___
Sugar	35	50	150	120	___
Complete 14-piece set	318	370	1400	1040	___

Child's tea set, Scotty on ivory: creamer, sugar, plate, cup & saucer.

LINCOLN INN
(1928-1929 Fenton Art Glass Company)

Lincoln Inn seems to be out . . . there . . . somewhere . . . but we couldn't find much. Yes, this is a plea for the opportunity to photograph a collection, so get in touch with us if you can bring yours "inn."

This is a sophisticated pattern with an intriguing design. The stems have a series of bulges of glass reminiscent of fine crystal stemware. Colors range from pink, green, ruby, Royal Blue, and even to Jade-ite. There are many offerings, but we have had a difficult time locating them.

LINCOLN INN	All Colors	Qty
Ashtray	25	___
Bonbon, handles square or oval	20	___
Bowl, finger	20	___
Bowl, 5" fruit	15	___
Bowl, 6" cereal	18	___
Bowl, 6" crimped	18	___
Bowl, 9"	30	___
Bowl, 9.25" footed	75	___
Bowl, 10.5" footed	65	___
Bowl, 1-handled olive	18	___
Comport plate	35	___
Comport, shallow	35	___
Creamer	30	___
Cup	20	___
Goblet, cocktail/wine	30	___
Goblet, water	30	___
Mint, flat	30	___
Mint, oval	30	___
Nut	30	___
Pitcher, 7.25"	1000	___
Plate to line finger bowl	10	___
Plate, 6" bread & butter	10	___
Plate, 8" salad	15	___
Plate, 9.25" dinner	45	___
Plate, 12"	40	___
Salt & pepper	350	___
Sandwich server w/ center handle	200	___
Saucer	8	___
Sherbet, 4.5" cone	20	___
Sherbet, 4.75" w/stem	25	___
Sugar	30	___
Tumbler, 4 oz. ftd. juice	30	___
Tumbler, 7 oz. ftd. water	30	___
Tumbler, 9 oz. flat water	30	___
Tumbler, 12 oz. ftd. ice tea	50	___
Tumbler, 12 oz. flat high ball high ball	30	___
Vase, 9.75"	150	___
Vase, 12"	175	___

Note: Black & Jade-ite salt & pepper, $500 each pair. Add 30% for items with fruit design pressed into center.

Above: Sugar, jade-ite salt & pepper, sugar. *Courtesy of Vic & Jean Laermans.*

Left: 8" salad plate. *Courtesy of Neil McCurdy - Hoosier Kubboard Glass.*

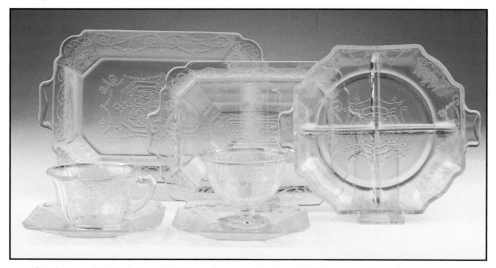

Back row: 11.5" platter, 9.75" oval vegetable bowl, 8" 4-part relish; *front:* cup & saucer, sherbet on 5.5" sherbet plate. *Courtesy of Brad & Tammy James.*

LORAIN

(1929-1932 Indiana Glass Company)

Green Lorain is more common, more popular, and less expensive than yellow. However, there are many loyal collectors of yellow. As with Horseshoe and Florentine No. 1 and 2, Lorain yellow is bright and cheerful.

Lorain plates were manufactured with a line of extra glass along the top surface near the outer edge. Naturally, this glass received bumps and is often nicked simply because it extends from the plate. Plates are much more available than bowls as reflected in the prices.

Collectors of Lorain are among the most resilient of any seekers of Depression Glass. They assume each dealer they meet won't have any Lorain but continue to search relentlessly anyway. Time and time again they optimistically inquire about their pattern and rejoice (often visibly!) when they have the good fortune of meeting up with some pieces.

Back row: 10.25" dinner plate, 8.25" luncheon plate, 7.75" salad plate; *front row:* 4.75" tumbler, creamer, sugar. *Courtesy of Brad & Tammy James.*

LORAIN	Green	Yellow	Qty
Bowl, 6" cereal	60	75	____
Bowl, 7.25" salad	50	60	____
Bowl, 8" deep berry	120	175	____
Bowl, 9.75" oval vegetable	50	60	____
Creamer	20	30	____
Cup	15	20	____
Plate, 5.5" sherbet	10	14	____
Plate, 7.75" salad	15	20	____
Plate, 8.25" luncheon	20	35	____
Plate, 10.25" dinner	75	100	____
Platter, 11.5"	35	55	____
Relish, 8", 4-part	25	40	____
Saucer	7	8	____
Sherbet	28	35	____
Sugar	20	30	____
Tumbler, 4.75"	25	35	____

Note: Crystal prices 1/2 of yellow, except for Snack Tray with colored trim, $50.

11.5" platter, 6" cereal bowl. *Courtesy of Diefenderfer's Collectibles & Antiques.*

MADRID
Reproduced
(1932-1938 Federal Glass Company)

Of all the patterns manufactured in amber, Madrid is among the most popular. Pieces needed to set a table and serve a meal are easily found and relatively affordable. There are elusive items such as the ashtray, gravy boat, and tray, and Lazy Susan. The 10.5" dinner plate is also difficult to find. However, it is reasonable to say that amber Madrid can be assembled with less frustration and a smaller investment than many other patterns.

Green Madrid is harder to find than amber. The cups, saucers, and sherbets are abundant, but additional items become increasingly challenging to locate. Pink is seen less than green. The 11" flared out console bowl is common and very popular with general collectors of pink Depression Glass who are often drawn to its unique, low shape. Other pieces of pink are more difficult to find. Blue Madrid is the most elusive color of all, which is reflected in the value of these items.

There are two Madrid sherbets. The 2.75" cone-shaped sherbet made with the Sylvan (Parrot) mold is extremely common. The 2.25" squatty sherbet is much harder to find. One could easily stumble upon fifty cone-shaped sherbets for each squatty sherbet.

This brings us to another interesting point regarding Madrid. As with several other Depression Glass patterns, Madrid came from previously used molds. Federal Glass Company manufactured Sylvan (Parrot) in 1931 and 1932. Although Sylvan is an extremely popular pattern today, Federal executives were dissatisfied with it, believing Sylvan had too much undecorated glass. Plain glass would show any of the inevitable scratching that occurred from use and these decision makers were concerned that homemakers would be unhappy with the long-term performance of the pattern. So, the directive came for the designers to develop a busier design that would fill the plate, thereby providing camouflage for potential scratching. Madrid resulted, and there are few patterns busier than Madrid.

Amber Madrid was reproduced in 1976. New collectors sometimes express concern over this, but there is no mystery to identifying reproduction pieces. Look for a "76" worked into the design near the outer edge of reproduced amber Madrid items. The photograph showing old and new Madrid side by side demonstrates the apparent differences: both in the "76" and the color variance. There is an *R* after any listed item that has been reproduced, and you can check the reproduction information provided to easily recognize new Madrid.

Above: *Back row:* 11.5" platter, 10.5" dinner plate; *front row:* 7" soup bowl, 6" sherbet plate, cup, 5.5" flat iced tea tumbler, 5.5" juice pitcher. *Courtesy of Corky & Becky Evans.*

Right: Common 2.75" sherbet (similar to Sylvan), more elusive 2.25" squatty sherbet.

Gravy boat on tray/under platter. *Courtesy of Corky & Becky Evans.*

Sugar & creamer. *Courtesy of Neil MᶜCurdy - Hoosier Kubboard Glass.*

Above: 8.75" luncheon plate, 6" sherbet plate, creamer.

Left: 5" hot dish coaster.

MADRID	Amber	Green	Pink	Blue	Qty
Ashtray	225	225			____
Bowl, 4.75" cream soup	25				____
Bowl, 5" dessert	10	10	10	35	____
Bowl, 7" soup	20	25			____
Bowl, 8" salad	20	22			____
Bowl, 9.25" berry	25		30		____
Bowl, 9.5" deep salad	40				____
Bowl, 10" oval vegetable	20	20	20	50	____
Bowl, 11" flared out console	20		20		____
Butter dish base	30	40			____
Butter dish lid *R*	50	60			____
Butter complete	80	100			____
Candlestick, ea. *R*	15		15		____
Cookie jar/lid	55		50		____
Creamer *R*	20	20		35	____
Cup	8	10	10	20	____
Gravy boat w/ 6" x 8.25" tray	3000				____
Hot dish coaster, 5"	75	75			____
Hot dish coaster w/indent	75	75			____
Jam dish, 7"	30	40		50	____
Jello mold, 2" high	18				____
Lazy Susan, wooden w/glass cold cut coasters	trtp*				____
Pitcher, 5.5", 36 oz., juice	50				____
Pitcher, 8", 60 oz., square w/applied handle		200		250	____
Pitcher, 8", 60 oz., square w/molded handle	50	150	50	200	____
Pitcher, 8", 80 oz., no ice lip	85	250			____
Pitcher, 8.5", 80 oz., with ice lip	85	250			____
Plate, 6" sherbet	7	7	5	15	____
Plate, 7.5" salad	15	15	12	25	____
Plate, 8.75" luncheon	10	15	12	25	____
Plate, 10.25" relish	25	25	18		____
Plate, 10.5" dinner	60	60		100	____
Plate, 10.5" grill *R*	10	20			____
Plate, 11.25" cake	20		20		____
Platter for under gravy boat	800				____
Platter, 11.5"	18	20	18	35	____
Salt & pepper, footed	140	145		175	____
Salt & pepper, flat *R*	50	75			____
Saucer	5	7	7	12	____
Sherbet, 2.75" cone (Similar to Sylvan sherbet)	5	12		18	____
Sherbet, 2.25", squatty	30				____
Sugar base *R*	20	20		35	____
Sugar lid	65	65		200	____
Tumbler, 4", 5 oz., juice, flat	18	35		45	____
Tumbler, 4", 5 oz., footed	30	45			____
Tumbler, 4.25", 9 oz., water, flat	18	25	20	40	____
Tumbler, 5.5", 12 oz., iced tea, 2 styles, flat	25	35		45	____
Tumbler, 5.5", 10 oz., footed	35	50			____

*trtp = too rare to price

Reproduction information: Amber Madrid that is just too dark and has "76" worked into the design is newly produced. Pink Madrid that is too pale is not old. Beware of the following items in pink: butter, shaker, pedestal cake plate, tumblers, goblets, vase, a 2-part plate, and candlesticks with extra glass in the holes to secure a taper in position. Teal is a new color. Any paneled items are new; old Madrid tumblers are round without "sides." Butter dish lid: old knob has horizontal seam mold, new mold line is vertical. Candlesticks: new have glass ridges to grasp a candle, old are smooth inside. Grill plates: old have 3 sections, new have 2 sections. Shakers: Short, chunky shakers are new. Creamer: new spouts are made by applying extra glass, old spouts are formed below top rim. Sugar & creamer: old handles form pointed pear shape where they meet the sides of the object. New handles meet and form an oval with no points.

Note: Crystal hot dish coaster, $40, 8" pitcher, $175. Iridescent items same price as Amber.

Above: *Back:* gravy boat on 6" x 8.25" tray/under platter, 8.5" pitcher w/ no ice lip; *front:* salt & pepper, 5" dessert bowl, creamer, sugar w/ lid. *Courtesy of Corky & Becky Evans.*

Right: Reproduction and original issue 10" oval vegetable bowls. (Note: reproduction is darker and has "76" worked into the design at the top of the item near the rim.)

MANHATTAN

(1939-1941 Anchor Hocking Glass Company)

Manhattan and Iris are the two most popular patterns of crystal Depression Glass. People in their twenties and thirties have discovered the Deco look of Manhattan and are collecting it with energy and devotion. Dealers know that this is a pattern hard to keep in stock.

Care must be taken when buying bowls in this pattern. One can find them throughout most antique malls, and sometimes with very reasonable prices. Manhattan bowls are often nicked along the rim and sellers who are unfamiliar with Depression Glass may not take note of this. Pitchers also require special attention as there may be a crack where the handle was applied. To really determine the condition of a pitcher hold it up to a light and twist and turn it carefully. While we're discussing pitchers we have learned that a Jadeite Manhattan pitcher exists! We have spoken to dealers who have seen it and mentioned a $3,500 selling price. We have chosen to value it as too rare to price as there seems to be only one in existence.

The sherbet style ashtray with a metal cover was created utilizing the center relish insert. "Center relish insert ashtray"

seemed too cumbersome of a name, so we have presented it with the name coined by the collector/owner. Note the notches in the glass allowing the metal cover to fit.

Pink is rarely seen beyond the creamer, sugar, and open candy dish with three feet. We have never owned a pink dinner plate. While working on this book we networked with many fine dealers and none of them have ever had one either. Where are they?

5.75" comport, 8" vase, 24 oz. tilted pitcher. *Courtesy of Michael & Kathleen Jones.*

Sugar, 10.25" dinner plate, tumbler. *Courtesy of Michael & Kathleen Jones.*

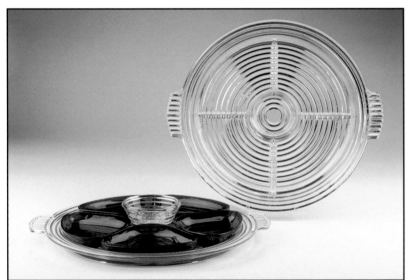

14" relish tray (no sections) w/ 5 outer ruby inserts and center insert having straight-sided base, 14" relish w/ 5 sections. *Courtesy of Michael & Kathleen Jones.*

Back: sherbet w/ bubble foot; *front row:* 5.25" cereal bowl, candlestick, cup.

MANHATTAN	Crystal	Pink	Ruby	Qty
Ashtray, sherbet style	35			____
Ashtray, 4" round	15			____
Ashtray, 4.5" square	18			____
Bowl, 4.5" sauce w/handles	10			____
Bowl, 5.25" berry w/handles	20	25		____
Bowl, 5.25" cereal	50	100		____
Bowl, 7.5" berry	15			____
Bowl, 8" w/handles	20	25		____
Bowl, 9" salad	25			____
Bowl, 9.5" fruit, w/foot & 2 open handles	45	45		____
Candlestick, 4.5" square, ea.	8			____
Candy dish, open w/3 feet		15		____
Coaster	15			____
Comport, 5.75"	35	45		____
Creamer	15	15		____
Cup	20	200		____
Insert for relish tray, outer	8	8	6	____
Insert for relish tray, center	10			____
Pitcher, 24 oz., tilted	35			____
Pitcher, 80 oz., tilted	45	75	450	____
Plate, 6" sherbet/saucer	10	75		____
Plate, 8.5" salad	20			____
Plate, 10.25" dinner	23	250		____
Plate, 14" sandwich	35			____
Salt & pepper, square	35	65		____
Sherbet, bubble foot	12	18		____
Sugar	15	15		____
Tray, 14" relish, 5 sections	18	35		____
Tray, 14" relish, no sections	18			____
Tumbler, bubble foot	20	24		____
Vase, 8", bubble foot	30			____

Note: Companion pieces by Anchor Hocking: Candy dish w/ lid, $45; Cocktail & Wine, 3.5", $12; Decanter w/stopper, $25.

Note: Ashtray w/advertisement, $15. Ruby 24 oz. Pitcher, $500. Green tumblers, $25 each. Iridized tumblers, $15 each. Jade-ite pitcher, too rare to price.

Sherbet style ashtray w/ metal cover, sherbet style ashtray showing notches for metal cover to fit. (Note: this is a center relish insert, not a sherbet.) *Courtesy of Michael Rothenberger/Mike's Collectables.*

Above: Ashtray w/ advertisement. *Courtesy of Michael & Kathleen Jones.*

Left: 80 oz. tilted pitcher, 4.5" sauce bowl w/ handles, open candy dish w/ 3 feet.

Manhattan look alikes: 5" flat tumbler, 10.25" bowl (4.5" deep) on 12.75" plate.

MAYFAIR "FEDERAL"
(1934 Federal Glass Company)

The look of Mayfair is reminiscent of the facets of gemstones, which were probably the inspiration for the designer who was also a jeweler. Federal Glass Company had advertised Mayfair prior to receiving patent rights. The patent was rejected because Hocking Glass Company already had claimed the name with their own Mayfair pattern. Federal redesigned the molds and changed the name to Rosemary. Shown are some transitional pieces which are a cross between the more decorative Mayfair produced briefly in 1934 and the more simple Rosemary manufactured in 1935 and 1936.

Due to the brief duration of manufacture, Mayfair is not commonly seen. Sometimes the limited supply of a line of glassware adds to its collectibility. Sylvan was only produced for one year and is very much in demand in amber and green. However, with Mayfair this is not the case: demand for this pattern in any color is limited. If you are looking for Mayfair talk to dealers. Many times they have additional pieces and patterns other than what is on display. Be sure to check the dealer directory in the back of this book!

Top: *Back row:* 5" sauce bowl, 6" cereal bowl, 12" platter; *front row:* 10" oval vegetable bowl. *Courtesy of Ardell & George Conn.*

Center: 4.5" tumbler, 9.5" grill plate, cup & saucer, cream soup bowl. *Courtesy of Ardell & George Conn.*

Right: 6.75" salad plate, 9.5" dinner, sugar, creamer. *Courtesy of Ardell & George Conn.*

MAYFAIR "FEDERAL"	Green	Amber	Crystal	Qty
Bowl, 5" sauce	15	10	5	____
Bowl, cream soup	20	18	10	____
Bowl, 6" cereal	10	15	5	____
Bowl, 10" oval vegetable	30	25	15	____
Creamer	20	15	5	____
Cup	15	10	5	____
Plate, 6.75" salad	12	10	5	____
Plate, 9.5" dinner	25	15	10	____
Plate, 9.5" grill	20	12	8	____
Platter, 12"	30	30	15	____
Saucer	8	5	4	____
Sugar, no handles	20	15	5	____
Tumbler, 4.5"	40	30	15	____

Back row: creamer & cream soup bowl in true Mayfair; *front row:* creamer & cream soup bowl in "transitional Mayfair." (Note: transitional has simpler pattern without lattice inside arches.) *Courtesy of Ardell & George Conn.*

MAYFAIR "OPEN ROSE"
Reproduced
(1931-1936 Hocking Glass Company)

Hocking Glass Company's Mayfair is among the most popular of all Depression Glass patterns and is desirable in all four colors. Although only produced for five years, the pattern was very popular in the 1930s, so Hocking produced large quantities then, particularly in pink. Today pink is most commonly seen, but even many of the pink pieces are challenging to locate. Just ask collectors of pink about the sugar lid of which there may be only ten in existence. Blue is easier to find than green and yellow, but most pieces are few and far between. The green sandwich server with the center handle is among the most common of the green pieces. Beyond this, finding other items in green becomes a real challenge. Yellow requires the ultimate commitment along with a huge dose of patience; anything yellow is extremely rare! Many serious Depression Glass collectors seek to own a few pieces of blue, green, and yellow Mayfair to display as special trophies of their diligence and perseverance, even if they have selected a different pattern as their main focus.

Satinized or frosted pieces are gaining in popularity. There was a time when many dealers avoided these items as the demand for them was so low. Collectors are renewing their interest in them, but the handpainted embellishments must be in near-perfect condition.

As with many popular patterns, contemporary manufacturers have opted to reproduce selected pieces. It is virtually impossible to avoid seeing cobalt blue Mayfair salt and pepper shakers in almost any catalogue featuring country collectibles. Make sure you utilize the reproduction information provided as many of the other reproductions will be much more subtle than these crude, dark blue shakers.

Back row: 9.5" grill plate. 9.5" dinner plate; *front row:* 8.5" luncheon plate, 6.5" round sherbet plate, 5.75" plate. *Courtesy of Dottie & Doug Hevener/The Quacker Connection.*

Back: 12" platter w/ open handles; *front row:* salt & pepper, creamer, sugar base, cup & saucer. *Courtesy of Dottie & Doug Hevener/The Quacker Connection.*

5" cream soup bowl, vase, sandwich server w/ center handle. *Courtesy of Dottie & Doug Hevener/The Quacker Connection.*

Back: 7" vegetable bowl; *front:* 9.5" oval vegetable bowl, 12" bowl. *Courtesy of Dottie & Doug Hevener/The Quacker Connection.*

3.25" footed juice tumbler, 5.25" footed iced tea tumbler, 6.5" footed iced tea tumbler. *Courtesy of Dottie & Doug Hevener/The Quacker Connection.*

Above: 7.25" goblet, 4.5" wine goblet, 4.25" goblet, 3.25" footed sherbet, 4" cocktail goblet. *Courtesy of Dottie & Doug Hevener/The Quacker Connection.*

Left: 5.25" flat iced tea tumbler, 4.25" flat water tumbler, 3.5" juice tumbler, 2.25" whiskey tumbler. *Courtesy of Dottie & Doug Hevener/The Quacker Connection.*

Decanter w/ stopper, 11.75" shallow fruit bowl. *Courtesy of Dottie & Doug Hevener/The Quacker Connection.*

10" vegetable bowl w/ 2 open handles (note the bowl does have a lid), 7.5" x 11" oval bowl w/ 2 open handles. *Courtesy of Dottie & Doug Hevener/The Quacker Connection.*

Above: Sugar w/ lid. *Courtesy of Vic & Jean Laermans.*

Left: 12" cake plate w/ handles, candy jar w/ lid, cookie jar w/ lid. *Courtesy of Dottie & Doug Hevener/The Quacker Connection.*

Satinized/frosted pieces: 10" vegetable bowl, 12" cake plate, candy dish w/ lid. *Courtesy of Charlie Diefenderfer.*

Shakers in blue and satinized/frosted pink. *Courtesy of Michael Rothenberger/Mike's Collectables.*

MAYFAIR "OPEN ROSE"	Pink	Blue	Green	Yellow	Qty
Bowl, 5" cream soup	60				____
Bowl, 5.5" cereal	30	65	100	125	____
Bowl, 7" vegetable w/tab handles	30	65	150	160	____
Bowl, 9" console w/3 legs	6000		6000		____
Bowl, 9.5" vegetable, oval	40	80	150	160	____
Bowl, 10" vegetable w/handles	30	80		160	____
Bowl, 11.75", shallow	70	100	75	250	____
Bowl, 12" scalloped fruit, "hat"	65	125	75	350	____
Butter dish base	30	100	300	400	____
Butter dish lid	50	250	1200	1300	____
Butter complete	80	350	1500	1600	____
Candy dish w/lid	75	350	700	600	____
Celery dish, 9", 2 sections			250	250	____
Celery dish, 10"	60	75	200	200	____
Celery dish, 10", 2 sections	275	75			____
Cookie jar/lid R	70	350	700	1000	____
Creamer	30	100	250	275	____
Cup, squarish	20	65	200	200	____
Cup, round	375				____
Decanter w/stopper	250				____
Goblet, 3.75" cordial	1300		1100		____
Goblet, 4" cocktail	100		450		____
Goblet, 4.25"	1100		1100		____
Goblet, 4.5" wine	120		500		____
Goblet, 5.25" claret	1300		1100		____
Goblet, 5.75" water	85		525		____
Goblet, 7.25"	300	250			____
Lid for 10" vegetable bowl	100	150	175	200	____
Pitcher, 6" R	70	175	600	625	____
Pitcher, 8", 60 oz.	85	200	600	600	____
Pitcher, 8.5" 80 oz.	130	330	800	800	____
Plate, 5.75"	15	30	100	100	____
Plate, 6.5" sherbet, round	20				____
Plate, 6.5" sherbet, round w/off center indent	50	60	150	150	____
Plate, 8.5" luncheon	30	65	150	150	____
Plate, 9.5" dinner	60	100	200	200	____
Plate, 9.5" grill	45	65	100	100	____
Plate, 10" cake w/feet & tab handles	40	85	200		____
Plate, 11.5" grill w/handles				150	____
Plate, 12" cake w/handles	70	100	100		____
Platter, 12" w/open handles, no feet	40	80	200	200	____
Platter, 12.5" w/closed handles			300	300	____
Relish, 8.5" w/4 sections	40	75	200	200	____
Relish, 8.5", not sectioned	300		375	375	____
Salt & pepper flat R	80	350	1300	1000	____
Salt & pepper, footed	trtp*				____

MAYFAIR "OPEN ROSE" (Cont.)	Pink	Blue	Green	Yellow	Qty
Sandwich server w/center handle	60	100	80	150	____
Saucer	45			150	____
Sherbet, 2.25" w/out stem or foot	300	300			____
Sherbet, 3.25" w/foot	25				____
Sherbet, 4.75" w/foot	85	100	200	200	____
Sugar base	30	100	250	275	____
Sugar lid	2000		2000	2000	____
Tumbler, 2.25" whiskey R	85				____
Tumbler, 3.25" juice, footed	100				____
Tumbler, 3.5" juice, flat R	60	150			____
Tumbler, 4.25" water, flat	50	150			____
Tumbler, 4.75" water, flat	225	150	250	250	____
Tumbler, 5.25" iced tea, footed	60	150		225	____
Tumbler, 5.25" iced tea, flat	80	300			____
Tumbler, 6.5" iced tea, footed	60	300	250		____
Vase	300	175	450		____

*trtp = too rare to price

Note: Satinized/frosted pink items worth the same as transparent pink pieces if the paint is in excellent condition. Crystal items 1/3 of pink prices.

Reproduction information: Whiskeys were only made in pink; new may be wrong shade. New have one stem for blossoms with veins molded in the leaves; old have branching stems and leaves have no veins. New bottoms have more glass than old ones. Cookie jar bottoms: new have indistinct design & bottom is totally smooth; old bottoms have pronounced 1.75" mold circle rim which is missing from the new ones. Cookie jar lids: new have curved edges of design, almost like a scallop, where design approaches outside edge of flat rim edge; old lids end the design in a straight line. Shakers: new are made in wrong colors and have opening smaller than the .75" opening of the old. New shakers have ridges on 4 corners that extend to the top of the shaker; old ones have ridges that only go about ½ way up. 6" pitchers: new have totally smooth bottoms missing the pronounced 2.25" mold circle rim found on the old. Handles misshapen, should be able to squeeze a dime between handle & shoulder of pitcher. Old spout does not extend beyond shoulder of pitcher, new spout is ½" beyond side of pitcher. 3.5" juice tumblers: reproduced in pink & blue. New are missing a smooth band near top of tumbler & have raised ridges around the blossoms. Old tumblers have blossoms inside the smooth band.

8.5" 80 oz. pitcher, 8" 60 oz. pitcher, 6" pitcher. *Courtesy of Paul Reichwein.*

6.5" round sherbet plate w/ off center indent & 2.25" sherbet. *Courtesy of Paul Reichwein.*

Vase, butter. *Courtesy of Donna L. Cehlarik.*

Back row: 9.5" dinner plate, 5.75" plate; *front:* creamer & sugar. *Courtesy of Paul Reichwein.*

Back row: 8.5" 4-sectioned relish, 9" divided celery; *front:* 10" celery. *Courtesy of Paul Reichwein.*

Reproduction whiskey tumblers. *Courtesy of Charlie Diefenderfer.*

Reproduction cookie jar. *Courtesy of Jane O'Brien.*

MISS AMERICA
Reproduced
(1933-1936 Hocking Glass Company)

Back row: 10.25" dinner plate, 5.75" sherbet plate, 10.25" grill plate; *front row:* sherbet, cup & saucer, 6.25" cereal bowl. *Courtesy of Diefenderfer's Collectibles & Antiques*.

Back row: 8.75" 4-sectioned relish, 8.5" salad plate; *front row:* 11.5" candy jar w/ lid, 10.5" oval celery. *Courtesy of Diefenderfer's Collectibles & Antiques*.

Pink Miss America is not only one of the most recognizable Depression Glass patterns, it is also one of most popular and therefore it was reproduced. Take advantage of the reproduction information provided for Miss America to determine the legitimacy of a piece you may be considering. Sometimes confusion exists between Miss America and English Hobnail. The points on Miss America are quite defined and not elongated. The starburst seen on some Miss America pieces forms a circle with no rays extending further than the others.

Pink is widely collected while crystal has a smaller following. Some dealers don't take crystal Miss America to shows because the requests for it are so few. If you are searching for crystal Miss America, don't hesitate to ask for it as many dealers have additional stock of all kinds that may include something you need. There are even fewer collectors searching for green as the selection is minimal and there are no dinner plates. On the other hand, Royal Ruby is treasured because it is quite rare and usually relatively expensive.

Prices on hard-to-find items have been rising sharply. In particular the butter dish and goblets have become almost impossible to find, and collectors are paying higher prices for the privilege of adding a rare piece to their collection. Many of these scarce items are in collections where they may remain for years. Remember, popularity creates competition and this pattern was only produced for a few years.

A variety of unique pieces have been found and we hope you enjoy seeing some of them here.

Factory workers probably loved this pattern as much as many of you so they opted to have a little fun with it, resulting in some rare and wonderful treasures. You won't want to miss Miss America!

4" juice tumbler, 4.5" water tumbler, 5.75" iced tea tumbler, 5.5" water goblet, 3.75" wine goblet. *Courtesy of Diefenderfer's Collectibles & Antiques*.

12" footed cake plate, 8" bowl. *Courtesy of Diefenderfer's Collectibles & Antiques*.

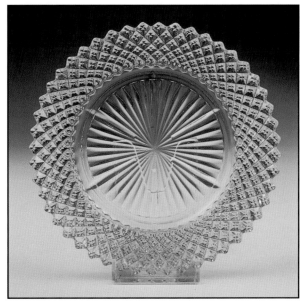

5.75" coaster. *Courtesy of Diefenderfer's Collectibles & Antiques*.

Far left: Butter. *Courtesy of Charlie Diefenderfer.*

Left: Salt & pepper. *Courtesy of Michael Rothenberger/ Mike's Collectables.*

8.5" pitcher w/ ice lip, 8" pitcher w/ no ice lip.
Courtesy of Diefenderfer's Collectibles & Antiques.

Note the hump of extra glass above where the handles are attached to these pitchers indicating these are not reproductions. *Courtesy of Diefenderfer's Collectibles & Antiques.*

Two creamers; one on the right is missing a spout. *Courtesy of Vic & Jean Laermans.*

MISS AMERICA	Pink	Crystal	Green	Ruby	Qty
Bowl, 4.5" berry			15		____
Bowl, 6.25" cereal	25	15	25		____
Bowl, 8", curves inward	110	65		600	____
Bowl, 8.75", straight sides	80	50			____
Bowl, 10" oval vegetable	35	15			____
Bowl, 11"				1000	____
Butter dish base (same as 6.25" cereal bowl)	25	15			____
Butter dish lid *R*	800	300			____
Butter dish complete	825	315			____
Candy jar w/lid, 11.5"	200	125			____
Coaster, 5.75"	35	20			____
Comport, 5"	30	20			____
Creamer	20	10		500	____
Cup	25	10	20	400	____
Goblet, 3.75" wine	100	25		400	____
Goblet, 4.75" juice	120	30		400	____
Goblet, 5.5" water	70	25		400	____
Pitcher, 8" w/no ice lip *R*	175	75			____
Pitcher 8.5" w/ice lip	225	85			____
Plate, 5.75" sherbet	15	8	12	65	____
Plate, 6.75"			10		____
Plate, 8.5" salad	45	10	12	225	____
Plate, 10.25" dinner	40	20			____
Plate, 10.25" grill	35	12			____
Plate, 10.5" oval celery	35	15			____
Plate, 12" footed cake	60	40			____
Platter, 12.25"	35	20			____
Relish, 8.75", 4 sections	30	15			____
Relish, 11.75", 5 sections	trtp*	50			____
Salt & pepper *R*	75	40	500		____
Saucer	10	6		80	____
Sherbet	20	10		225	____
Sugar	20	10		500	____
Tumbler, 4" juice *R*	70	25		400	____
Tumbler, 4.5" water *R*	45	20	35		____
Tumbler. 5.75" iced tea *R*	100	35			____

Reproduction information: Anything in cobalt is new. Butter lids: pronounced curve near bottom, inside area where knob touches lid is filled with glass (old lid has hollow area where knob and lid meet). Look for a pronounced "star" with distinct points when looking from the underside of the lid through the knob as evident in only the old lids. Shakers: new measure 3.25" and old are actually a bit taller; old allow one to insert a finger inside and reach almost to the bottom with an absence of extra glass at the base that is found in new. New approx. 2" deep; old approx. 2.5" deep. Old shakers have neat ridges with which to screw & unscrew the lids; new have rounded off ridges that overlap. Points of the Miss America design are sharper and consistent in quality with other pieces on old; new are more rounded. Pitchers without ice lip: old have a hump of extra glass above where the handle is attached; new are perfectly even around the rim. Tumblers: new have 2 vertical mold marks, old have 4. New have approx. ½" glass on bottom; old have approx. 1/4".

*trtp = too rare to price

Note: Ice blue pieces 10 times the price of pink.

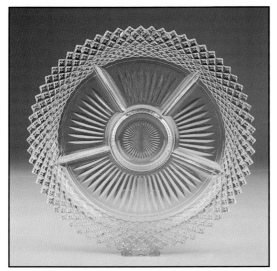

11.75" 5-section relish.

Sugar w/ metal lid & creamer. *Courtesy of Vic & Jean Laermans.*

Creamer & sugar. *Courtesy of Vic & Jean Laermans.*

4.5" jade-ite water tumbler, too rare to price. *Courtesy of Charlie Diefenderfer.*

8.75" straight-sided bowl in smoked iridescence (sold for $1300 in early 1998). *Courtesy of Charlie Diefenderfer.*

Reproduction shakers. (Don't be fooled by the legitimately old shaker tops.) *Courtesy of Charlie Diefenderfer.*

MODERNTONE
(1934-early 1950s Hazel-Atlas Glass Company)

Blue glass lovers are drawn to Moderntone. This ranks among the most sought after patterns of cobalt blue Depression Glass along with Royal Lace. The styles are totally different though. Collectors looking for a simple design or looking to accent their blue China place settings buy Moderntone. It is rare to have collectors interested in both of these wonderful patterns.

Basic dinnerware pieces are abundant which means it will not take a major investment to amass multiple place settings. A handful of items are more expensive including certain bowls and tumblers as shown on the price list. The 10.5" sandwich plate is almost impossible to find in excellent, scratch-free condition and competition for this plate has escalated as collectors select this as their dinner plate, replacing the diminutive 8.75" dinner plate. Another item that has become virtually impossible to find is the 5" ruffled nut/cream soup bowl.

The metal lid on the sugar is one of the correct lids, and these are not easily found. There were several metal lids made to accompany the sugar bases. After completing the photography for this book we had an interesting piece come into a friend's shop. We have described it here and hopefully will have a picture of it along with a more detailed description for the next book. It is a set that includes a circular chrome tray with the Moderntone creamer, sugar with a metal lid, shakers, and a bowl resembling American Pioneer covered with a chrome lid. The original owner stated that he had purchased the items together just as he had brought them in.

Sugar w/ metal lid. *Courtesy of Charlie Diefenderfer*.

Back row: 12" platter, 11" platter; *front row:* salt & pepper, sugar, creamer. *Courtesy of David G. Baker*.

Back row: 10.5" sandwich plate, 8.75" dinner plate, 7.75" luncheon plate; *front row:* cup & saucer, sherbet on 5.75" sherbet plate. *Courtesy of David G. Baker.*

8.75" berry bowl, 4.75" cream soup bowl, 5" ruffled nut/cream soup bowl, custard. *Courtesy of David G. Baker.*

Amethyst, originally called "Burgundy," is harder to find than cobalt. It also seems to have suffered far more abuse as most pieces are quite scratched. Collectors have recently begun asking for Amethyst with greater frequency. Often an increased level of interest results in higher prices as items get even more difficult to locate.

Owners of Platonite are very enthusiastic about their collections, but by and large dealers know that these customers are few in number. The colors are varied, the pieces easy to find, and the prices are reasonable. Perhaps in time there will be a renewed interest in these lively pieces.

The bridge set (seen on page 150) was an Internet find. This is the first one we had seen and we bought it solely for inclusion in this book. We hope you enjoy seeing it as we were just delighted with it!

Back: 8.75" dinner plate; *front:* cup & saucer, 7.75" luncheon plate, sugar base, creamer. *Courtesy of Marie Talone & Paul Reichwein.*

Back row: 5.75" sherbet plate, 8.75" dinner plate, 7.75" luncheon plate; *middle row:* cup & saucer, 3.75" juice tumbler, 4.25" water tumbler; *front row:* 4.75" cream soup bowl, 1.5 oz. whiskey tumbler, creamer, sugar w/ metal lid. *Courtesy of Charlie Diefenderfer.*

MODERNTONE	Cobalt	Amethyst	Platonite-pastels	Platonite-others	Qty
Ashtray, 7.75"	175				____
Bowl, 4.75" cream soup	25	25	8	20	____
Bowl, 5" berry	35	30	8	15	____
Bowl, 5" deep cereal, w/white			8		____
Bowl, 5" deep cereal, no white			12		____
Bowl, 5" ruffled nut/cream soup	100	55			____
Bowl, 6.5" cereal	100	85			____
Bowl, 7.5" soup	200	150			____
Bowl, 8", rim			15	35	____
Bowl, 8", no rim			20		____
Bowl, 8.75" berry	65	50		35	____
Butter dish complete w/metal cover	150				____
Cheese dish complete w/metal cover	500				____
Creamer	15	12	10	20	____
Cup	15	15	5	15	____
Custard	25	20			____
Plate, 5.75" sherbet	10	8	5	8	____
Plate, 6.75" salad	15	12			____
Plate, 7.75" luncheon	15	12			____
Plate 8.75" dinner	20	15	8	20	____
Plate, 10.5" sandwich	100	65	20		____
Platter, 11"	50	50		30	____
Platter, 12"	100	80	15	40	____
Salt & pepper	45	45	20		____
Saucer	5	5	3	4	____
Sherbet	15	15	6	12	____
Sugar base	15	12	10	20	____
Sugar lid (metal)	60				____
Tumbler, 1.5 oz. whiskey	50				____
Tumbler, 3.75" juice	65	45			____
Tumbler, 4.25" water	45	35	12		____
Tumbler, 5.5" iced tea	150	125			____

Note: Items in pink and green 1/2 price of cobalt EXCEPT pink cup, $100, & pink saucer, $35. Items in crystal 1/4 of cobalt.

Above: Red Willow Platonite. *Back row:* 7.75" luncheon plate, 8.75" dinner plate, 5" berry bowl; *front row:* sherbet, cup & saucer, creamer, sugar. *Courtesy of Charlie Diefenderfer.*

Right: Platonite Bridge Set consisting of one 10.5" sandwich plate, four 7.75" luncheon plates, four cups, four saucers, one creamer, and one sugar. $125 for set as shown.

Pastel Platonite. *Back row:* 8.75" dinner plate, 5" berry bowl; *front row:* salt & pepper, 5" cereal w/ white interior, sherbet. *Courtesy of Bob & Cindy Bentley.*

Platonite. *Back row:* 8" bowl w/ rim, 12" platter; *front row:* sherbet, 5" berry bowl, cup & saucer, 4.75" cream soup bowl. *Courtesy of Bob & Cindy Bentley.*

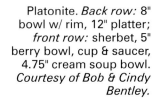

Shakers in a variety of colors. *Courtesy of Michael Rothenberger/ Mike's Collectables.*

"Little Hostess Party Dishes:" complete 16-piece set in burgundy, chartreuse, gray, and green. *Courtesy of Charlie Diefenderfer.*

MOONDROPS

(1932-1940s   New Martinsville Glass Manufacturing Company)

New Martinsville created spectacular glass including Moondrops. Some magnificent examples are presented courtesy of Debora and Paul Torsiello, Debzie's Glass. Look for them in the dealer directory at the back of the book.

Moondrops, marketed as "No. 37 Line," was in production for more than a decade, a relatively long time when compared to other Depression Glass patterns. This explains the lengthy list of offerings in a rainbow of colors including amber, blue (Ritz blue), crystal, evergreen, green, jade, rose (pink), and ruby. There are multiple offerings of bowls, candle holders, plates, tumblers, and even decanters and vases. Moondrops is not commonly seen in antique malls; so if you wish to add some of these dramatic pieces to your collection, Depression Glass shows and sales would be a great source. Dealers love showcasing their best wares at shows and any piece of Moondrops earns this exclusive rating.

This listing of Moondrops includes an additional item: the 9.25" bowl. It is amazing how new pieces of Depression Glass continue to be found.

Butter. *Courtesy of Debora & Paul Torsiello, Debzie's Glass.*

2.75" sugar, 4" compote, 2.75" creamer. *Courtesy of Debora & Paul Torsiello, Debzie's Glass.*

Two 8.25" 53 oz. pitchers, two 4.75" tumblers. *Courtesy of Michael Rothenberger/Mike's Collectables.*

Previously unlisted 9.25" etched bowl. *Courtesy of Michael Rothenberger/Mike's Collectables.*

Creamer & sugar on 7.5" x 2.75" tray. *Courtesy of Vic & Jean Laermans.*

9.75" oval bowl w/ handles, 5" candle holders. *Courtesy of Debora & Paul Torsiello, Debzie's Glass.*

5.25" candle holder (holds 3 tapers), 5.25" tumbler. *Courtesy of Debora & Paul Torsiello, Debzie's Glass.*

Moondrops

Left: Creamers & sugars in various colors. *Courtesy of Vic & Jean Laermans.*

Below: 2.75" creamer & 2.75" sugar on 7.5" tray, cocktail shaker w/ out metal lid, cup & saucer. *Courtesy of Vic & Jean Laermans.*

MOONDROPS	Red & Cobalt	Ice Blue	Other colors	Qty
Ashtray	40	35	20	____
Bottle, perfume ("rocket")	300	250	200	____
Bowl, cream soup	125	100	50	____
Bowl, 5.25" berry	25	20	15	____
Bowl, 5.25" mayonnaise	75	60	40	____
Bowl, 6.75" soup	125	100	50	____
Bowl, 7.5" pickle	35	25	20	____
Bowl, 8.25" concave top	65	50	35	____
Bowl, 8.5" relish, divided w/3 feet	50	35	20	____
Bowl, 9.25"			75	____
Bowl, 9.5" ruffled w/3 legs	80	75	45	____
Bowl, 9.75" casserole (base only)	80	75	50	____
Bowl, 9.75" oval vegetable	60	45	35	____
Bowl, 9.75" oval w/2 handles	75	60	45	____
Bowl, 11.5" celery, boat shape	45	35	25	____
Bowl, 12" casserole w/3 feet	100	85	45	____
Bowl, 13" console	150	135	85	____
Butter dish base	150	125	100	____
Butter dish lid	400	325	250	____
Butter dish complete	550	450	350	____
Candle holder, 2" ruffled, ea.	40	35	30	____
Candle holder, 4.5", ea.	35	30	25	____
Candle holder, 5" ruffled, ea.	35	30	25	____
Candle holder, 5", ea.	75	60	45	____
Candle holder, 5.25", holds 3, ea.	100	75	50	____
Candle holder, 8.5" metal stem, ea.	30	25	20	____
Candy dish, 8"	50	40	30	____
Cocktail shaker, may or may not have handle	80	70	50	____
Compote, 4"	35	30	25	____
Compote, 11.5"	75	65	45	____
Creamer, 2.75"	25	20	15	____
Creamer, 3.75"	20	18	12	____
Cup	20	18	12	____
Decanter w/stopper, 7.75"	80	70	50	____
Decanter w/stopper, 8.5"	90	75	60	____
Decanter w/stopper, 10.25" ("rocket")	500	450	400	____
Decanter w/stopper, 11.25"	150	125	75	____
Goblet, 2.75" liquor/cordial	50	40	30	____
Goblet, 4" wine	30	25	20	____
Goblet, 4.25" wine ("rocket")	70	60	40	____
Goblet, 4.75"	30	25	20	____
Goblet, 5.25" wine w/metal stem	25	20	15	____
Goblet, 5.5" wine w/metal stem	25	20	15	____
Goblet, 6.25" water w/metal stem	35	30	20	____
Gravy	150	125	100	____

MOONDROPS (Cont.)	Red & Cobalt	Ice Blue	Other colors	Qty
Lid for 9.75" casserole	125	100	75	____
Mug	50	40	30	____
Pitcher, 6.75", 22 oz.	180	160	120	____
Pitcher, 8", 50 oz. (with ice lip)	200	175	130	____
Pitcher, 8.25", 32 oz.	190	170	135	____
Pitcher, 8.25", 53 oz. (no ice lip)	200	175	130	____
Plate, 5.75" bread & butter	15	12	10	____
Plate, 6" sherbet w/off-center indent	18	15	12	____
Plate, 6.25" sherbet	12	10	8	____
Plate, 7.25" salad	18	15	12	____
Plate, 8.5" luncheon	18	15	12	____
Plate, 9.5" dinner	35	30	20	____
Plate, 14" sandwich	45	40	30	____
Plate, 14" sandwich w/2 handles	60	50	30	____
Platter, 12"	45	40	30	____
Powder jar w/3 feet	400	350	250	____
Saucer	10	8	5	____
Sherbet, 2.5"	20	18	15	____
Sherbet, 4.5"	40	30	25	____
Sugar, 2.75"	20	18	15	____
Sugar, 4"	22	18	15	____
Tray, 7.5" for 2.75" creamer & sugar	50	40	30	____
Tumbler, 2.75" whiskey	20	18	15	____
Tumbler, 2.75" whiskey w/handle	20	18	15	____
Tumbler, 3.75" w/foot	20	18	15	____
Tumbler, 3.75" flat	18	15	12	____
Tumbler, 4.25", 7 & 8 oz.	20	18	15	____
Tumbler, 4.75" w/handle	35	30	20	____
Tumbler, 4.75"	25	20	15	____
Tumbler, 5.25"	40	35	20	____
Vase, 7.75"	80	75	65	____
Vase, 8.5" ("rocket")	300	275	200	____
Vase, 9.25" ("rocket")	275	250	175	____

MOONSTONE
(1942-1946 Hocking Glass Company)

Moonstone is very available and quite popular on the East Coast. Large collections are frequently showing up at auctions and in shops. Due to the design of this pattern having no thin, delicate edges, an abundance seems to have survived since its debut during World War II. The groupings pictured are a fairly complete representation of this pattern. Some Moonstone pieces were also manufactured in transparent green. These items are rarely seen and are worth four times their crystal counterparts.

Back row: 6.5" crimped edge bowl w/ handles, 9.5" crimped edge bowl; *front row:* 5.5" crimped edge dessert bowl, 7.5" crimped edge bowl. *Courtesy of Connie & Bill Hartzell.*

Back row: cloverleaf bowl, 10.75" sandwich plate; *front row:* bonbon, 5.5" vase, 7.75" divided relish bowl. *Courtesy of Connie & Bill Hartzell.*

Back: 5.5" berry bowl, sugar; *front row:* candle holders, creamer. *Courtesy of Connie & Bill Hartzell.*

Back row: sherbet on 6.25" sherbet plate, 8.25" luncheon plate;
front row: cup, saucer & goblet. *Courtesy of Connie & Bill Hartzell.*

Back: 4.75" round puff box w/ cover;
front: cigarette jar w/ cover, candy
jar w/ cover. *Courtesy of Connie &
Bill Hartzell.*

MOONSTONE	Crystal w/bluish white	Qty
Bonbon, heart-shaped w/one handle	15	____
Bowl, 5.5" berry	18	____
Bowl, 5.5" dessert, crimped edge	10	____
Bowl, 6.5" crimped edge w/handles	10	____
Bowl, 7.75", crimped edge	12	____
Bowl, 7.75" relish, divided	10	____
Bowl, 9.5" crimped edge	20	____
Bowl, cloverleaf (3 sections)	12	____
Candleholder, ea.	8	____
Candy jar w/cover	30	____
Cigarette jar w/cover	25	____
Creamer	8	____
Cup	8	____
Goblet	15	____
Plate, 6.25" sherbet	5	____
Plate, 8.25" luncheon	15	____
Plate, 10.75" sandwich	30	____
Puff box w/cover, 4.75" round	30	____
Saucer	5	____
Sherbet	5	____
Sugar	8	____
Vase, 5.5"	10	____

Note: Items in green 4 times prices of crystal

MT. PLEASANT
(Early 1930s L.E. Smith Glass Company)

The majority of Mt. Pleasant collectors are only interested in cobalt. Pink and green pieces are rarely seen or requested. There is some interest in amethyst and black, and pieces in these colors are still quite easy to locate.

L.E. Smith Glass Company created many lines of glassware similar to Mt. Pleasant including Do-Si-Do, No. 55, and Kent. They also produced a plethora of unnamed footed bowls, vases, ashtrays, and more that were reminiscent of Mt. Pleasant, but not officially part of the line. Collectors of this pattern rarely care whether or not an item is actually Mt. Pleasant. If it is L.E. Smith glassware in their chosen color there is a good chance a purchase will be made.

Mt. Pleasant was susceptible to two types of damage: scratching, which is extremely evident on amethyst and black pieces, and wear to the trim, which is apparent on cobalt blue Mt. Pleasant. In general trimmed pieces are less popular, and when the gold is only partially visible due to wear, the item may be even more difficult to sell.

Back row: 9" grill plate, 6" mint plate w/ center handle; *front row:* 6" square bowl w/ handles on 8" plate w/ handles, tumbler, cup & saucer, shaker.

Above: Double candlestick, single candlestick, 8" leaf plate, bonbon w/ 2 handles and foot.

Left: *Back row:* 10.5" cake plate w/ 2 handles, 7.25" vase; *front row:* ashtray, 5.5" mayonnaise bowl, 7" bowl.

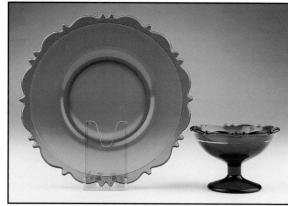

8" plate,
sherbet.

8" square bowl
w/ handles.

8" plate.

MT. PLEASANT	Cobalt	Other colors	Qty
Ashtray	30	25	____
Bonbon w/2 handles & foot	35	25	____
Bonbon, 7" w/rolled-up edges & handles	30	20	____
Bowl, 4" opening w/rolled-in edges (rose bowl)	35	25	____
Bowl, 4.75" square w/foot	30	20	____
Bowl, 5.5" mayonnaise w/3 feet	35	20	____
Bowl, 6" square w/handles	35	20	____
Bowl, 7" rolled-out edge w/3 feet	30	20	____
Bowl, 8" scalloped w/2 handles	40	20	____
Bowl, 8" square w/2 handles	40	20	____
Bowl, 9" scalloped w/foot	40	20	____
Bowl, 9.25" square w/foot	45	25	____
Bowl, 10" scalloped	50	35	____
Bowl, 10" rolled-up edge w/2 handles	50	35	____
Candlestick, single ea.	25	15	____
Candlestick, double ea.	35	20	____
Creamer	25	15	____
Cup	15	10	____
Plate, 6" mint w/center handle	30	20	____
Plate, 7" scalloped w/2 handles	15	10	____
Plate, 8" scalloped (no handles)	15	10	____
Plate, 8" square (no handles)	15	10	____
Plate, 8" w/2 handles	15	10	____
Plate, 8" leaf	25		____
Plate, 8.25" square w/cup indent	15	10	____
Plate, 9" grill	15	10	____
Plate, 10.5" cake w/2 handles	35	15	____
Plate, 10.5" cake, 1.25" high	45	15	____
Plate, 11.25" leaf	35		____
Plate, 12" w/2 handles	45	15	____
Plate, sandwich server w/ center handle	45	15	____
Salt & pepper, 2 styles	65	45	____
Saucer	10	5	____
Sherbet, 2 styles	20	12	____
Sugar	25	15	____
Tumbler	30		____
Vase, 7.25"	35	15	____

Back: 11" platter, 5.5" flat tumbler; *front:*
6" sherbet plate, shaker, sugar base.

NEW CENTURY

(late 1920s-early 1930s
Hazel-Atlas Glass Company)

Looking at the listing for this pattern one can see that green is much more dominant than cobalt blue. However, more people collect cobalt blue than green, pink, or crystal (clear). Cobalt is a universally appreciated color and was used in only a handful of Depression Glass patterns adding to the appeal of New Century. Amethyst glass aficionados are enthusiasts of the New Century offerings as well.

There are many reasonably priced items in this Hazel-Atlas pattern. If you are looking for a green pattern, New Century is one you may wish to consider. Keep in mind that lower prices usually mean higher availability; this is not the case with New Century. Many pieces are quite difficult to find as you can see from our layout.

NEW CENTURY	Green & Crystal	Amethyst & Pink	Cobalt	Qty
Ashtray/coaster, 5.25"	30			___
Bowl, 4.5" berry	35			___
Bowl, 4.75" cream soup	25			___
Bowl, 8" berry	30			___
Bowl, 9" casserole base	30			___
Bowl, 9" casserole w/lid	75			___
Butter dish base	30			___
Butter dish lid	45			___
Butter dish complete	75			___
Creamer	12			___
Cup	10	15	20	___
Decanter w/stopper	85			___
Goblet, 2.5 oz. wine	40			___
Goblet, 3.25 oz. cocktail	40			___
Pitcher, 7.75" w/or w/out ice lip	45	45	60	___
Pitcher, 8" w/or w/out ice lip	45	45	70	___
Plate, 6" sherbet	5			___
Plate, 7.25" breakfast	12			___
Plate, 8.5" salad	12			___
Plate, 10" dinner	25			___
Plate, 10" grill	15			___
Platter, 11"	30			___
Salt & pepper	45			___
Saucer	5	10	15	___
Sugar base	12			___
Sugar lid	28			___
Tumbler, 2.5" whiskey, 1.5 oz. flat	35			___
Tumbler, 3.5", 5 oz. flat	15	20	22	___
Tumbler, 3.5", 8 oz. flat	25			___
Tumbler, 4", 5 oz. footed	30			___
Tumbler, 4.25", 9 oz. flat	15	20	22	___
Tumbler, 4.75", 9 oz. footed	30			___
Tumbler, 5", 10 oz. flat	20	25	28	___
Tumbler, 5.25", 12 oz. flat	30	35	40	___

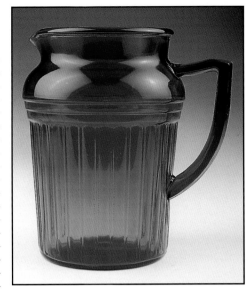

Left: 8" pitcher w/ no ice lip. *Courtesy of Diefenderfer's Collectibles & Antiques.*

Below: 3.5" 5 oz. flat tumbler, 5" flat tumbler, 3.5" 5 oz. tumbler. *Courtesy of Marie Talone & Paul Reichwein.*

NEWPORT

(mid-1930s Hazel-Atlas Glass Company)

Cobalt is the most popular Newport color; however, amethyst also has a strong following. The fired-on pieces are quite vibrant, but, as with other fired-on glass, these items are not particularly popular at this time. The pink is a paler, lighter shade than other patterns of Depression Glass and is therefore often overlooked by those who favor the color.

Hazel-Atlas manufactured just enough variety in this line to meet dining requirements. If you have already accumulated an array for yourself you were quite smart and are very fortunate as Newport has become difficult to find. There was a time one could count on finding several pieces while combing the markets, but this is no longer the case. The 11.5" sandwich plate, 11.75" platter, and 8.25" berry bowl will pose the greatest difficulty.

Back: 8.75" dinner plate, 11.5" sandwich plate, 6" sherbet plate; *front:* 4.5" tumbler, sherbet, creamer, sugar, cup & saucer. *Courtesy of Charlie Diefenderfer.*

Shakers in two colors. *Courtesy of Michael Rothenberger/Mike's Collectables.*

Back: 11.75" platter; *front:* 4.25" berry bowl, 4.75" cream soup bowl, 8.25" berry bowl, salt & pepper, 5.25" cereal bowl. *Courtesy of Charlie Diefenderfer.*

5.25" cereal bowl. *Courtesy of Vic & Jean Laermans.*

NEWPORT	Cobalt	Amethyst	Fired-on colors	Qty
Bowl, 4.25" berry	25	20	8	____
Bowl, 4.75" cream soup	25	25	10	____
Bowl, 5.25" cereal	45	40		____
Bowl, 8.25" berry	50	50	15	____
Creamer	20	18	8	____
Cup	15	12	8	____
Plate, 6" sherbet	10	8	5	____
Plate, 8.5" luncheon	20	15	8	____
Plate, 8.75" dinner	35	35		____
Plate, 11.5" sandwich	50	45	15	____
Platter, 11.75"	50	45	15	____
Salt & pepper	65	65	30	____
Saucer	5	5	2	____
Sherbert	18	15	10	____
Sugar	20	18	8	____
Tumbler, 4.5"	50	45	15	____

Note: Pink pieces 1/2 price of Amethyst. Crystal pieces 1/2 price of fired-on colors.

Two sherbets, cup, creamer & sugar. *Courtesy of Debora & Paul Torsiello, Debzie's Glass*.

4.25" berry bowls in fired-on colors. *Courtesy of Charlie Diefenderfer.*

NORMANDIE
(1933-1939 Federal Glass Company)

Normandie is one of the most popular amber (originally called "Golden Glow") patterns, joining the ranks of Madrid and Patrician. The availability of Normandie is high with the sugar lid being the most difficult item to locate. Even the pitcher, though pricy compared to the rest of this pattern, is not too challenging to find. The pieces are durable and many have survived in great condition since their manufacture in the 1930s.

Pink is not as popular as amber and a lot more difficult to find. Cups are very common and are often seen without saucers. Luncheon plates and 5" berry bowls are also abundant. Finding the rest of this pattern in pink will require time to hunt and search. The dinners are quite rare and many people are not willing to invest large sums of money into dinners. Assuming one is building a service for eight, pink Normandie dinners become a serious investment if not prohibitive. The rarity of this color has not created a greater demand as is sometimes the case. Normandie is primarily a pattern collected in amber.

Virtually every piece of iridescent (originally called "Sunburst") Normandie ever made must have been distributed in New England. The shops are full of relatively complete sets and additional ones continue to be consigned to auctions there. The prices at these auctions remain low which may be an indication of the demand—low.

Pitchers, 4.5" tumblers. *Courtesy of Michael Rothenberger/Mike's Collectables.*

Creamers & sugars in various colors. *Courtesy of Vic & Jean Laermans.*

Back: 9.25" luncheon plate, pitcher; *front:* 5" berry bowl, sherbet, cup & saucer. *Courtesy of Marie Talone & Paul Reichwein.*

NORMANDIE	Amber	Pink	Iridescent	Qty
Bowl, 5" berry	8	12	4	____
Bowl, 6.5" cereal	20	35	8	____
Bowl, 8.5" berry	25	40	15	____
Bowl, 10" oval vegetable	25	50	15	____
Creamer	15	20	10	____
Cup	10	15	8	____
Pitcher	95	195		____
Plate, 6" sherbet	8	12	4	____
Plate, 7.75" salad	25	15	50	____
Plate, 9.25" luncheon	25	15	10	____
Plate, 11" dinner	65	150	10	____
Plate, 11" grill	18	45	8	____
Platter, 11.75"	40	35	15	____
Salt & pepper	65	100		____
Saucer	8	12	2	____
Sugar base	15	20	10	____
Sugar lid	125	500		____
Tumbler, 4"	50	125		____
Tumbler, 4.5"	40	90		____
Tumbler, 5"	65	150		____

Back: 8" mint tray, 7.25" vase; *front:* 6" olive dish, 4.5" bowl, 6.5" bowl. *Courtesy of Michael Rothenberger/Mike's Collectables.*

OLD CAFE
(1936-1938 Hocking Glass Company)

Having been made for a brief period of time, many pieces of Old Cafe were produced in small quantities. The pricing, particularly in pink, reflects the availability of various pieces. Both pitchers are hard to find, and the dinners pose a challenge. If you plan to build a set that includes dinners, it may take a great deal of effort. On the other hand, several pink items are quite abundant as these were manufactured as premiums. They were ordered and produced in larger quantities than many of the other pieces of Old Cafe.

The pieces of ruby that were produced will not permit one to completely set a table. Often Royal Ruby collectors will buy several Old Cafe items to enhance their collections.

Crystal (clear) is of relatively little consequence at this time. Iris and Manhattan dominate the crystal Depression Glass market.

Back: 6" sherbet plate, 10" dinner plate; *front:* sherbet, 3" juice tumbler, 4" tumbler. *Courtesy of Michael Rothenberger/Mike's Collectables.*

Candy jar w/ lid. *Courtesy of Joan Kauffman.*

OLD CAFE	Pink	Ruby	Crystal	Qty
Bowl, 3.75" berry	10	12	5	____
Bowl, 4.5" w/handles	12		6	____
Bowl, 5.5" cereal	25	18	10	____
Bowl, 6.5" w/handles	30			____
Bowl, 9" w/handles	15	20	8	____
Candy jar w/lid (crystal or pink base, ruby lid)	30	20	20	____
Cup	10	12	5	____
Lamp	35	50	25	____
Mint tray, 8" low & flared	12	18	6	____
Olive dish, 6" oval	12			____
Pitcher, 6", 36 oz.	100			____
Pitcher, 80 oz.	125			____
Plate, 6" sherbet	8		2	____
Plate, 10" dinner	65			____
Saucer	8		2	____
Sherbet, 3.75"	18	20	5	____
Tumbler, 3" juice	20	25	8	____
Tumbler, 4"	22	30	8	____
Vase, 7.25"	35	45	20	____

OLD COLONY
(1935-1938 Hocking Glass Company)

Old Colony is one of the most popular patterns of pink Depression Glass, but it is also one of the most troublesome. First there is the issue of the name having been incorrectly identified as "Lace Edge" and "Open Lace." Next there is the concern regarding condition. The lacy loops of glass encircling most pieces are extremely delicate. Often there are cracks and chips in these loops diminishing the value of a piece. Confusion with other patterns is also a consideration as similar patterns were manufactured by Imperial, Lancaster, and Westmoreland glass companies. Finally inconsistencies in design make several pieces difficult to identify for those less familiar with Old Colony.

For the sake of clarity, some of the design inconsistencies will be discussed. First, the 8.25" bowl is crystal, but *every* other piece of Old Colony is either transparent pink or satin finished pink, except for the fish bowl and the green cereal bowl. Next, the 9.5" ribbed bowl is the only bowl that is not smooth. There are three versions of the 13" plate, all with solid lace. Solid lace has no openings or holes. The scalloped edges are molded with lines reminiscent of the open lace, but there are no openings. Finally, the tumblers don't quite look like they belong to this pattern. Old Colony tumblers are expensive and, if you don't know what to look for, you might miss some bargains or confuse them with Coronation tumblers, which are very similar, but less valuable.

Added to the listing is an ashtray that was verified by someone who had owned one. Hopefully we will be able to picture the item in a future book.

Along side the pink sherbet is one in white that is 100% identical. It is not known whether or not it is a true Old Colony item.

Back row: 10.5" dinner plate, 10.5" grill plate, 8.25" luncheon plate; *front:* cup & saucer. *Courtesy of Bryan & Marie James.*

Back row: 13" 4-part solid lace plate, 10.5" 3-part relish, 12.75" 5-part platter; *front:* 7.5" 3-part relish. *Courtesy of Bryan & Marie James.*

Back: 9.5" salad bowl w/ ribs, 9.5" smooth bowl; *front:* 6.5" cereal bowl, 10.5" bowl w/ 3 feet. *Courtesy of Bryan & Marie James.*

4.25" flat tumbler, 5" footed tumbler that resembles Coronation tumbler. *Courtesy of Staci & Jeff Shuck/Gray Goose Antiques & Neil McCurdy - Hoosier Kubboard Glass.*

Back: 12.75" platter; *front:* ribbed flower bowl w/ crystal frog, sherbet, 7" comport. *Courtesy of Bryan & Marie James.*

Butter, ribbed candy jar w/ lid, 7" comport w/ lid, cookie jar w/ lid. *Courtesy of Bryan & Marie James.*

Sherbets in pink & white ($25). *Courtesy of Diefenderfer's Collectibles & Antiques.*

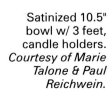

Satinized 10.5" bowl w/ 3 feet, candle holders. *Courtesy of Marie Talone & Paul Reichwein.*

OLD COLONY	Pink	Qty
Ashtray	trtp*	___
Bowl, 6.5" cereal	30	___
Bowl, 6.5" cereal satin finish	20	___
Bowl, 7.75" salad w/ribs	35	___
Bowl, 8.25" (in crystal)	12	___
Bowl, 9.5" smooth	30	___
Bowl, 9.5" w/ribs	35	___
Bowl, 9.5" satin finish	25	___
Bowl, 10.5" w/3 feet	350	___
Bowl, 10.5" w/3 feet satin finish	50	___
Bowl, ribbed flower w/crystal frog	40	___
Bowl, fish (in crystal; similar to cookie jar base)	40	___
Butter dish base	40	___
Butter dish lid	60	___
Butter complete	100	___
Candle holder, ea.	225	___
Candle holder, ea. satin finish	30	___
Candy jar w/lid, ribbed	80	___
Comport, 7"	35	___
Comport, 7" satin finish	25	___
Comport w/lid, 7"	80	___
Comport, 9"	trtp*	___
Cookie jar w/lid	100	___
Cookie jar w/lid satin finish	50	___
Creamer	35	___
Cup	30	___
Plate, 7.25" salad	35	___
Plate, 8.25" luncheon	30	___
Plate, 10.5" dinner	40	___
Plate, 10.5" grill	25	___
Plate, 13" solid lace	60	___
Plate, 13" solid lace, 4-part	60	___
Plate, 13" solid lace w/satin finish, 4-part	30	___
Platter, 12.75"	50	___
Platter, 12.75", 5-part	45	___
Relish, 7.5", 3-part	100	___
Relish, 10.5", 3-part	30	___
Saucer	18	___
Sherbet	165	___
Sugar	35	___
Tumbler, 3.5" flat	225	___
Tumbler, 4.25" flat	40	___
Tumbler, 5" w/foot	100	___
Vase, 7"	650	___
Vase, 7" satin finish	65	___

Note: 6.5" green cereal bowl, $100.

*trtp = too rare to price

OLD ENGLISH
(1926-1929 Indiana Glass Company)

Our presentation of this pattern needs the help of someone who has accumulated a collection of Old English. We had a great deal of difficulty locating a good representation for this book; it seems a pattern you just don't find.

Dealers have reported that even at shows this is a very hard pattern to sell with the exception of the pitcher with the cover.

11" footed fruit bowl, candlesticks. *Courtesy of Paul Reichwein.*

Far left: 5.5" & 4.5" tumbler. *Courtesy of Staci & Jeff Shuck/Gray Goose Antiques.*

Left: Sugar w/ lid. *Courtesy of Vic & Jean Laermans.*

Above: Sherbet.

Left: 9.5" bowl. *Courtesy of Charlie Diefenderfer.*

OLD ENGLISH	All colors	Qty
Bowl, 4"	25	___
Bowl, 9" w/foot	35	___
Bowl, 9.5" flat	50	___
Bowl, 11" fruit, w/foot	50	___
Candlestick, ea.	30	___
Candy jar w/lid	75	___
Comport, 3.5", 2 styles	35	___
Creamer	25	___
Egg cup (only in crystal)	12	___
Goblet, 5.75"	40	___
Pitcher	80	___
Pitcher cover	120	___
Sandwich server w/ center handle	75	___
Sherbet, 2 styles	25	___
Sugar base	25	___
Sugar lid	40	___
Tumbler, 4.5"	30	___
Tumbler, 5.5"	40	___
Underplate for comport	30	___
Vase, 5.25" fan	60	___
Vase, 8"	60	___
Vase, 8.25"	60	___
Vase, 12"	75	___

11" bowl, pair of candlesticks. *Courtesy of Debora & Paul Torsiello, Debzie's Glass.*

6.75" comport. *Courtesy of Debora & Paul Torsiello, Debzie's Glass.*

ORCHID
(1929-1930s Paden City Glass Manufacturing Company)

The exquisite quality of Paden City Glass is evident in the beautiful Orchid pattern. As with other lines of glass manufactured by Paden City during the 1930s, the Orchid shapes were used elsewhere. The basic mold was advertised as "Line No. 300." Etchings were applied to these pieces thus creating masterpieces like Orchid. There are several orchid designs that have been applied by Paden City artists, and most collectors are content with any design they are fortunate enough to discover.

Orchid was produced in the colors that helped to create Paden City's excellent reputation: Cheri-glo (pink), crystal, Golden Glow (amber), and green as well as amethyst, black, cobalt blue, and red. Interesting to note, Paden City was one of the few manufacturers to use the term "cobalt blue" during the 1930s.

There is nothing easy about collecting Orchid. No color is particularly easy to find, and not one item is common. Even searches in antique malls tend to yield poor results. Despite its scarcity, sellers who are unfamiliar with Depression Glass still recognize the superb quality of Orchid and price their merchandise accordingly. If you are seeking Orchid try attending Depression Glass shows and sales, and contacting the dealers listed in the directory at the back of the book.

ORCHID	Black, Cobalt blue, & Red	Other colors	Qty
Bowl, 4.75"	65	30	____
Bowl, 8.5" w/handles	150	100	____
Bowl, 8.75"	150	100	____
Bowl, 10" w/foot	200	125	____
Bowl, 11"	200	100	____
Cake stand	175	100	____
Candlestick, 5.75" ea.	220	120	____
Candy box w/cover (square shape)	220	120	____
Candy box w/cover (3-leaf clover shape)	220	120	____
Comport, 3.25" tall	65	30	____
Comport, 6.75" tall	150	75	____
Creamer	100	60	____
Ice Bucket, 6"	220	120	____
Mayonnaise, 3-piece set	200	120	____
Plate, 8.5"	85		____
Sandwich server w/ center handle	125	75	____
Sugar	100	60	____
Vase, 5"	300		____
Vase, 8.25" elliptical	280	120	____
Vase, 10"	325	150	____

Two 10" vases, 5" vase, 8.25" elliptical vase. *Courtesy of Debora & Paul Torsiello, Debzie's Glass.*

OVIDE
(1930-1935 Hazel-Atlas Glass Company)

The color schemes on Ovide platonite are endless. Several combinations are presented here, but these represent a sampling of the vast array of possibilities.

As with most other fired-on patterns, Ovide is not particularly popular with the vast majority of today's collectors. At this time Ovide is an inexpensive pattern. So, if you are interested in collecting a service, it won't require a serious financial commitment. On the other hand, as Ovide is not in great demand, it is a line of glassware that normally won't be available at Depression Glass shows. Don't be afraid to ask for it as most dealers have an abundance of inventory other than what you currently see on display.

Creamer & sugar.

14-piece boxed set including four 9" dinner plates, four cups, four saucers, one creamer, and one sugar.

Cup.

Sugar.

OVIDE	Decorated	Deco	Black	Green	Qty
Bowl, 4.75" berry	10				___
Bowl, 5.5" cereal	15				___
Bowl, 8" berry	25				___
Candy dish w/lid	35		50	20	___
Cocktail, stemmed			8	4	___
Creamer	15	85	10	4	___
Cup	10	60	8	3	___
Plate, 6" sherbet	5			3	___
Plate, 8" luncheon	10	45		4	___
Plate, 9" dinner	20				___
Platter, 11"	25				___
Salt & pepper	35		35	30	___
Saucer	5	18	5	3	___
Sherbet	12	50	8	3	___
Sugar	15	85	10	4	___
Tumbler	25	85			___

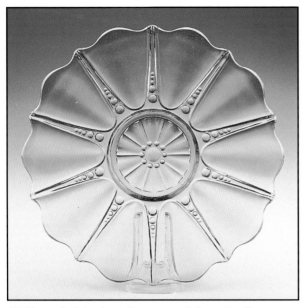

13.5" sandwich plate. *Courtesy of Joan Kauffman.*

OYSTER AND PEARL
(1938-1940   Anchor Hocking Glass Corporation)

The only offerings available in this relatively commonly-seen pattern are serving pieces and candlesticks. There are no cups, saucers, plates for eating, or tumblers. However, there are some charming occasional pieces that are pleasantly designed and affordable within most budgets, particularly in pink.

Ruby is the most difficult color of Oyster and Pearl to locate. Royal Ruby collectors often appreciate the design of these pieces because so much made in Royal Ruby has no design whatsoever.

Added to the list is the 10.5" x 7.75" tray made in all four fired-on colors—blue, green, peach, and yellow—and pictured with the fired-on candlesticks and bowl.

Back: two 10.25" oval 2-part relishes; *front row:*
two 6.5" bonbons. *Courtesy of Jane O'Brien.*

Candle holders, 10.5" console bowl. *Courtesy of Jane O'Brien & Tanya Poillucci.*

OYSTER & PEARL	Ruby	Pink	Crystal, other colors, & fired-on	Qty
Bowl, 5.25" jelly, heart-shaped w/1 handle	25	15	8	___
Bowl, 5.5" round w/1 handle	25	15		___
Bowl, 6.5" bon bon, deep	30	18		___
Bowl, 10.5" console	60	30	15	___
Candle holder, 3.5" ea.	30	20	10	___
Plate, 13.5" sandwich	60	25		___
Relish, 10.25" oval, 2-part		18		___
Tray, 10.5" x 7.75"			15	___

Fired-on pieces: 10.5" console bowl, 10.5" x 7.75" tray, candle holders.

PARK AVENUE

(1941-early 1970s   Federal Glass Company)

There is little interest in this little pattern. However, Park Avenue tumblers are fairly common and you may have questions as to what you are looking at. Like Peanut Butter Glasses and Swanky Swigs, some Park Avenue tumblers were marketed with a food product inside. The pry-off top was removed, the contents consumed, and a "free" glass was added to the cupboard. Collectors buying Park Avenue usually either have a sentimental attachment to these tumblers or appreciate buying something reasonably priced with a bit of age to it.

4.75" dessert bowls in a variety of colors.
Courtesy of Charlie Diefenderfer.

PARK AVENUE	Crystal & Amber	Qty
Ashtray, 3.5"	5	___
Ashtray, 4.5"	5	___
Bowl, 4.75" dessert	5	___
Bowl, 8.5" vegetable	10	___
Candle holder, 5" each	10	___
Tumbler, 2.25" whiskey, 1.25 oz.	4	___
Tumbler, 3.5" juice, 4.5 oz.	4	___
Tumbler, 3.75", water 9 oz.	4	___
Tumbler, 4.75", water 10 oz.	6	___
Tumbler, 5.25" iced tea, 12 oz.	6	___

Note: 4.75" dessert bowls in frosted colors $8 each.

8.5" vegetable bowl,
4.75" dessert bowl,
3.5" 4.5 oz. tumbler.

Back row: 10.5" grill plate, 10.5" dinner plate, 9" luncheon plate; *middle row:* 8.25" pitcher, 10" oval vegetable bowl, 5.5" flat tumbler, 4.75" cream soup bowl, 8.25" pitcher; *front row:* 6" cereal bowl, cup & saucer, salt & pepper. *Courtesy of Marie Talone & Paul Reichwein.*

PATRICIAN

(1933-1937 Federal Glass Company)

Although amber ("Golden Glow") Patrician is less valuable than green ("Springtime Green") or pink, it is the color of choice for most Patrician collectors and fortunately the easiest color to locate. While it is true that collectors of amber Depression Glass usually select Patrician or Madrid as their pattern based on favoring the color, the 10.5" dinner plate appeals to many who buy Depression Glass with the intention of using it. Dinners in many patterns are difficult to find, and in some cases dinner plates were never produced, but the Patrician dinner plate remains affordable and available at a considerably larger dimension than dinner plates in other patterns. This combination of being accessible and affordable is often an influence on committing to collect a pattern, especially if a service of eight or ten or twelve is being planned.

The pricing accurately reflects the availability of the pieces and colors. Thus far, the demand for amber can be met and prices have not risen a great deal in recent years.

Patrician plates were molded with a severe edge where the rim meets the eating surface. Prior to buying, one should take the time to run a fingernail along this inner rim as it is prone to being damaged.

PATRICIAN	Green	Pink	Amber & Crystal (see Notes at bottom)	Qty
Bowl, 4.75" cream soup	22	20	17	____
Bowl, 5" berry	15	14	14	____
Bowl, 6" cereal	30	26	26	____
Bowl, 8.5" berry	45	35	45	____
Bowl, 10" vegetable	40	35	30	____
Butter dish base	75	150	65	____
Butter dish lid	50	75	35	____
Butter complete	125	225	100	____
Cookie jar/lid	600		100	____
Creamer	18	15	12	____
Cup	12	12	10	____
Jam dish, 6"	50	40	35	____
Pitcher, 8" molded handle	130	125	120	____
Pitcher, 8.25" applied handle	160	140	160	____
Plate, 6" bread & butter	10	10	10	____
Plate, 7.5" salad	18	18	18	____
Plate, 9" luncheon	15	12	12	____
Plate, 10.5" dinner	45	20	10	____
Plate, 10.5" grill	18	15	14	____
Platter, 11.5"	35	35	30	____
Salt & pepper	75	95	65	____
Saucer	12	10	10	____
Sherbet	18	15	12	____
Sugar base	18	15	12	____
Sugar lid	65	65	65	____
Tumbler, 4" flat	35	35	30	____
Tumbler, 4.5" flat	30	30	30	____
Tumbler, 5.25" w/foot	75		65	____
Tumbler, 5.5" flat	45	40	45	____

Note: Crystal same as Amber EXCEPT: complete butter, $125; 8.25" pitcher w/applied handle, $175; 10.5" dinner plate, $25.

Above: Butter. *Courtesy of Michael Rothenberger/Mike's Collectables.*

Right: 5.25" footed tumbler. *Courtesy of Charlie Diefenderfer.*

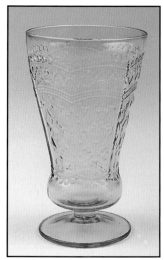

PATRICK
(1930s   Lancaster Glass Company)

This pattern was quite a challenge for us to locate. Patrick, could you please phone home so we can take your picture?

It is easy to identify Lancaster glass, especially in yellow. Lancaster Glass Company produced a "signature" pure, bright yellow that was called topaz. Pink (rose) was also produced and is even more difficult to find than yellow. Glassware made by this company has smooth rims and edges. There are no troubling edges of extra glass as seen in Lorain and Horseshoe.

Frustrated Patrick collectors will occasionally buy other Lancaster Glass Company items such as Jubilee just for the gratification of making a purchase. Conversely, Jubilee collectors rarely buy Patrick. Of course, there is very little Patrick to be found.

Detail of pattern. *Courtesy of Michael Rothenberger/Mike's Collectables.*

PATRICK	Pink	Yellow	Qty
Bowl, 9" fruit w/handles	200	150	____
Bowl, 11.5" low console	180	140	____
Candlestick, ea.	85	85	____
Candy bowl w/cover	200	175	____
Cheese & cracker	200	175	____
Creamer	90	50	____
Cup	85	50	____
Goblet, 4" stemmed cocktail	100	100	____
Goblet, 4.75" juice	100	100	____
Goblet, 6" water	100	100	____
Mayonnaise, 3-piece set	240	220	____
Plate, 7" sherbet	30	20	____
Plate, 7.5" salad	40	30	____
Plate, 8" luncheon	60	40	____
Plate, 9"	60		____
Plate, 11" sandwich w/handles	90	70	____
Saucer	25	15	____
Sherbet, 4.75" w/stem	80	65	____
Sugar	90	50	____
Tray, 11" sandwich w/center handle	175	140	____

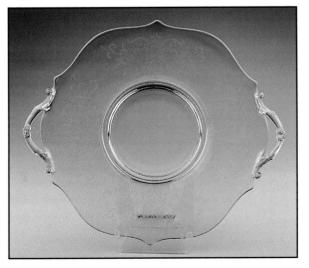

Above: Creamer, two sugars, 8" luncheon plate, cup & saucer. *Courtesy of Vic & Jean Laermans.*

Left: 11" sandwich plate w/ handles. *Courtesy of Michael Rothenberger/Mike's Collectables.*

Detail of pattern. *Courtesy of Debora & Paul Torsiello, Debzie's Glass.*

12" vase. *Courtesy of Debora & Paul Torsiello, Debzie's Glass.*

PEACOCK & ROSE

(1928-1930s Paden City Glass Manufacturing Company)

Peacock and Rose is another fine example of the expert craftsmanship of Paden City Glass Manufacturing Company. The blanks, Line No. 300, were used in other patterns such as Cupid to create magnificent glassware.

Although easier to find than Orchid and Cupid, the "Peacocks" will require a committed collector (who may feel a need to be "committed" for taking on this daunting challenge). As with so much of Paden City's glassware, there are no bargains to be had and finding anything can be quite a challenge. Paden City is not for the faint of heart. One needs tenacity to maintain the hunt and control to remain relatively calm at that inspirational moment of discovery! If you have risen to the challenge of hunting for Peacock and Rose look for pieces in amber, black, cobalt blue, blue, crystal (clear), green, pink, and red.

Back: 8.5" oval bowl; *front:* 10" footed bowl w/ rolled edge, 9.5" footed bowl. *Courtesy of Michael Rothenberger/Mike's Collectables.*

6.25" comport, 2" tall rolled edge candlestick (this is Nora Bird, $100 ea.), 14" rolled edge console bowl. *Courtesy of Michael Rothenberger/Mike's Collectables.*

PEACOCK & ROSE

	Any color	Qty
Bowl, 8.5" flat	130	____
Bowl, 8.5" oval	200	____
Bowl, 8.75" w/foot	200	____
Bowl, 9.5" w/center handle	175	____
Bowl, 9.5" w/foot	200	____
Bowl, 10" w/foot	200	____
Bowl, 10.5" w/center handle	175	____
Bowl, 10.5" w/foot	200	____
Bowl, 10.5" flat	200	____
Bowl, 11" console, rolled edge	180	____
Bowl, 14" console, rolled edge	220	____
Cake plate, 11" w/foot	150	____
Candlestick, 5" across, ea.	85	____
Candy box w/lid, 7"	200	____
Cheese and cracker	200	____
Comport, 3.25" tall	130	____
Comport, 6.25" tall	150	____
Ice bucket, 6"	200	____
Ice tub, 4.75"	200	____
Mayonnaise, 3 piece set	130	____
Pitcher, 5"	265	____
Relish, 6.25"	130	____
Tray, 10" sandwich	150	____
Tumbler, 2.25"	100	____
Tumbler, 3"	80	____
Tumbler, 4"	80	____
Tumbler, 4.75" ftd.	80	____
Tumbler, 5.25"	100	____
Vase, 8.25", elliptical	400	____
Vase, 10" 2 styles	275	____
Vase, 12"	300	____

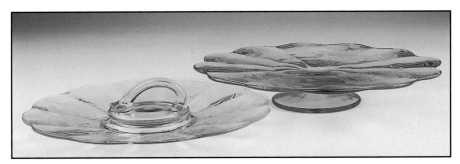

Above: 10" sandwich tray, 11" footed cake plate. *Courtesy of Debora & Paul Torsiello, Debzie's Glass.*

Left: 10" vase, ice bucket. *Courtesy of Michael Rothenberger/ Mike's Collectables.*

10" vases in a variety of colors. *Courtesy of Debora & Paul Torsiello, Debzie's Glass.*

PEACOCK REVERSE
(1930s   Paden City Glass Manufacturing Company)

Back: 6" vase; *front:* 5" candlesticks, 9.25" bowl w/ center handle. *Courtesy of Michael Rothenberger/ Mike's Collectables.*

Forever using and reusing molds, Paden City created Peacock Reverse by etching a lovely motif on the blanks from Crow's Foot and "Penny" Line. Crow's Foot is featured in this book, but if you have "Penny" Line, No. 991, please drop us a line! The Crow's Foot pieces are easy to detect as they have telltale footprints.

Paden City Glass Manufacturing Company created pieces with a quality that was superior to much of the other glass from the 1930s. Artistically, the designs were spectacular, and the glass itself was carefully finished with no rough seams or mold lines. There was such an impressive palette of colors that Paden City earned distinction even during the time of production. Look for this pattern in amber, black, cobalt blue, crystal (clear), green, pink, red, and yellow.

Peacock Reverse, like much of Paden City glassware, is difficult to find. A big thank you to Michael Rothenberger/Mike's Collectables for much of the Paden City glassware presented. You can contact Mike by using the dealer directory in the back of the book.

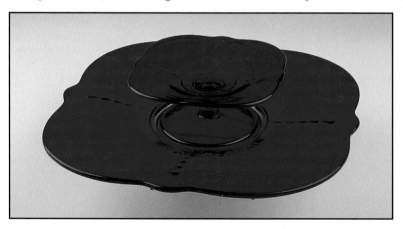

Cheese & cracker. *Courtesy of Debora & Paul Torsiello, Debzie's Glass.*

Sugar & creamer. *Courtesy of Vic & Jean Laermans.*

PEACOCK REVERSE	Any color	Qty
Bowl, 4.75"	50	____
Bowl, 8.75"	125	____
Bowl, 8.75" w/handles	125	____
Bowl, 9.25" w/center handle	150	____
Bowl, 11.75", console	150	____
Candlestick, ea., 5" tall	85	____
Candy box w/lid	200	____
Cheese & cracker	200	____
Comport, 3.25" tall	85	____
Comport, 4.25" tall	85	____
Creamer, 2.75"	90	____
Cup	85	____
Plate, 5.75" sherbet	25	____
Plate, 8.5" luncheon	70	____
Plate, 10.5" w/handles	100	____
Plate, sandwich w/center handle	85	____
Saucer	25	____
Sherbet, 2 sizes	75	____
Sugar, 2.75"	90	____
Tumbler, 4"	100	____
Vase, 10"	200	____

PETALWARE

(1930-1940 Macbeth-Evans Glass Company)

Petalware is one of the most undervalued patterns of Depression Glass available. It was manufactured by Macbeth-Evans Glass Company, the source for American Sweetheart and Dogwood. The same delicate quality of these two patterns is also seen on Petalware, but Petalware is not collected with the same enthusiasm as other Macbeth-Evans patterns.

Petalware is collected in all colors, but crystal (clear) gets minimal attention. Iris and Manhattan do an efficient job of monopolizing most of the crystal market. The pink is a true powder pink, not orangish as some patterns of Depression Glass, and all of the colors are molded into light-weight, relatively inexpensive pieces. From our own experience, if we take Petalware to a show it always sells, but usually to a new collector.

This pattern was produced for a decade, which was a long time compared to many other Depression Glass patterns, so Petalware is plentiful. If you are seeking a pattern this is one you may wish to consider. Just keep in mind the tumblers were only made in crystal.

We have had a chance to do some careful measurements of this glassware, so you will find changes from the listings in *Mauzy's Comprehensive Handbook of Depression Glass Prices*. As these adjustments are primarily 0.25" we trust that there is no confusion.

Above: *Back row:* 7" soup bowl, 13" platter; *front row:* cream soup bowl, 6" dessert/cereal bowl, 9" berry bowl. *Courtesy of Bob & Cindy Bentley.*

Left: 3-tier & 2-tier tidbits. *Courtesy of Bob & Cindy Bentley.*

Lamp shade (one of many shapes). *Courtesy of Bob & Cindy Bentley.*

Back row: 9" dinner plate, 11" salver, 8" salad plate; *front row:* cup & saucer, sherbet on 6" bread & butter plate, sugar & creamer. *Courtesy of Bob & Cindy Bentley.*

Above: *Back:* 9" dinner plate, 6" bread & butter plate, 9" berry bowl; *front:* cream soup bowl, condiment.

Right: Decorated 8" salad plates, cup & saucer.

Decorated 8" salad plates. *Courtesy of Bob & Cindy Bentley.*

Creamer & two sugars. *Courtesy Of Vic & Jean Laermans.*

PETALWARE	Pink	Monax & Cremax (plain)	Decorated & Ivrene	Crystal	Qty
Bowl, cream soup, 4.5"	20	15	15	5	____
Bowl, 5.75" dessert/cereal	15	10	15	5	____
Bowl, 7" soup		60	75		____
Bowl, 8.5" berry	30	25	35	12	____
Creamer, 3.25"	15	10	15	5	____
Cup	10	8	10	5	____
Lamp shade (multiple shapes)		25			____
Pitcher				25	____
Plate, 6.25" bread & butter	8	8	12	4	____
Plate, 8.25" salad	12	10	15	4	____
Plate, 9" dinner	20	15	24	6	____
Plate, 11" salver	20	15	25	8	____
Plate, 12" salver	20	20			____
Platter, 13"	25	20	30	10	____
Saucer	5	5	5		____
Sherbet, 4"		22			____
Sherbet, 4.25"	15	15	18	5	____
Sugar, 3.5"	15	10	15	5	____
Tidbits, 2- or 3-tier servers, several sizes	30	25	25	15	____
Tumbler, 3 sizes				12	____

Note: Cobalt Blue condiment, $10; add $5 for metal lid with wooden knob; add $8 for metal lid with Bakelite knob. Cobalt 9" berry bowl, $50; 4.5" sherbet, $30.

"PHILBE"
FIRE-KING DINNERWARE
(1940   Hocking Glass Company)

. . . and the award for "Most Rare Pattern of All" goes to . . . Philbe! What a challenge it is to locate Philbe. With only one year of production few pieces are available and many of them are in collections. It is rare to find Philbe in antique malls. Listings do appear on Internet auctions and the prices shown here reflect the prices individuals are paying to add Philbe to their collections.

Often glass companies used the same molds to create several lines of glassware. Hocking Glass Company produced Cameo from 1930 through 1934. The molds were then resurrected in 1940 for Philbe as the creamer clearly demonstrates.

Collectors of Philbe are usually seeking any item they can find rather than looking specifically for a particular color. Even crystal (clear) becomes an important color as it is not easily found. Philbe blue is a unique shade that is not often seen in Depression Glass, and if you don't appreciate this hue perhaps you can appreciate its rarity.

Above: Two 10" oval vegetable bowls, 4" water tumbler, 4.75" stemmed sherbet. *Courtesy of Staci & Jeff Shuck/Gray Goose Antiques.*

Left: Creamer. *Courtesy of Neil McCurdy - Hoosier Kubboard Glass.*

PHILBE	Blue	Pink & Green	Crystal	Qty
Bowl, 5.5" cereal	180	100	35	___
Bowl, 7.25" salad	300	120	50	___
Bowl, 10" oval vegetable	500	200	100	___
Candy jar w/lid, 4"	2000	1500	500	___
Cookie jar w/lid	trtp*	trtp*	trtp*	___
Creamer, 3.25"	300	200	65	___
Cup	300	200	100	___
Goblet, 7.25"	600	300	150	___
Pitcher, 6" juice	2200	1200	500	___
Pitcher, 8.5"	4000	2500	600	___
Plate, 6" sherbet	200	100	50	___
Plate, 8" luncheon	180	100	40	___
Plate, 10" heavy sandwich	350	200	50	___
Plate, 10.5" salver	250	125	50	___
Plate, 10.5" grill	250	125	50	___
Plate, 11.5" salver	300	125	50	___
Platter, 12" w/tab handles	500	300	80	___
Saucer/sherbet plate	200	100	50	___
Sherbet, 4.75" stemmed	1500	500		___
Sugar	300	200	65	___
Tumbler, 3.5" juice w/foot	500	350	80	___
Tumbler, 4" water, no foot	400	300	80	___
Tumbler, 5.25" w/foot	300	200	80	___
Tumbler, 6.5" iced tea w/foot	300	200	80	___

*trtp = too rare to price

Cup, 11.5" salver, 6.5" footed iced tea tumbler.

9.5" plate w/ center indent, 4" water tumbler.
Courtesy of Diefenderfer's Collectibles & Antiques.

PINEAPPLE AND FLORAL
Reproduced
(1932-1937 Indiana Glass Company)

In order to make this book easier to use, Pineapple and Floral is listed by its commonly used nickname rather than its true name—No. 618.

There is not a great deal of competition for this pattern which makes it interesting to note that Indiana Glass Company reissued the 7.5" berry bowl. It is a practical size, but did the demand warrant this action?

As with other patterns with a smaller legion of devotees, you may need to talk to dealers in order to locate needed objects. Pineapple and Floral is heavy and may be left elsewhere when dealers pack for shows.

Back: platter, 3-part relish; *front:* sugar, creamer, diamond-shaped comport.

Back: 9.5" dinner plate, 6" sherbet plate, sherbet; *front:* cream soup bowl.

PINEAPPLE & FLORAL	Crystal, Fired-on red, & Amber	Qty
Ashtray, 4.5"	10	___
Bowl, cream soup	10	___
Bowl, 4.75" berry	12	___
Bowl, 6" oatmeal	14	___
Bowl, 7.5" berry *R*	5	___
Bowl, 10" oblong vegetable	10	___
Comport, 6.25" diamond shaped *R*	4	___
Creamer	5	___
Cup	5	___
Plate, 6" sherbet	3	___
Plate, 8.5" salad	5	___
Plate, 9.5" dinner	10	___
Plate, 9.5" w/center indent	10	___
Plate, 11.5" cake	8	___
Plate, 11.5" w/center indent	10	___
Platter	8	___
Relish, 11.5" 3-part	10	___
Saucer	2	___
"Servitor" 2-tier 8" & 11" plates	15	___
"Servitor" 2-tier 6" & 9" plate	15	___
Sherbet	10	___
Sugar	5	___
Tumbler, 4"	20	___
Tumbler, 4.5" iced tea	25	___
Vase, 12"	35	___
Vase holder (metal)	35	___

Reproduction information: Other fired on colors, light pink.

Note: Green dinner plate, $15

PRETZEL

(1930s-1970s Indiana Glass Company)

Pretzel, officially named No. 622, is a pattern of contradictions. As common as the 10.25" celery bowl is, just try to find a pitcher! The pattern was primarily issued in crystal (clear), but Indiana Glass Company produced a few items in teal, one of the least-used colors in Depression Glass.

Pretzel is durable and the pieces are quite practical. Several Pretzel serving pieces are quite common and may be found scattered about antique malls being offered by sellers who may have no idea they are peddling a Depression Glass pattern. These familiar objects include the celery, 8.5" pickle bowl, and 7" leaf plate which were items Indiana added to the line in the 1970s. One can place "vintage" glassware on the table for a minimal investment.

PRETZEL	Crystal	Qty
Bowl, 4.5" fruit cup	10	____
Bowl, 7.5" soup	12	____
Bowl, 8.5" oblong pickle w/handles	8	____
Bowl, 9.5" berry	20	____
Bowl, 10.25" oblong celery	5	____
Creamer	10	____
Cup	8	____
Leaf, 7" olive	8	____
Pitcher	trtp*	____
Plate, 6"	4	____
Plate, 6" w/tab (fruit cup plate or cheese plate)	5	____
Plate, 7.25" square snack plate w/cup indent	12	____
Plate, 7.25" 3-part square	12	____
Plate, 8.25" salad	8	____
Plate, 9.25" dinner	12	____
Plate, 11.5" sandwich/cake	15	____
Saucer	2	____
Sugar	10	____
Tray, 10.25" oblong celery	5	____
Tumbler, 3.5"	75	____
Tumbler, 4.5"	75	____
Tumbler, 5.5"	100	____

*trtp = too rare to price
Note: Teal cup, $125; saucer, $45. Plates with center design twice those with plain center.

Back: 9.25" dinner plate, 11.25" sandwich/cake plate, saucer; *middle:* 4.5" tumbler, 9.5" berry bowl, cup; *front:* creamer, sugar, 4.5" fruit cup bowl. *Courtesy of Paul Reichwein.*

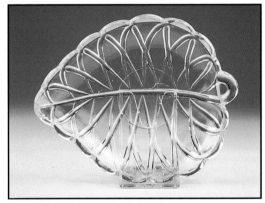

7" leaf (olive).

PRIMO

(1932 United States Glass Company)

United States Glass Company produced Primo for only one year. Not many pieces were manufactured and this shortage is evident in our book. We would love to hear from a "Primo-donna" who could assist us with the next edition.

If you choose to do an Internet search for this pattern, look under the nickname "Paneled Aster." Searching for Primo will bring up all kinds of things having nothing to do with Depression Glass.

All of the basic items needed to set the table and serve the meal are available in both yellow and green, but you may have a long wait until you can do so. This is a difficult pattern to find, and locating items in satisfactory condition requires even more effort. Due to the molding having an extra rim of glass, Primo is susceptible to damage.

5.75" tumbler, 5.25" x 4.75" coaster/ashtray. *Courtesy of Staci & Jeff Shuck/Gray Goose Antiques.*

PRIMO	Yellow	Green	Qty
Bowl, 4.5"	22	18	____
Bowl, 7.75"	35	30	____
Bowl, 11" footed console bowl	45	35	____
Cake plate, 10"	35	30	____
Coaster or ashtray, 5.25" x 4.75"	15	12	____
Creamer	20	15	____
Cup	15	12	____
Plate, 6.25"	12	10	____
Plate, 7.5"	12	10	____
Plate, 10" dinner	25	22	____
Plate, 10" grill	20	15	____
Saucer	5	4	____
Sherbet	18	15	____
Sugar	20	15	____
Tumbler, 5.75"	25	22	____

10" grill plate, cup & saucer.

PRINCESS
Reproduced
(1931-1934   Hocking Glass Company)

Princess perfectly exemplifies that a blanket statement can't be made that one particular color is "better" than another. Pink and green Princess are collected equally, sharing the same level of popularity. One can find both colors in the marketplace. Yellow and topaz are harder to find, but they are in less demand than the other colors. Some yellow items, more so than topaz, which was limited to fewer pieces, are extremely hard to find augmenting their value. So, you will notice when scanning the price columns the numbers go up and down.

The bowl commonly called "hat shaped" was actually listed by Hocking Glass Company as an "orange or flower" bowl. This particular item is extremely popular, and shoppers unfamiliar with Depression Glass looking for a gift often select this for their purchase.

Adam, Lorain, Madrid, Mayfair "Open Rose," and Princess are among the only patterns to have square-shaped plates. This is important to keep in mind if someone is attempting to identify an unknown pattern or object.

There is no true saucer for Princess cups as the cups sit on sherbet plates. This is sometimes confusing to collectors expecting a saucer.

Satinized items are in low demand at this time. The following pieces may be found with a satinized finish: 9.5" orange or flower bowl, candy jar and lid, cookie jar and lid, creamer, 10.25" sandwich plate with two closed handles, salt and pepper shakers, sugar and lid, and 8" vase. Some of these items have become relatively scarce, and tastes change, so it is always possible that in the future the value of these pieces could increase dramatically.

We would love to sing the blues in the next book, so if you have blue Princess please let us know!

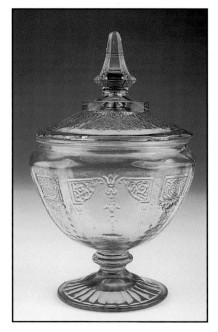

Above: 5.5" oatmeal bowl, 8.25" salad plate, 9.5" dinner plate, 6.5" footed iced tea tumbler. *Courtesy of Diefenderfer's Collectibles & Antiques.*

Right: Candy jar w/ lid. *Courtesy of Bryan & Marie James.*

PRINCESS	Pink & Green	Topaz & Apricot	Qty
Ashtray, 4.5"	85	120	____
Bowl, 4.5" berry	25	50	____
Bowl, 5.5" oatmeal	40	35	____
Bowl, 9" salad, octagonal	65	150	____
Bowl, 9.5" orange or flower (hat shaped)	75	150	____
Bowl 10" vegetable	35	65	____
Butter dish base	50	*trtp	____
Butter dish lid	75	*trtp	____
Butter complete	125	*trtp	____
Cake stand, 10"	35		____
Candy jar w/lid *R*	70		____
Coaster	85	120	____
Cookie jar/lid	75		____
Creamer	20	20	____
Cup	15	10	____
Pitcher, 6" no foot	70	700	____
Pitcher, 7.5" w/foot	750		____
Pitcher, 8" no foot	60	125	____
Plate, 5.5" sherbet or saucer	10	5	____
Plate, 8.25" salad	20	20	____
Plate, 9.5" dinner	30	20	____
Plate, 9.5" grill	16	8	____
Plate, 10.25" sandwich w/closed handles (add 1" if measuring handles)	30	175	____
Plate, 10.5" grill w/closed handles	15	10	____
Platter, 12"	30	65	____
Relish, 7.5" divided	30	100	____
Relish, 7.5"	200	250	____
Salt & pepper, 4.5"	65	85	____
Spice shaker, 5.5" ea	25		____
Saucer or sherbet plate	10	5	____
Sherbet	25	35	____
Sugar base	20	20	____
Sugar lid	25	20	____
Tumbler, 3" juice	30	30	____
Tumbler, 4" water	30	30	____
Tumbler, 4.75" square foot	65		____
Tumbler, 5.25" iced tea	40	30	____
Tumbler, 5.5" round foot	30	25	____
Tumbler, 6.5" iced tea, round foot	125	175	____
Vase, 8"	45		____

Reproduction information: Candy jar in green: crude & foot missing rays. In pink the new foot is smooth & missing rays. Old knobs have 2 flat sides & two round sides; new knobs are flat on all 4 sides. All blue candy jars are new.

Note: Satinized pieces 1/2 value of transparent items in same color.

*trtp = too rare to price

Note: Items in	Ice Blue	Qty:
Cookie jar w/lid	1000	____
Cup	175	____
Plate, 5.5" sherbet/saucer	175	____
Plate, 9.5" grill	175	____

Back: 10" cake plate; *middle:* 8" pitcher, 9.5" orange or flower bowl (hat shaped), 8" pitcher; *front:* 5.5" tumbler, sherbet, cookie jar w/ lid. *Courtesy of Marie Talone & Paul Reichwein.*

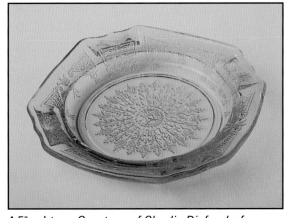

4.5" ashtray. *Courtesy of Charlie Diefenderfer.*

Reproduction candy jar w/ lid.

4.5" shakers in various colors. *Courtesy of Michael Rothenberger/Mike's Collectables.*

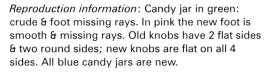

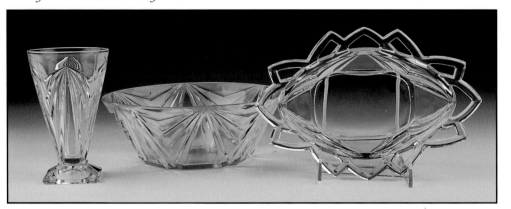

5.5" 8 oz. tumbler, 8.5" berry bowl, 9.5" oval bowl.

PYRAMID

(1928-1932...see note below
Indiana Glass Company)

The actual name of this pattern is "No. 610," but most collectors and dealers use the nickname "Pyramid." To simplify using our books we have opted to list this pattern by its more frequently used nickname.

The strong, geometric forms of Pyramid make this a truly unique pattern. Tea Room is the only other Depression Glass line that resembles Pyramid in any way and newbies to the wonderful world of Depression Glass may get confused early on until they learn to discern the very dynamic differences.

The demand for Pyramid has remained steady in green, pink, and yellow. The prices of crystal (clear) aren't necessarily a reflection of availability, but of demand, as there is generally considerably less interest in crystal than the other colors. However, the crystal pitcher and tumblers are so difficult to locate they are equal in value to the yellow ones.

Note that the 8 ounce tumblers are 5.5" tall. They may be found with bases 2.25" square and 2.5" square and are equal in value.

PYRAMID	Green	Pink	Yellow	Crystal	Qty
Bowl, 4.75" berry	30	30	35	15	___
Bowl, 8.5" berry	45	45	75	25	___
Bowl, 9.5" oval	45	45	65	25	___
Bowl, 9.5" oval pickle w/handles & rounded edges	50	50	65	25	___
Creamer	30	35	45	20	___
Ice tub	125	125	250	50	___
Ice tub cover				trtp*	___
Pitcher	300	300	550	550	___
Relish, 4-part	60	60	75	25	___
Sugar	30	35	45	20	___
Tray w/center handle for creamer & sugar	30	30	65	30	___
Tumbler, 8 oz., 5.5" tall w/2.25" or 2.5" base	60	60	95	95	___
Tumbler, 11 oz.	80	80	120	120	___

*trtp = too rare to price
Note: Black and blue made in 1970s.

Creamers & sugars on center-handled trays. *Courtesy of Debora & Paul Torsiello, Debzie's Glass.*

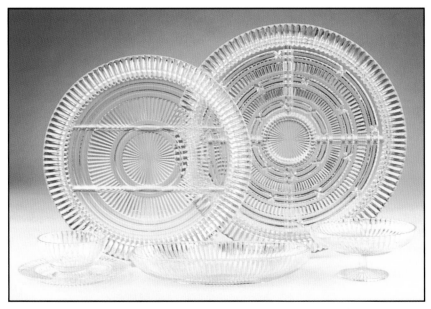

QUEEN MARY

(1936-1939 Hocking Glass Company)

Although Queen Mary is predominantly a pink collector's pattern, and pink was introduced first, there is still enough interest in crystal (clear) that it would behoove dealers to keep crystal in stock. The linear motif recalls Manhattan, which was manufactured by the same glass company, but the strong Deco look of Manhattan is not present in this pattern. Crystal Manhattan is generally more popular than crystal Queen Mary.

Back row: 12" 3-part relish, 14" 4-part relish; *front row:* sherbet on 6" sherbet plate, 5" x 10" celery/pickle, 5.75" comport. *Courtesy of Eunice A. Yohn.*

Back row: 14"
sandwich
plate, 12"
sandwich
plate, 10"
dinner plate;
front row: 4"
bowl, cup &
saucer.
*Courtesy of
Eunice A. Yohn.*

Pink dinner plates have become quite scarce, and they do readily sell for $60 each. Even crystal dinners are disappearing, and if one intends to use this glassware, dinner plates are essential. Most collectors know how rare Queen Mary dinners have become and are pleased to find any even at this relatively expensive price.

It is important to note that there are two creamers and two sugars. The flat creamer and sugar are easy to find and are much less valuable than those with a foot. Note that although there is a metal lid for the butter base, a glass one worth considerably more money is also available. Most collectors opt for an all-glass butter and delay making a purchase until they find one.

There are two cup sizes, one being a bit larger than the other. Some collectors don't care which cup they buy as long as it is consistent with the size they already have. Because the smaller cups fit well on the saucer, and the larger ones rest on the 6" sherbet plate some collectors prefer the smaller cups. The arrangement with the larger cup is the same as the Princess cups and saucers, another Hocking pattern.

Most Queen Mary offerings are relatively easy to find. This is a line worthy of one's consideration if seeking a pattern with a generous selection of pieces in a geometric as opposed to a floral design. Just remember to check the multitude of edges on each piece prior to making a purchase.

6.5" plate, 6" sherbet plate, creamer & sugar.
Courtesy of Eunice A. Yohn.

Back: candy jar w/ lid, butter, 5" footed tumbler; *front:*
cigarette jar (missing lid), 3.5" round coaster/ashtray,
ashtray, salt & pepper. *Courtesy of Eunice A. Yohn.*

6" cereal bowl, 8.75" berry bowl, 4.5" berry bowl,
7" bowl. *Courtesy of Eunice A. Yohn.*

Candlesticks, 5.5" bowl w/ handles.
Courtesy of Eunice A. Yohn.

Butter w/ metal lid. *Courtesy of Michael
Rothenberger/Mike's Collectables.*

Shakers in various colors. *Courtesy of Michael
Rothenberger/Mike's Collectables.*

QUEEN MARY	Pink	Crystal	Qty
Ashtray, 2 styles	7	5	____
Bowl, 4" w/ or w/out single handle	8	5	____
Bowl, 4.5" berry	8	5	____
Bowl, 5" berry	15	8	____
Bowl, 5.5" w/handles	15	8	____
Bowl, 6" cereal	30	10	____
Bowl, 7"	15	8	____
Bowl, 8.75" berry	20	10	____
Butter dish base	30	10	____
Butter dish metal lid	35		____
Butter complete w/metal lid	65		____
Butter dish glass lid	120	20	____
Butter complete w/glass lid	150	30	____
Candy Jar w/lid	55	25	____
Candlestick, 4.5" ea.		8	____
Celery/pickle, 5" x 10"	40	15	____
Cigarette Jar, 2" x 3" oval w/metal lid	20	10	____
Coaster, 3.5" round	8	5	____
Coaster/ashtray, 4.25" sq.	8	5	____
Comport, 5.75"	30	15	____
Creamer w/foot	75	25	____
Creamer, flat	15	8	____
Cup, 2 sizes	12	6	____
Plate, 6" sherbet	10	4	____
Plate, 6.5"	10	4	____
Plate, 8.5" salad		6	____
Plate, 10" dinner	60	25	____
Plate, 12" sandwich	30	15	____
Plate, 12" 3-part relish	40	20	____
Plate, 14" sandwich	40	25	____
Plate, 14" 4-part relish	40	25	____
Punch Bowl Set:Ladle & bowl w/metal ring on which rests 6 cups	trtp*	trtp*	____
Salt & pepper		28	____
Saucer	10	4	____
Sherbet	15	8	____
Sugar w/foot	75	25	____
Sugar, flat	15	8	____
Tumbler, 3.5" juice	20	8	____
Tumbler, 4" water	22	8	____
Tumbler, 5" w/foot	80	30	____

*trtp = too rare to price

Note: Royal Ruby: candlesticks, trtp*; 3.5"
round ashtray, $10. Forest Green: 3.5" round
ashtray, $8.

RADIANCE
(1936-1939 New Martinsville Glass Company)

Debora and Paul Torsiello/Debzie's Glass (they are listed in the dealer directory in the back of the book) generously brought huge tubfuls of New Martinsville glass into the studio and here are some of their treasures. When all of the ice blue Radiance was arranged it was simply breathtaking. We hope you enjoy seeing it as much as we enjoyed the privilege of photographing it.

Radiance is very typical of the extraordinary glass created by New Martinsville Glass Company. The design of the glass was so strong and lovely that surface embellishments were simply unnecessary. Much of the glassware produced by this company has undecorated glass, but these items could never be called plain. They are simple but stunning, as demonstrated by Radiance. Some pieces of Radiance were etched and listed in the New Martinsville Glass Company catalogue as "Etched No. 26 Pattern." However, this embellishment was not needed to make Radiance more attractive; it simply created additional lovely pieces.

The pricing reflects the challenge one will have in locating Radiance. Items with multiple parts such as lids and stoppers command high prices. Finding both pieces of any two-part glassware can be extremely difficult. The candlesticks with prisms are extremely rare as few survived. Please note the pricing for all candlesticks in this book is for each and not for a pair.

Fewer collectors buy crystal (clear) Radiance than the other colors, and amber is in less demand than cobalt blue, emerald green, ice blue, pink, and red. New Jersey and New York seem to have more Radiance than some locations, so happy hunting!

10" flared footed bowl, butter/cheese, 12" flared shallow bowl. *Courtesy of Debora & Paul Torsiello, Debzie's Glass.*

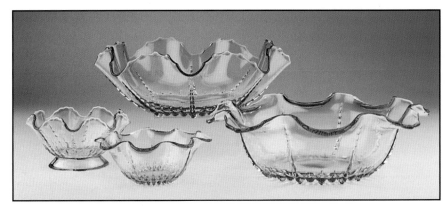

Back: 10" crimped bowl; *front:* 6" crimped footed compote, 6" crimped open bonbon, 12" crimped bowl. *Courtesy of Debora & Paul Torsiello, Debzie's Glass.*

Back: pitcher, 10" crimped bowl w/ short stem; *front:* 8" footed salver, mayonnaise w/ under plate & spoon. *Courtesy of Debora & Paul Torsiello, Debzie's Glass.*

Back row: cheese & cracker, 8" salad plate; *front row:* 6" crimped open bonbon, 9 oz. tumbler, 5" mint w/ handles. *Courtesy of Debora & Paul Torsiello, Debzie's Glass.*

Punch bowl, 14" plate, ladle & cup. *Courtesy of Debora & Paul Torsiello, Debzie's Glass.*

RADIANCE	Pink, Red, Ice Blue	Amber	Qty
Bon Bon, 6" ftd. open	50	25	____
Bon Bon, 6" flared open	50	25	____
Bon Bon, 6" crimped open	50	25	____
Bon Bon, 6" highly crimped open	50	25	____
Bon Bon, 6" covered	130	60	____
Bowl, 5" nut	30	15	____
Bowl, 10" flared w/foot	60	30	____
Bowl, 10" crimped	60	30	____
Bowl, 10" w/short stem crimped	60	30	____
Bowl, 10" w/short stem flared	60	30	____
Bowl, 12" crimped, 2 styles	60	30	____
Bowl, 12" flared (shallow)	60	30	____
Bowl, 12" flared fruit	60	30	____
Bowl, Punch	250	150	____
Butter/Cheese base	200	80	____
Butter/Cheese lid	300	170	____
Butter/Cheese complete	500	250	____
Candelabra, 2 lights w/prisms ea.	250	100	____
Candlestick, 6" ruffled ea.	120	60	____
Candlestick, 8" 1 light w/prisms ea.	200	75	____
Candlestick, 2 lights, no prisms ea.	80	40	____
Candy Box w/ cover	250	150	____
Celery, 10"	40	20	____
Cheese & Cracker	90	60	____
Compote/Mint 5" stemmed	60	30	____
Compote, 6" crimped ftd.	60	30	____
Compote, 6"	60	30	____
Condiment set, 5 pieces: tray, 2 cruets, salt & pepper	295	165	____
Creamer	30	20	____
Cruet	80	40	____
Cup, coffee	20	14	____
Cup, punch	16	10	____
Decanter w/stopper	200	120	____
Goblet, 1 oz. Cordial	50	30	____
Honey jar w/lid	250	150	____
Ladle (for Punch Bowl)	150	120	____
Lamp, 12"	125	75	____
Mayonnaise w/under plate and spoon	120	80	____
Mint, 5" w/handles, 2 styles	30	15	____
Pickle, 7"	45	30	____

Back row: 8" 3-part crimped relish, 12" crimped vase, 7" 2-part flat rimmed relish; *front:* 10" celery. *Courtesy of Debora & Paul Torsiello, Debzie's Glass.*

Left: 8" 1-light candlesticks w/ prisms. (Note how prisms are on a removable ring.) *Courtesy of Debora & Paul Torsiello, Debzie's Glass.*

Below: "Service Set" consisting of tray, sugar & creamer, salt & pepper, and 2-light candlesticks. *Courtesy of Debora & Paul Torsiello, Debzie's Glass.*

RADIANCE (Cont.)	Pink, Red, Ice Blue	Amber	Qty
Pitcher	300	200	____
Plate, 8" salad	20	12	____
Plate, 8" ftd salver	60	30	____
Plate, 11"	60	30	____
Plate, 14"/Punch bowl liner	90	50	____
Relish, 7" 2-part crimped	45	25	____
Relish, 7" 2-part flared	45	25	____
Relish, 7" 2-part flat rim	45	35	____
Relish, 8" 3-part	50	30	____
Relish, 8" 3-part crimped	50	30	____
Relish, 8" 3-part flared	50	30	____
Salt & pepper	125	75	____
Saucer	10	7	____
Service Set, 5 pieces:tray, creamer, sugar, salt & pepper	195	125	____
Sugar	30	20	____
Tray for sugar & creamer	35	20	____
Tumbler	50	35	____
Vase, 10" crimped	100	80	____
Vase, 10" flared	100	80	____
Vase, 12" crimped	125	100	____
Vase, 12" flared	125	100	____

Note: Cobalt Blue is twice the price of Red, Pink, and Ice Blue. Emerald Green: 9" punch bowl, $200; 14" punch bowl liner, $150. Crystal: 1/2 amber values.

6" compote, 8" salad plate, cup & saucer, honey jar w/ lid. *Courtesy of Debora & Paul Torsiello, Debzie's Glass.*

6" ruffled candlesticks, cruets, 12" flared fruit bowl. *Courtesy of Debora & Paul Torsiello, Debzie's Glass.*

RAINDROPS
(PEBBLE OPTIC will be used in future)
(1927-1932 Federal Glass Company)

Federal Glass Company produced this abbreviated pattern early in the history of Depression Glass. It became known as "Raindrops," but we will be reviving the original name "Pebble Optic" in future books.

Confusion sometimes exists between Raindrops, Hex Optic, and Thumbprint. All three patterns are presented in this reference, and hopefully the pictures and measurements will add clarity to the situation. Federal Glass Company imprinted a signature "F" inside a shield on the bottom of much of their glassware. Look for this symbol to help distinguish Raindrops from Hex Optic which was made by Jeannette Glass Company. Because Thumbprint is also a Federal line, one needs to recognize the uniqueness of these two patterns. Raindrops indents are much smaller and almost circular, while Thumbprint indents are considerably larger and elongated.

Above: 6" cereal bowl w/ distinctive Federal marking. *Courtesy of Neil McCurdy - Hoosier Kubboard Glass.*

Right: *Back row:* 6" sherbet plate, 4.5" fruit bowl; *front row:* sugar w/ lid, creamer, 3" tumbler.

RAINDROPS	Green	Qty
Bowl, 4.5" fruit	8	____
Bowl, 6" cereal	12	____
Bowl, 7.5" berry	30	____
Creamer	10	____
Cup	8	____
Plate, 6" sherbet	4	____
Plate, 8" luncheon	8	____
Salt & pepper	trtp*	____
Saucer	4	____
Sherbet	10	____
Sugar base	10	____
Sugar lid	125	____
Tumbler, 1.75" whiskey	10	____
Tumbler, 2.25"	10	____
Tumbler, 3"	10	____
Tumbler, 3.75"	10	____
Tumbler, 4.25"	10	____
Tumbler, 5"	10	____
Tumbler, 5.25"	12	____

*trtp = too rare too price

1.75" whiskey tumbler.

RIBBON

(1930-1931 Hazel-Atlas
Glass Company)

There are many Ribbon look-alike pieces, but true Ribbon has a strong indent to the pattern and not just a weak indication of some design. Ribbon is predominantly a green pattern and many of these pieces that cause confusion are also green. It is certainly fine to purchase them, but disappointing if one intended to buy Ribbon and later discovers an error. Not all sellers of glass are Depression Glass dealers, so take care and depend on your own knowledge and intelligence as glassware does get unintentionally incorrectly identified on price tags.

Ribbon was designed as a luncheon set and all the necessary pieces are available except for a serving plate or platter. The shapes are very reminiscent of other Hazel-Atlas Glass Company patterns like Cloverleaf and Ovide. Glass companies were able to get a lot of mileage from the same molds by reworking their designs. Interesting to note, all three of these Hazel-Atlas patterns were introduced in 1930.

Bowls and shakers create the biggest dilemma in assembling a collection of Ribbon. Collectors of green Depression Glass are attracted to the charming size and shape of the candy jar. This is one of the items frequently selected by shoppers buying a gift for a friend who is really the collector.

Back row: 8" luncheon plate, 6.25" sherbet plate; *front row:* sugar, creamer, cup & saucer, 3" sherbet.

RIBBON	Green	Black	Pink	Qty
Bowl, 4" berry	30			____
Bowl, 5" cereal	40			____
Bowl, 8"	40	40		____
Candy jar w/cover	40			____
Creamer, 3.5"	18			____
Cup	5			____
Plate, 6.25" sherbet	4			____
Plate, 8" luncheon	5	10		____
Salt & pepper	35	50	50	____
Saucer	3			____
Sherbet, 3"	5			____
Sugar, 3.5"	18			____
Tumbler, 5.5"	25			____

RING

(1927-1933 Hocking Glass Company)

Here are some clarifications on two patterns often confused by collectors: distinguish Ring by groupings of four rings; Circle has only one larger group of rings encircling each piece. The shapes of many of the pieces in these two patterns are not the same even though they were both produced by Hocking Glass Company. Green Ring is much harder to find than green Circle. So, if one locates a quantity of green glass with some kind of circles or rings, it will probably be Circle. Both patterns have been presented in this reference and examining the photographs should prove helpful.

The most popular version of this pattern is the crystal decorated with bands of colors. Collectors looking for barware have been selecting this not only because they enjoy the contemporary look, but Ring has many tumblers, a decanter, a cocktail shaker, and even an ice bucket. The order of the colored stripes varies and most people are loyal to one arrangement. Collectors, you may want to write down the color sequence of your glassware to avoid confusion while shopping.

A new Ring item is being presented, a black amethyst open candy with three feet. It is always exciting to discover new pieces!

Creamer & sugar.

3.5" 3 oz. cone-shaped footed juice tumbler, 8" luncheon, 4.75" 10 oz. flat tumbler, 7.25" goblet, 6.5" 14 oz. cone-shaped footed iced tea tumbler. *Courtesy of David G. Baker*.

Ice bucket, 4.25" 9 oz. flat tumbler, cocktail shaker w/ aluminum top, 3" 3 oz. flat tumbler. *Courtesy of Michael Rothenberger/ Mike's Collectables*.

8" luncheon plate, 3.5" 3 oz. cone-shaped footed juice tumbler.

Cup & saucer. *Courtesy of Jane O'Brien.*

8" luncheon plate, 8.5" pitcher.

RING	Crystal w/ Colors	Green	Crystal	Qty
Bowl, 5" berry	8	6	2	____
Bowl, 5.25" divided	40	35	15	____
Bowl, 7" soup	20	15	8	____
Bowl, 8"	18	15	8	____
Butter tub/ice bucket	40	35	20	____
Cocktail shaker w/ aluminum top	40	30	25	____
Creamer	10	8	5	____
Cup	10	6	2	____
Decanter w/stopper	50	40	30	____
Goblet, 3.75" cocktail plain foot	20	15	8	____
Goblet, 4.5" wine	20	15	8	____
Goblet, 7.25"	20	15	8	____
Ice bucket	35	25	15	____
Pitcher, 8"	40	35	20	____
Pitcher, 8.5"	40	35	20	____
Plate, 6" sherbet	7	5	2	____
Plate, 6.5" sherbet w/off-center indent	8	6	3	____
Plate, 8" luncheon	8	6	2	____
Plate, 11" sandwich	18	14	8	____
Salt & pepper	45	60	15	____
Sandwich server w/open handle	28	24	18	____
Saucer	5	3	2	____
Sherbet (fits 6.5" sherbet plate)	18	12	5	____
Sherbet, 5" stemmed	12	8	4	____
Sugar	10	8	5	____
Tumbler, 2" whiskey, 1.5 oz.	15	12	5	____
Tumbler, 3" flat, 3 oz.	10	7	3	____
Tumbler, 3.5" flat, 5 oz.	10	7	3	____
Tumbler, 3.5" footed juice (cone-shaped), 3 oz.	12	10	5	____
Tumbler, 4.25" flat, 9 oz.	10	7	3	____
Tumbler, 4.75" flat, 10 oz.			5	____
Tumbler, 5.25" flat iced tea, 10 oz.	10	7	5	____
Tumbler, 5.5" footed water (cone-shaped), 10 oz.	12	10	5	____
Tumbler, 6.5" footed iced tea (cone-shaped), 14 oz.	18	15	7	____
Vase, 8"	35	30	20	____

Note: Distinguish this pattern from similar ones by looking for bands of **4** rings.

Note: Pink pitcher, $35. Red & Blue: cup, $65; 8" luncheon, $25. Green salt & pepper, $60 for the pair. Black amethyst open candy, 7.75", w/3 feet, $50.

7.25" goblet. *Courtesy of Verna C. Rothenberger.*

Above: Decanter w/ stopper. *Courtesy of Diefenderfer's Collectibles & Antiques.*

Left: Previously unlisted 7.75" dia. 3-footed black amethyst open candy 1.25" tall ($50). *Courtesy of Charlie Diefenderfer.*

Fancy tankard pitcher, 12 oz. iced tea tumbler, 11" vase. *Courtesy of Michael Rothenberger/ Mike's Collectables & Robert Tulanowski.*

ROCK CRYSTAL FLOWER
(1922-1931 McKee Glass Company)

Oh, the fun we had photographing Rock Crystal Flower! Although there were countless stands and pedestals, we had two very special stands that seemed to be the most versatile. While photographing this pattern the weight of a piece broke one of these stands. Blair, a photographer with Bruce, has been able to recognize this pattern ever since.

Rock Crystal Flower was originally issued in crystal (clear) explaining why crystal is more abundant than amber, amethyst, blue, green, milk glass, pink, yellow, or red. Ruby was only made in 1930 and 1931, the shortest run of any color. If you are looking for crystal at a Depression Glass show and sale, be sure to ask for it as dealers often refrain from carrying heavy items to a show, but may have the pieces you need elsewhere. As for the other colors, Rock Crystal Flower is out and about no matter what direction your travels may take you. The more expensive items reflect the pieces that are a greater challenge to find. Several of the bowls, the candlesticks, the lamp, and the tankard pitcher are quite scarce.

This is one of the most complete patterns of Depression Glass with numerous options in many categories. If you are frustrated at your inability to locate one particular tumbler, you may want to substitute it with another one.

The original McKee Glass Company catalog designated the two different edges as "s.e." for scalloped edge and "p.e." for plain edge. The same abbreviations are used in the pricing lists.

Above: 7 oz. goblet.

Right: *Back:* 12 oz. iced tea tumbler, creamer; *middle:* 6 oz. low footed sundae, 9 oz. tumbler, sugar; *front:* cup & saucer. *Courtesy of Marie Talone & Paul Reichwein.*

ROCK CRYSTAL FLOWER	Red	Cobalt	Other Colors	Crystal	Qty
Bon bon, 7.5" s.e.	60	50	30	20	____
Bowl, 4" s.e., sauce	35	30	20	10	____
Bowl, 4.5" s.e., fruit	35	30	20	10	____
Bowl, 5" s.e., fruit	45	35	25	15	____
Bowl, 5" p.e., finger	60	50	40	20	____
Bowl, 7" s.e., salad	65	55	35	25	____
Bowl, 8" s.e., salad	80	60	40	30	____
Bowl, 8.5" p.e., open center handle	250				____
Bowl, 9" s.e., salad	120	100	50	25	____
Bowl, 10.5" s.e., salad	100	80	50	25	____
Bowl, 12.5" s.e., "Center Bowl", ftd.	300	200	150	75	____
Butter dish base				200	____
Butter dish lid				150	____
Butter complete				350	____
Cake stand, 11"	125	100	60	40	____
Candelabra, 2-lite, ea.	150	75	60	20	____
Candelabra, 3-lite, ea.	185	85	70	30	____
Candlestick, flat w/stem, ea.	70	60	40	20	____
Candlestick, 5.5", ea.	100	70	40	20	____
Candlestick, 8.5", ea.	225	175	80	40	____
Candy w/lid, 7"	250	200	80	60	____
Candy w/lid, 9.25"	275	225	100	70	____
Comport, 7"	100	80	50	40	____
Creamer, s.e., flat				30	____
Creamer, s.e., ftd., 4.25"	70	50	30	20	____
Cruet w/stopper, 6 oz.				100	____
Cup	70	50	20	15	____
Devilled egg plate				65	____
Goblet, 4 oz., 3.75"				15	____
Goblet, 7.5 oz	60	50	25	15	____
Goblet, 8 oz.	60	50	25	15	____
Goblet, 8 oz., "Large Footed	60	50	25	15	____
Goblet, 11 oz. iced tea	70	50	20	15	____
Ice Dish, 3 designs				35	____
Jelly, 5" s.e.	50	40	30	15	____
Lamp	750	600	350	225	____
Parfait, 3.5 oz.	80	60	40	20	____

ROCK CRYSTAL FLOWER (Cont.)	Red	Cobalt	Other	Crystal Colors	Qty
Pitcher, 1 qt., s.e., "Squat Jug"			250	175	____
Pitcher, ½ gal., 7.5" s.e., "Squat Jug			200	130	____
Pitcher, 9" covered	750	600	325	200	____
Pitcher, fancy tankard	1000	800	600	250	____
Plate, 6" s.e., bread & butter	20	18	12	8	____
Plate, 7" p.e., under plate for finger bowl	20	18	12	8	____
Plate, 7.5" p.e. & s.e., salad	20	18	12	8	____
Plate, 8.5" p.e. & s.e., salad	30	20	18	10	____
Plate, 9" s.e., cake	65	45	25	20	____
Plate, 10.5" s.e., cake (small center design)	65	45	35	25	____
Plate, 10.5" s.e., dinner (large center design)	180	100	80	60	____
Plate, 11.5" s.e., cake	60	40	30	20	____
Punch bowl, 14", 2 styles				400	____
Punch bowl base, 2 styles				200	____
Relish, 11.5" p.e., 2-part		70	60	40	____
Relish, 14" p.e., 6-part			100	80	____
Relish, 7-part w/closed handles, p.e.				80	____
Salt & pepper			140	85	____
Salt dip				30	____
Sandwich server, center handle	150	100	60	40	____
Saucer	20	18	12	8	____
Sherbet/Egg, 3 oz.	70	50	30	15	____
Spooner				50	____
Stemmed 1 oz. cordial	70	50	50	25	____
Stemmed 2 oz. wine	60	40	30	20	____
Stemmed 3 oz. wine	60	40	30	20	____
Stemmed 3.5" cocktail	50	30	25	20	____
Stemmed 6 oz. champagne/ tall sundae, 4.5"	40	30	25	20	____
Stemmed 7 oz. goblet	60	40	30	20	____
Stemmed 8 oz. goblet	60	40	30	20	____
Sugar base	50	40	30	20	____
Sugar lid	150	120	50	40	____
Sundae, 6 oz., low foot	40	30	20	15	____
Syrup w/metal lid	800			200	____
Tray, 7" s.e., Pickle or Spoon				70	____
Tray, 12" s.e., Celery	90	60	50	30	____
Tray, 13" p.e., Roll	125	100	75	35	____
Tumbler, 2.5 oz. whiskey	70	50	30	20	____
Tumbler, 5 oz. tomato juice	60	50	30	20	____
Tumbler, 5 oz. old fashioned	60	50	30	20	____
Tumbler, 9 oz., 2 styles	60	50	30	20	____
Tumbler, 12 oz., 2 styles, iced tea	70	60	40	30	____
Vase, cornucopia			100	80	____
Vase, 11"	200	175	125	65	____
Vase, 12" w/square top	200	175	125	65	____

Note: Red slag 12.5" footed bowl, $450. Cobalt: 12.5" footed bowl, $450; 2-light candelabra, $450.

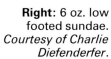

Right: 6 oz. low footed sundae. *Courtesy of Charlie Diefenderfer.*

Below: *Back:* 6" scalloped edge bread & butter plate, 8.5" salad plate; *front:* butter, 3 oz. sherbet/egg. *Courtesy of Charlie Diefenderfer.*

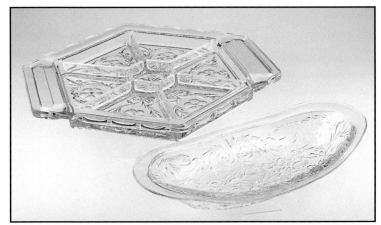

14" 6-part relish, 13" roll tray. *Courtesy of Michael Rothenberger/Mike's Collectables.*

3.5" cocktail, 11.5" 2-part relish, 4.5" fruit bowl
on 7" under plate for finger bowl.

4.5" 6 oz. champagne/tall sundae
w/ unusual round foot. *Courtesy
of Charlie Diefenderfer.*

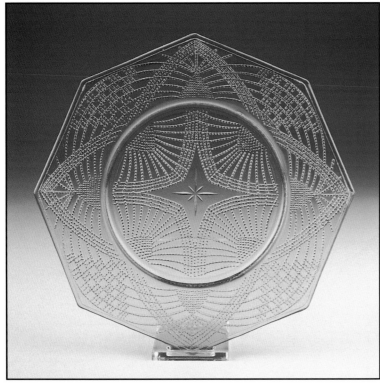

8" octagonal plate.

ROMANESQUE
(Late 1920s   L.E. Smith Glass Company)

This little-known pattern is not often seen. If you are looking for Romanesque, the Internet is an excellent source. We have found more online doing a single search than in walking through countless shops.

The unusual octagonal shape of many Romanesque pieces causes the pattern to stand apart from many other Depression Glass lines. Unlike etched glass, the Romanesque design stands up, away from the glass. The design, which resembles dewdrops on a spider web, is on the underside of each piece to avoid damage that surely would have occurred even during the most careful use.

As you can see, for the next book, this is a pattern that would greatly benefit from collectors' contributions. Please let us know if you have Romanesque.

ROMANESQUE	All colors*	Qty
Bowl, 10.5" flat	40	____
Bowl, 10.5" w/foot	40	____
Cake plate w/2 open handles	30	____
Candlestick, ea., 2.5"	20	____
Plate, 5.5", octagonal	10	____
Plate, 7", octagonal	10	____
Plate, 8", octagonal	10	____
Plate, 8", round	10	____
Plate, 10", octagonal	15	____
Sherbet, round rim	12	____
Sherbet, crimped rim	12	____
Vase, 7.5" fan	35	____

*Made in Amber, Black, Crystal, Green, & Yellow.

ROSE CAMEO

(1931 Belmont Tumbler Company)

Belmont Tumbler Company created one of the Depression Glass patterns having the fewest items of all with charming Rose Cameo. Limited to a small variety of pieces, available only in green, the pattern allows one to set the table for simple meals or dessert. Without the benefit of having dinner plates or serving pieces, the demand for this pattern has diminished.

The 5" footed tumbler may or may not have a flare at the rim. Discerning collectors will want the style that matches their previous purchases.

5" footed tumbler, 7" luncheon plate, 5.5" straight sided bowl, sherbet.

ROSE CAMEO	Green	Qty
Bowl, 4.5" berry	15	____
Bowl, 5" cereal	20	____
Bowl, 5.5", straight sided	35	____
Plate, 7" luncheon	15	____
Sherbet	15	____
Tumbler, 5", 2 styles	23	____

ROSEMARY

(1935-1936 Federal Glass Company)

Rosemary evolved from Federal Glass Company's Mayfair pattern. Federal Glass created and advertised Mayfair in 1934 not realizing that Hocking Glass Company already had a patent on the Mayfair name. Federal's Mayfair pattern was simplified and renamed Rosemary; it enjoyed a two-year production period in 1935 and 1936. Transitional pieces are available that show a lovely blending of the two Federal Glass patterns, as seen on the tumbler. Other transitional items are provided in Mayfair "Federal."

Most often seen in amber, Rosemary is not one of the most popular Depression Glass patterns. The lower demand has resulted in the affordability of the older glass manufactured in amber, green, and pink. Pricing reflects availability meaning that the pink tumbler is the hardest piece to find. This pattern is worthy of consideration if you are looking for Depression Glass that will require a relatively small investment. It is unlikely that the prices will change dramatically in the near future.

Above: *Back:* 6" cereal bowl, 10" oval bowl; *front:* 5" berry bowl, cup & saucer, cream soup bowl. *Courtesy of Connie & Bill Hartzell.*

Left: 12" platter. *Courtesy of Neil McCurdy - Hoosier Kubboard Glass.*

ROSEMARY	Amber	Green	Pink	Qty
Bowl, 5" berry	5	7	10	____
Bowl, cream soup	15	20	25	____
Bowl, 6" cereal	35	30	35	____
Bowl, 10" oval	15	30	35	____
Creamer	8	14	18	____
Cup	5	7	10	____
Plate, 6.75" salad	5	7	10	____
Plate, 9.5" dinner	8	16	22	____
Plate, 9.5" grill	8	16	24	____
Platter, 12"	20	24	30	____
Saucer	4	4	5	____
Sugar, 4", no handles	8	14	18	____
Tumbler, 4.25"	25	30	40	____

Above: *Back:* 12" platter, 9.5" dinner plate, 9.5" grill plate; *front:* 6.75" salad plate, creamer & sugar. *Courtesy of Connie & Bill Hartzell.*

Right: 4.5" transitional tumbler as Federal changed their Mayfair pattern to Rosemary. *Courtesy of Connie & Bill Hartzell.*

Above: Saucer, sherbet.

Right: 9.5" fruit bowl. *Courtesy of Charlie Diefenderfer.*

ROULETTE

(1936-1937   Hocking Glass Company)

Although manufactured in pink and crystal (clear), Roulette is a pattern collected almost exclusively in green. Roulette had a brief period of production, but several items such as the 8.5" luncheon plate and sherbet are still commonly seen. The pitcher and tumblers create the biggest challenge in any color.

Roulette's green is similar to the color of Colonial "Knife and Fork," with a definite yellow tint in a color formulation rarely used by Hocking Glass Company.

There are adequate green Roulette pieces to serve a meal. Although there are no true dinner plates, the 8.5" luncheon would do. For hearty appetites, the 12" sandwich plate would work well. The less common yellow-green glass will be difficult to mix and match with a dinner plate from another pattern and achieve a satisfactory look. However, one can gamble on Roulette as it is both relatively available and pleasant to see.

ROULETTE	Green	Pink	Crystal	Qty
Bowl, 9.5" fruit	15		7	___
Cup	5		5	___
Pitcher, 8"	45	45	30	___
Plate, 6" sherbet	6		3	___
Plate, 8.5" luncheon	8		4	___
Plate, 12" sandwich	18		8	___
Saucer	5		2	___
Sherbet	8		3	___
Tumbler, 2.5" whiskey, 1.5 oz.	20	20	10	___
Tumbler, 3.25" old-fashioned, 7.5 oz.	40	40	20	___
Tumbler, 3.5" juice, 5 oz.	30	30	12	___
Tumbler, 4" water, 9 oz.	30	30	10	___
Tumbler, 5" iced tea, 12 oz.	30	30	10	___
Tumbler 5.5" footed, 10 oz.	25		10	___

Above: 8" pitcher. *Courtesy of Diefenderfer's Collectibles & Antiques.*

Left: 4" 9 oz. water tumbler, 2.5" whiskey tumbler. *Courtesy of Diefenderfer's Collectibles & Antiques.*

ROUND ROBIN

(Late 1920s   Unknown manufacturer)

An unknown manufacturer created this charming luncheon set commonly called Round Robin. There are two unique features worth noting. First, the cup has a foot, a design element rarely seen in Depression Glass. Second, as abbreviated as this pattern is, a Domino tray was included. Cameo has two Domino trays, but this particular item is a piece not found in other patterns. Finding the Domino tray will be the greatest challenge in assembling this set.

Most Round Robin pieces were made in green and iridescent; however, green is the color in greatest demand. As for iridescent round Robin, there is little interest and therefore it remains extremely low in value.

Cup & saucer, sherbet.

7.5" domino tray. *Courtesy of Vic & Jean Laermans.*

ROUND ROBIN	Green	Iridescent	Qty
Bowl, 4" berry	10	3	___
Creamer	10	4	___
Cup	5		___
Domino tray (Sugar cube tray), 7.5" w/3" indent	50		___
Plate, 6" sherbet	3	2	___
Plate, 8" luncheon	6	3	___
Plate, 12" sandwich	15	5	___
Saucer	2		___
Sherbet	10	4	___
Sugar	10	4	___

Right: 5.5" plate, sherbet.

Below: Saucer, 4.5" x 2.5" bowl.

ROXANA
(1932 Hazel-Atlas Glass Company)

So many short patterns were made in green that it is refreshing to see one in yellow. Roxana was produced for only one year making all of the pieces a bit challenging to locate. The sherbet is the most commonly found item with the 5.5" plate and 6" sherbet plate right behind. The options in Roxana make it difficult to use for any specific purpose. There is no cup or saucer, so dessert is eliminated. The lack of a luncheon plate speaks for itself. The yellow is not quite the same brilliant hue of the Florentines, or Hazel-Atlas patterns, so Roxana is a poor match to accessorize other patterns. It must be collected for the shear pleasure of owning a delicate array of Depression Glass.

ROXANA	Yellow	White	Qty
Bowl, 4.5" x 2.5"	25	20	____
Bowl, 5" berry	15		____
Bowl, 6" cereal	20		____
Plate, 5.5"	12		____
Plate, 6" sherbet	12		____
Sherbet	12		____
Tumbler, 4"	25		____

Back: 9.75" dinner plate w/ gold trim (rare!), 9.75" dinner plate; *front:* straight edge candle holders, 10" straight edge bowl. *Courtesy of Donna L. Cehlarik.*

ROYAL LACE
Reproduced
(1934-1941 Hazel-Atlas Glass Company)

Many collectors consider cobalt blue Royal Lace to be the elite Depression Glass color-pattern combination, and when a large quantity is assembled it is truly breathtaking.

Here's a little insight from our part of the world—south central Pennsylvania. Relatively speaking, blue Royal Lace is not difficult to find here. We always have a large quantity for sale and have had numerous opportunities to purchase complete sets. Several customers provided information that explains the profusion of this usually difficult-to-find glass. During the 1930s the Strand Theatre in Reading, Pennsylvania, gave away blue Royal Lace with the purchase of a ticket.

Tom Inglis, a Canadian collector, called to verify the existence of the 68 ounce, 8" pitcher with an ice lip in green! At the time we sent this book to press we had no picture, but have listed the value as too rare to price. Look for either a photograph in the next book or else a blank will appear at this item's value and we'll assume the hunt for this green pitcher is still in progress.

There is a nut bowl for your viewing pleasure. It is like a 10" round bowl that has been reduced in size.

Prices on the candle holders continue to escalate. Remember that the prices shown are for individual holders, not for pairs. Console sets, a pair of candle holders with a matching bowl, will command higher prices when offered together and are very much in demand.

Cookie jar prices have remained stable. Perhaps many who have sought to own a cookie jar have done so already. More cookie jar bottoms were made than cookie jar lids as the bottoms were used in toddy sets. Finding a lid is next to impossible, so you might want to rethink purchasing a bottom with the intention of eventually locating the lid. Remember, the lid is being reproduced.

Royal Lace was designed with a hard edge where the rim ends and meets the surface of a plate. This inner rim was extremely susceptible to damage just from normal use. Royal Lace collectors are often quite forgiving of small nicks and flea bites along the inner rim.

Blue is the most desired color of Royal Lace. Collectors are fairly evenly divided between green and pink. Although crystal (clear) Royal Lace is the least popular color, there are still many, many collectors interested in it. Depression Glass enthusiasts who love a challenge know how extremely elusive the crystal 10" rolled-edge console bowl and crystal straight-sided pitcher are. There are only a few items in amethyst (burgundy), and they are all quite prized.

Royal Lace is truly the royalty of Hazel-Atlas glassware.

Back: 10" round bowl, sugar w/ lid, creamer; *front:* cup & saucer, cream soup bowl, 5" berry bowl. *Courtesy of Donna L. Cehlarik.*

Back: 13" platter; *front:* sherbet w/ chrome base on 6" sherbet plate, all glass sherbet, rolled edge candle holders, 10" rolled edge bowl. *Courtesy of Donna L. Cehlarik.*

Back: 8.5" luncheon plate, 9.75" grill plate; *front row:* 10" ruffled edge bowl, ruffled edge candle holders. *Courtesy of Donna L. Cehlarik.*

Back row: 11" oval bowl, cookie jar w/ lid; *front:* salt & pepper, butter. *Courtesy of Donna L. Cehlarik.*

Back row: 8.5" 96 oz. pitcher w/ ice lip, 8" 86 oz. pitcher w/ no ice lip; *front:* 8" 68 oz. pitcher w/ ice lip, 8" 64 oz. pitcher w/ no ice lip, straight pitcher. *Courtesy of Donna L. Cehlarik.*

Straight pitchers in all four colors. *Courtesy of Charlie Diefenderfer.*

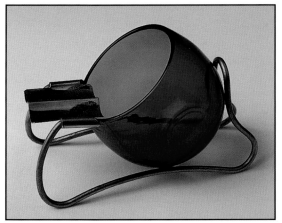

Unusual ashtray utilizing the cobalt roly poly from the toddy set ($45).

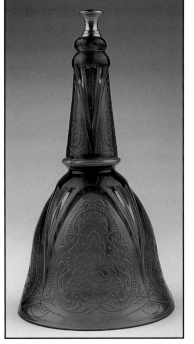

Bell seemingly composed of an inverted handless sugar bowl w/ a shaker for a handle. *Courtesy of Michael Rothenberger/Mike's Collectables*.

Reproduction 3.5" tumbler (no design on the bottom).

ROYAL LACE	Blue	Green	Pink	Crystal	Qty
Bowl, nut	trtp*	trtp*	trtp*	trtp*	____
Bowl, cream soup, 4.5"	50	40	28	15	____
Bowl, 5" berry	135	100	75	50	____
Bowl, 10" round	85	75	65	30	____
Bowl, 10" straight edge	100	80	65	45	____
Bowl, 10" rolled edge	1200	400	200	400	____
Bowl, 10" ruffled edge	1400	300	200	100	____
Bowl, 11" oval	95	85	75	45	____
Butter dish base	450	250	150	75	____
Butter dish lid	350	200	100	50	____
Butter complete	800	450	250	125	____
Candle holder, ea., straight edge	110	80	70	40	____
Candle holder, ea., rolled edge	250	150	140	85	____
Candle holder, ea., ruffled edge	300	150	140	75	____
Cookie jar/lid *R*	450	125	75	40	____
Creamer	65	45	25	15	____
Cup	40	30	20	10	____
Pitcher, straight	180	150	120	375	____
Pitcher, 64 oz., 8" no ice lip	350	225	125	75	____
Pitcher, 68 oz., 8" with ice lip	500	trtp*	125	100	____
Pitcher, 86 oz., 8" no ice lip	500	300	200	125	____
Pitcher, 96 oz., 8.5" with ice lip	600	275	225	150	____
Plate, 6" sherbet	18	15	12	8	____
Plate, 8.5" luncheon	60	40	35	20	____
Plate, 9.75" dinner	45	40	35	25	____
Plate, 9.75" grill	35	30	25	15	____
Platter, 13"	75	65	50	30	____
Salt & pepper	350	200	125	75	____
Saucer	18	15	12	8	____
Sherbet, all glass	55	45	30	20	____
Sherbet w/chrome base	40			8	____
Sugar base	65	45	25	15	____
Sugar lid	200	150	100	75	____
Toddy set, cookie jar w/metal lid & tray, 8 plain cobalt rolypolies, ladle	400				____
Tumbler, 3.5" *R*	65	60	60	25	____
Tumbler, 4"	50	45	35	20	____
Tumbler, 4.75"	225	125	125	75	____
Tumbler, 5.25"	150	95	110	75	____

Reproduction cookie jar lid missing mold seams across the knob and down two sides. *Courtesy of Marie Talone.*

Reproduction information: Reproductions only in Cobalt. Tumblers: new have smooth bottoms with no design; color too dark. Cookie jar lid: new missing mold seam across knob & down 2 sides.

*trtp = too rare to price

Note: Amethyst: 10" rolled edge console bowl, $2000; rolled edge candlesticks, $1000 ea.; sherbet w/chrome base, $65; Toddy set, $500.

Reproduction cookie jar w/ crude design and slightly darker color. *Courtesy of Marie Talone.*

Above: 5.25" tumbler, 4.75" tumbler, 4" tumbler w/ panels (unusual!), 4" tumbler, 3.5" tumbler. *Courtesy of Donna L. Cehlarik.*

Right: Amethyst toddy set. *Courtesy of Donna L. Cehlarik.*

Below: Nut bowl, 10" round bowl. (Note: the design is the same less the medallion not found in the center base of the nut bowl.) *Courtesy of Donna L. Cehlarik.*

"S" PATTERN
(1930-1932 & Fired-on red 1934-1935
Macbeth-Evans Glass Company)

The thinness of the glass and slightly uneven outer rim of the plates help to identify this as another Macbeth-Evans Glass Company pattern. As with Petalware, "S" Pattern is quite underrated and somewhat overlooked by many collectors at this time. Most pieces were never produced in pink or green, so "S" Pattern is a bit out of the mainstream for collectors. Topaz is a midway shade that is neither light enough to be yellow nor deep enough to be amber, which limits the options for mixing it with other colored glass. The crystal (clear) both with and without decorations receives minimal attention from collectors. With only five items in fired-on red, one can't create much of a collection or place setting.

With few requests for this pattern, dealers may avoid keeping it in stock. However, tastes change and perhaps someday "S" Pattern will score an "A."

Back row: 8" luncheon plate w/ platinum trim, 8" luncheon plate; *front row:* cup & saucer w/ platinum trim, cup & saucer, 4" water tumbler. *Courtesy of Charlie Diefenderfer.*

8.5" berry bowl.

4.75" tumbler, sherbet.

"S" PATTERN	Topaz	Crystal w/variations	Crystal	Red (Fired-on)	Qty
Bowl, 5.5" cereal	8	4	2	16	___
Bowl, 8.5" berry	18	9	5		___
Creamer, 2.75" thin & 3" thick	8	4	3	16	___
Cup, 2 styles	6	3	2	12	___
Pitcher, round sides		60	50		___
Pitcher, straight sides	125	50	40		___
Plate, 6" bread & butter	4	2	1		___
Plate, 8" luncheon	6	3	2	40	___
Plate, 9.25" dinner	8	6			___
Plate, 10.5" grill	8	4	3		___
Plate, 11.75" cake	40	20	15		___
Plate, 13" cake	60	30	20		___
Saucer	4	2	1		___
Sherbet	6	3	2		___
Sugar, 2.5" thin & 3" thick	8	4	3	16	___
Tumbler, 3.5" juice	10	5	5		___
Tumbler, 4" water	8	4	4		___
Tumbler, 4.75"	8	4	4		___
Tumbler, 5"	12	6	6		___

Note: Monax: 6" sherbet plate, $8; 8" luncheon, $10. Amber 11.75" cake plate, $80. Green & Pink: Pitcher, $600; 4" tumbler, $65.

SANDWICH
Reproduced
(1940s-1960s Anchor Hocking Glass Company)

9" dinner plate, cup & saucer. *Courtesy of Diefenderfer's Collectibles & Antiques.*

3.5" juice tumbler, 4" water tumbler, cookie jar, 4.25" bowl, custard w/ smooth rim. *Courtesy of Charlie Diefenderfer.*

Boxed set including four 9" dinner plates, four 4.75" bowls, four cups & four saucers. *Courtesy of Michael Rothenberger/Mike's Collectables.*

The Sandwich glass produced by Anchor Hocking was available in a rainbow of colors, but today's collectors are primarily interested in Forest Green. Collectors of Forest Green glass tend to be purists. If Sandwich is the chosen pattern, it is unlikely that another line such as Charm will also be collected. Forest Green was not a successful color when originally introduced as the overall consensus was food was unattractive and unappetizing when served on this color. Today Forest Green is in demand, particularly for use at Christmas time.

The most common Forest Green pieces, 4.25" bowl with a smooth rim, custard with a smooth rim, custard liner/under plate, 3.5" 5 ounce juice tumbler, and 4" 9 ounce water tumbler, were given away free inside a package of oatmeal. The quantity made was tremendous and availability today continues to be fine so prices have remained low. The remainder of the Forest Green pieces increase in value somewhat dramatically. Dinner plates are very much in demand and certainly essential if one intends to use these dishes. The two pitchers are rarely seen, especially the half-gallon water pitcher. The green cookie jar resembles a vase, but, as noted in the pricing, it is open and never had a lid. There is no vase in this pattern.

Crystal (clear) Sandwich is one of the most recognized pattern-color combinations. It was available in Woolworth's for pennies a piece and many items became part of households particularly in the late 1940s and 1950s. Bowls are the most frequently seen commodity; however, the 6.5" scalloped cereal bowl is particularly rare, and the 4.75" crimped dessert is also difficult to find. As with Forest Green, crystal pitchers are not common, but they are much easier to locate than green. The punch bowl and salad bowl are one and the same. Adding the elusive punch bowl stand transforms the salad bowl into a punch bowl.

Amber Sandwich is less in demand than green and crystal, partially because there are fewer pieces available with which to create a table setting. The hue is deeper and somewhat browner than the amber of many Depression Glass lines.

Pink, white, and ivory pieces are few and far between. Pink sells well as shoppers are often drawn to unique pink items as gifts. Ivory and white punch bowls are abundant and often overlooked.

1/2 gallon pitcher, juice pitcher.
Courtesy of Connie & Bill Hartzell.

7" salad bowl, 9.75" salad/punch bowl on 12" sandwich plate. *Courtesy of Connie & Bill Hartzell.*

Back: 9" plate w/ indent for cup; *front row:* 9" salad bowl, cup, 4.25" bowl, sherbet. *Courtesy of Connie & Bill Hartzell.*

Back row: sugar w/ lid, cookie jar w/ lid; *front row:* creamer, butter dish, cup & saucer. *Courtesy of Connie & Bill Hartzell.*

Back: 8.25" bowl, 7.5" bowl; *front:* 6.5" bowl, 5.25" bowl. *Courtesy of Connie & Bill Hartzell.*

Back: 12" sandwich plate; *middle:* 9" dinner plate, 8" plate; *front:* 7" dessert plate. *Courtesy of Connie & Bill Hartzell.*

3.25" juice tumbler, 3.5" juice tumbler, 4" water tumbler, 9 oz. footed water tumbler. *Courtesy of Connie & Bill Hartzell.*

SANDWICH (Anchor Hocking)	Crystal	Forest green	Amber	Qty
Bowl, 4.25" w/smooth rim	6	5		____
Bowl, 4.75" dessert w/ crimped rim	25		5	____
Bowl, 4.75" w/smooth rim	6		6	____
Bowl, 5.25" w/scalloped rim	8			____
Bowl, 6.5" w/smooth rim	8		6	____
Bowl, 6.5" scalloped	8	50	30	____
Bowl, 6.75"cereal w/scalloped rim	100	50		____
Bowl, 6.75" cereal	35		14	____
Bowl, 7" salad	8			____
Bowl, 7.5" salad w/scalloped rim	8	60		____
Bowl, 8.25" w/scalloped rim	10	80		____
Bowl, 8.25" oval w/scalloped rim	12			____
Bowl, 9" salad	25		30	____
Bowl, 9.75" punch/salad	30			____
Butter dish base	20			____
Butter dish lid	25			____
Butter complete	45			____
Cookie jar open, never had lid		20		____
Cookie jar w/lid *R*	40		45	____
Creamer	8	35		____
Cup, coffee	4	20	5	____
Cup, punch	4			____
Custard w/ smooth rim	4	4		____
Custard w/crimped rim	15	25		____
Custard liner/under plate	20	4		____
Pitcher, 6" juice	70	175		____
Pitcher, 1/2 gallon	90	475		____
Plate, 7" dessert	14			____
Plate, 8"	7			____
Plate, 9" dinner	30	140	12	____
Plate, 9" w/indent for cup	8			____
Plate, 12" sandwich	25		15	____
Punch bowl (salad bowl), 9.75"	30			____
Punch bowl stand	40			____
Saucer	3	18	4	____
Sherbet	8			____
Sugar base	8	35		____
Sugar lid	18			____
Tumbler, 3.25" juice, 3 oz., flat	20			____
Tumbler, 3.5" juice, 5 oz., flat	8	8		____
Tumbler, water, 9 oz., flat, 4"	8	12		____
Tumbler, water w/foot, 9 oz.	35		250	____

Reproduction information: New cookie jar is taller & wider than old. New measures 10.25" tall; old measures 9.75" tall. New measures 5.5" across at opening; old measures 4.75".

Note: Ruby items: 4.75" bowl, $20; 5.25" bowl, $25; 6.5" bowl, 30; 8.25" bowl, $80. Pink items: 4.75" bowl, $8; 5.25" bowl, $10; 8.25" bowl, $20; 6" juice pitcher, $275. Ivory & white: punch bowl, $20; punch bowl base, $25; punch cup, $3.

Back row: 4.75" dessert w/ crimped rim, 8.25" oval bowl w/ scalloped rim; *front row:* custard w/ crimped rim on custard liner/under plate, 6.75" cereal, custard w/ smooth rim on custard liner/under plate. *Courtesy of Connie & Bill Hartzell.*

SANDWICH
Reproduced
(1920s-1980s Indiana Glass Company)

In general, Indiana's Sandwich is less popular than Anchor Hocking Sandwich. Many of the pieces have been remade or were added later as production on original molds continued into the 1980s.

Old green Sandwich will glow under a black light. Included is a new green butter dish photographed at West Wall Auction in Fulton, Illinois. Charlie Diefenderfer, the auctioneer, was eager to use his black light to determine the legitimacy of this piece. The sign of a reputable dealer or auctioneer is someone like Charlie who has the knowledge, tools, and willingness to accurately identify a piece of glass. (You can reach Charlie by using the dealer directory in the back of this reference.) Keep in mind the following green items are all recent additions: creamers, cups, saucers, sugars, and water goblets.

Other colors have also had newer production runs. Red was made in 1969, amber was made in 1970, and crystal (clear) was made in 1978. Because the same molds were used, discerning old from new becomes exceedingly challenging. The new wine goblet is a different mold and the dimensions are provided in the reproduction information. These later additions and reissues have severely damaged the collectibility of Indiana's Sandwich.

Back: 10.5" dinner plate; *front row:* 6" bowl, salt & pepper, 12 oz. footed iced tea tumbler. *Courtesy of Charlie Diefenderfer.*

Creamer. *Courtesy of Vic & Jean Laermans.*

Diamond-shaped creamer & sugar on tab-handled tray. *Courtesy of Vic & Jean Laermans.*

Reproduction butter dish. *Courtesy of Charlie Diefenderfer.*

SANDWICH (Indiana)	Amber & Crystal	Teal	Red	Pink & Green	Qty
Ashtrays shaped in 4 suits for bridge parties	5				____
Basket, 10"	35				____
Bowl, 4.25" berry	4				____
Bowl, mayonnaise w/foot	15			30	____
Bowl, 6" round	4				____
Bowl, 6", hexagonal	5	20			____
Bowl, 8.5"	10				____
Bowl, 9" console	18			40	____
Bowl, 11.5" console	18			50	____
Butter dish base *R*	10	75			____
Butter dish lid*R*	20	100			____
Butter complete *R*	30	175			____
Candlestick, 3.5" ea.	10			25	____
Candlestick, 7" ea.	15				____
Celery	18				____
Creamer	10		50		____
Creamer, diamond-shaped	10	12			____
Cruet w/stopper	30	150		175	____
Cup	4	9	30		____
Decanter w/stopper *(R in green)*	30		80	120	____
Goblet, 4 oz. wine, 3" *R*	8		15	28	____
Goblet, 9 oz.	14		50		____
Pitcher	30		130		____
Plate, 6" sherbet	4	8			____
Plate, 7" bread & butter	4				____
Plate, 8" oval w/cup indent	5	12			____
Plate, 8.25" luncheon	5		20		____
Plate, 10.5" dinner	12			30	____
Plate, 13" sandwich	14	28	38	28	____
Puff box	18				____
Salt & pepper	30				____
Sandwich server w/center handle	24		50	35	____
Saucer	3	5	8		____
Sherbet	7	15			____
Sugar base	10		50		____
Sugar, diamond-shaped	10	12			____
Sugar lid	20				____
Tray w/tab handles for diamond-shaped creamer & sugar	10				____
Tumbler, 3 oz. cocktail w/ft.	10				____
Tumbler, 8 oz. water w/foot	10				____
Tumbler, 12 oz. iced tea w/foot	10				____

Reproduction information: Green & pink items that are too light in color are new. Items not shown in this list are new. Wine goblet: old measures 2" across top; new is larger, about 2.75" across top. Butter dish, as well as other items, made new using old molds. Beware! Old green will glow under black light.

Back: cake plate; *front row:* butter, sherbet, candy jar w/ lid. *Courtesy of Sylvia A. Brown.*

Back row: 12.5" platter, 9" pitcher w/ no ice lip; *front row:* 8.5" berry bowl, cream soup bowl, 5" berry bowl. *Courtesy of Sylvia A. Brown.*

Back row: 9.5" dinner plate, 6" bread & butter plate, sugar w/ lid; *front:* cup & saucer, creamer. *Courtesy of Sylvia A. Brown.*

SHARON
Reproduced
(1935-1939 Federal Glass Company)

Distribution for Sharon must have been fairly wide as pieces are found throughout the country and many people recognize and collect it. Unlike patterns having one particular color in great demand, green, pink, and amber are all popular Sharon colors.

Several items are expensive, but even with recent price increases basic Sharon dinnerware remains plentiful and affordable. A cup, saucer, and dinner plate won't require a second mortgage. Tumblers in all colors are getting difficult to find as reflected in the pricing. Thick tumblers are more consistent with the glass used on other Sharon pieces, and thin tumblers are considerably more delicate than the rest of the collection. Flat tumblers were part of the original production line, and footed tumblers were added a year later.

Sugar bowls were marketed with and without lids; therefore, there are more bases than lids. If owning a sugar lid is important to you, then you may want to buy the two pieces together. Most dealers do not sell lids separately. If they gain possession of a lid, they normally match it to a base they may already have in stock or may wait to acquire the appropriate bottom. As a result, if you purchase only a bottom, it is unlikely that you will find the lid for sale.

Reproductions of this pattern initially had a negative affect on the demand, but many collectors and dealers have come to see how crude and easy to recognize these reproductions are. The reproduction butter dish demonstrates that although the new resembles the old there are specific details that should serve as red flags. Be sure to check the reproduction information provided for Sharon and all other reproduced Depression Glass patterns.

The amber 8.5" berry bowl is the single most common item of this line regardless of color. Some dealers avoid them because at $5 most savvy collectors are still not interested. You can find these bowls scattered throughout antique malls with all kinds of prices. Here's a line from "Gone With the Wind" that Barbara loves to repeat: "Askin' ain't gettin'!"

Shakers in various colors. *Courtesy of Michael Rothenberger/Mike's Collectables.*

SHARON	Green	Pink	Amber	Qty
Bowl, 5" berry	18	15	10	____
Bowl, cream soup	60	50	30	____
Bowl, 6" cereal	30	30	25	____
Bowl, 7.75" flat soup		55	55	____
Bowl, 8.5" berry	38	35	5	____
Bowl, 9.5" oval	38	35	22	____
Bowl, 10.5" fruit	50	50	28	____
Butter dish base *R* 7.5" x 1.5"	45	25	15	____
Butter dish lid *R*	75	40	30	____
Butter complete *R*	120	65	45	____
Cake plate	65	45	20	____
Candy jar w/ lid *R*	180	65	50	____
Cheese dish base *R* 7.25" x .75" w/rim		1500	200	____
Cheese dish lid *R* (Butter dish lid)		40	30	____
Cheese dish complete		1540	230	____
Creamer *R*	25	20	16	____
Cup	20	15	7	____
Jam dish, 7.5"	75	250	50	____
Pitcher, 9" ice lip	450	200	150	____
Pitcher, 9" no ice lip	500	180	150	____
Plate, 6" bread & butter	10	8	5	____
Plate, 7.5" salad	28	28	18	____
Plate, 9.5" dinner	25	24	12	____
Platter, 12.5"	35	30	22	____
Salt & pepper *R*	70	70	30	____
Saucer	12	12	5	____
Sherbet	38	18	14	____
Sugar base *R*	25	20	16	____
Sugar lid *R*	45	35	25	____
Tumbler, 4" thick, flat	75	50	35	____
Tumbler, 4" thin (blown), flat	80	50	35	____
Tumbler, 5.25" thick, flat	100	100	65	____
Tumbler, 5.25" thin (blown), flat	120	50	55	____
Tumbler, 6.5" footed		65	150	____

Note: Items in Crystal: 11.5" cake plate, $10; 7.5" salad plate, $10; 6.5" footed tumbler, $15.

Reproduction information: Butter: new lid has easy-to-grasp knob as it is about 1"; new base has true rim with a hard edge in which lid fits. Old lid's knob is about .75" high and the base has rounded, smooth rim for lid. No blue butters are old. Cheese dish: new base too thick, not flat enough but rather bowl shaped. Creamer: new pink is too pale, mold seam is not centered on spout. Sugar: new handles meet bowl in a circle; new lid missing extra glass from mold seam around the middle. Shakers: crude flowers with 4 petals rather than a bud with 3 leaves. Candy dish: thick glass, poor quality. Old foot is 3.25" in diameter; new foot is just under 3". If you find a piece of Sharon in an odd color, beware!

*trtp = too rare to price

6.5" footed tumbler, 5.25" thin flat tumbler, 4" thick flat tumbler, 4" thin flat tumbler. *Courtesy of Diefenderfer's Collectibles & Antiques.*

Butters in various colors. *Courtesy of Michael Rothenberger/Mike's Collectables.*

Reproduction butter showing knob on lid that protrudes higher than on older lids making lid easier to grasp. *Courtesy of Charlie Diefenderfer.*

Reproduction butter showing crudeness of pattern design. *Courtesy Of Charlie Diefenderfer.*

SHIPS
(WHITE SHIP will be used in future)
(Late 1930s Hazel-Atlas Glass Company)

Back row: 8" salad plate, 9" dinner plate, 6" sherbet plate; *front:* cup & saucer. (Note: this is also the Moderntone cup and has no details.) *Courtesy of Bob & Cindy Bentley.*

"White Ship" is the actual Hazel-Atlas name for this pattern and our future references and handbooks will have this pattern listed as such.

White Ship is a dynamic pattern. The cobalt blue contrasted with the simplicity of a sailboat skimming waves creates a look unique to this line of glass. Molds for White Ship are from Moderntone and the cup is the Moderntone cup as White Ship cups have no ship motif.

The cocktail mixer and ice tub are shown in the bottom left photograph. The mixer was designed for mixing drinks utilizing a glass stirrer. It is taller, has thicker glass than most of the other pieces in this collection, and is wider at the top than the bottom. The ice tub is about as thick as any tumbler, has straight sides, and was meant to be a reservoir for ice cubes.

The assortment of tumblers indicates the versatility provided to a home bartender. Most of the pieces from White Ship are somehow related to imbibing.

There are many variations of the ship design. Shown are some cocktail shakers and a collection of "Windmills." All designs are extremely popular and in great demand. Cocktail shakers are selling for close to $200 in California!

Pitcher w/ ice lip, pitcher w/ ice lip and ribs at neck, pitcher w/ no ice lip. *Courtesy of Bob & Cindy Bentley.*

Cocktail mixer, cocktail shaker, ice tub. *Courtesy of Bob & Cindy Bentley.*

Tray. *Courtesy of Bob & Cindy Bentley.*

Ashtray w/ metal sailboat, blotter ("go along" item $50), box w/ 3 sections & lid. *Courtesy of Bob & Cindy Bentley.*

2.25" shot glass, roly poly tumbler, heavy rounded bottom tumbler, 3.5" old fashion tumbler, 3.75" straight water tumbler. *Courtesy of Bob & Cindy Bentley.*

3.5" whiskey tumbler, 3.75" juice tumbler, 4.5" straight water tumbler, 4.75" 10 oz. iced tea tumbler, 5" 12 oz. iced tea tumbler. *Courtesy of Bob & Cindy Bentley.*

5" "go along" tumbler ($25). *Courtesy of Diefenderfer's Collectibles & Antiques.*

Four different "go along" cocktail shakers ($60 each).
Courtesy of Paula Apperson McNamara.

SHIPS	Blue glass w/white details	Qty
Ashtray, 2 styles	65	___
Ashtray w/metal sailboat	125	___
Box, 3 sections	250	___
Cocktail mixer	45	___
Cocktail shaker	45	___
Cup (no details)	15	___
Ice bowl (7" mixingbowl in metal holder w/tongs), complete	45	___
Ice tub	35	___
Pitcher, no ice lip or ribs at neck	65	___
Pitcher with ice lip and ribs at neck	85	___
Pitcher with ice lip, 80 oz.	75	___
Plate, 6" sherbet	35	___
Plate, 8" salad	35	___
Plate, 9" dinner	40	___
Saucer	35	___
Tray, 2 sizes	145	___
Tumbler, 2.25" shot glass	225	___
Tumbler, 3.5" whiskey	45	___
Tumbler, heavy rounded bottom	30	___
Tumbler, 3.75" juice	15	___
Tumbler, roly poly	10	___
Tumbler, 3.5" old fashion	22	___
Tumbler, 3.75" straight water	18	___
Tumbler, 4.5" straight water	16	___
Tumbler, 4.75" 10 oz. iced tea	18	___
Tumbler, 12 oz. iced tea, 5"	25	___

"Windmills" variation: cocktail mixer, roly poly tumbler, heavy rounded bottom tumbler (prices same as White Ship). *Courtesy of Diefenderfer's Collectibles & Antiques.*

SIERRA

(1931-1933   Jeannette Glass Company)

9" dinner plate, 6.5" pitcher. *Courtesy of Diefenderfer's Collectibles & Antiques.*

The greatest of care must be taken when selecting a piece of Sierra. There are many points and edges susceptible to damage. One needs to examine these pieces right side up, upside down, and along every rim-point. It is the fragile nature of Sierra that makes it hard to find, as well as that after only two years of production the Jeannette Glass Company ceased production of Sierra when they became aware of the ease at which the rim-points chipped. In an industry that used and reused molds, Sierra molds were not utilized after 1933.

The short production time and delicate nature of the glass result in Sierra being a bit more expensive than many other Depression Glass patterns. Pricing clearly reflects availability, and pitchers are the hardest items to locate in either color.

Here is a description of the Adam-Sierra combination butter dish. The bottom of the butter dish will be either Sierra or Adam. The key is the top which has both the Sierra motif and the Adam motif. The Sierra pattern is on the inside of the lid and the Adam pattern is on the outside of the lid. This item is too rare to price.

Added to the list are an ultramarine cup and 5.5" cereal bowl.

Back row: 10.25" sandwich tray w/ open handles, sugar w/ lid; *front:* saucer, creamer.

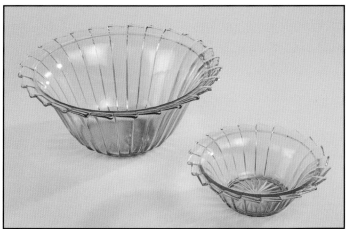

8.5" berry bowl, 5.5" cereal bowl. *Courtesy of Marie Talone & Paul Reichwein*.

Back row: 9.25" oval vegetable bowl, 9" dinner plate; *front:* butter. *Courtesy of Diefenderfer's Collectibles & Antiques*.

SIERRA	Pink	Green	Qty
Bowl, 5.5" cereal	20	25	____
Bowl, 8.5" berry	40	40	____
Bowl, 9.25" oval vegetable	80	175	____
Butter dish base	40	50	____
Butter dish lid	40	50	____
Butter complete	80	100	____
Butter w/Sierra bottom & Adam/Sierra lid	trtp*		____
Creamer	28	28	____
Cup	15	15	____
Pitcher, 6.5"	120	150	____
Plate, 9" dinner	30	30	____
Platter, 11" oval	60	70	____
Salt & pepper	60	60	____
Saucer	10	10	____
Sugar base	28	28	____
Sugar lid	28	28	____
Tray, 10.25" sandwich w/2 open handles	25	25	____
Tumbler, 4.5"	70	90	____

Note: Ultra-marine: cup, $175; 5.5" cereal bowl, $225.
*trtp= too rare to price

Shakers in both colors. *Courtesy of Michael Rothenberger/Mike's Collectables*.

SPIRAL
(1928-1930 Hocking Glass Company)

Back row: 3" flat tumbler, 8" luncheon plate, pitcher; *front row:* sherbet, cup & saucer, creamer. *Courtesy of Charlie Diefenderfer.*

Spiral is one of the few Depression Glass patterns originating in the 1920s and typical of these earliest patterns the design is simple. However, discerning actual Spiral pieces may not be simple! There were many patterns produced with some kind of spiraling design such as Diana, Swirl, Twisted Optic, and U.S. Swirl. There were also a variety of occasional pieces manufactured with a similar design. This plethora of spiraling glassware may create a bit of confusion.

Several Spiral pieces resemble Cameo items, which is a clue for identification. Spiral production ended in 1930, the year Cameo production began, and one can easily determine that at least some Spiral molds became Cameo molds.

One would assume that it would be difficult to locate a pattern made for a brief duration of time, and this is partially true. There are a few pieces that are hard to find: the batter bowl (especially undamaged), the pitchers, the preserve, and the vase. Conversely, many Spiral items that are the easiest to find are $15 or less. There are no dinner plates in this pattern, but the luncheon plates are abundant and remain a bargain at $5, even seventy years after production.

SPIRAL	Green	Qty
Bowl, 4.75" berry	7	____
Bowl, 7" mixing	12	____
Bowl, 8" berry	14	____
Bowl, batter w/spout & 1 handle	50	____
Candy w/lid	35	____
Creamer, 2.5" & 3"	10	____
Cup	6	____
Ice bucket	35	____
Pitcher, 3 styles	45	____
Plate, 6" sherbet	5	____
Plate, 8" luncheon	5	____
Platter, 12"	30	____
Preserve w/notched lid (for spoon)	50	____
Salt & pepper	40	____
Sandwich server w/open center handle	18	____
Saucer	3	____
Sugar, 2.5" & 3"	10	____
Syrup pitcher	65	____
Tumbler, 3" flat	8	____
Tumbler, 5" flat	10	____
Tumbler, flat iced tea	15	____
Tumbler, 5.75" footed	18	____
Vase, 5.75"	50	____

Note: Pink pieces worth twice green, crystal pieces worth 1/4.

Ice bucket. *Courtesy of Michael Rothenberger/Mike's Collectables.*

Shaker. *Courtesy of Michael Rothenberger/Mike's Collectables.*

STARLIGHT
(1938 Hazel-Atlas Glass Company)

Dealers who appreciate finding obscure and challenging pieces and patterns seem a bit more interested in Starlight than collectors. There are only three pink pieces and one in cobalt blue. All four are serving pieces, so individuals interested in a unique piece of pink or blue Depression Glass may be drawn to this pattern. Except for tumblers, one can set a table and serve a meal in crystal (clear). Few are choosing to do so, and Starlight remains a bargain.

2 dinners, 4.75" bowl w/ closed handles.

Creamer & sugar. *Courtesy of Diefenderfer's Collectibles & Antiques.*

Salt & pepper. *Courtesy of Michael Rothenberger/Mike's Collectables.*

STARLIGHT	Pink	Cobalt	White, Crystal	Qty
Bowl, 4.75" w/closed handles			10	____
Bowl, 5.5" cereal w/closed handles	14		7	____
Bowl, 8.5" w/closed handles	20	40	10	____
Bowl, 11" salad			20	____
Bowl, 12"			20	____
Creamer			7	____
Cup			7	____
Plate, 6" bread & butter			4	____
Plate, 8.5" luncheon			4	____
Plate, 9" dinner			10	____
Plate, 13" sandwich	25		18	____
Relish dish			10	____
Salt & pepper			30	____
Saucer			2	____
Sherbet			10	____
Sugar			7	____

12" bowl on 13" sandwich plate. *Courtesy of Marie Talone.*

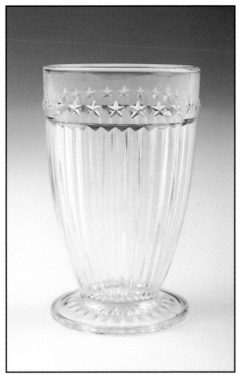

STARS & STRIPES
(1942 Anchor Hocking Glass Company)

The recent surge of Fire-King enthusiasm has resulted in a renewed interest in Anchor Hocking glassware and Stars and Stripes has benefited.

The only three pieces in this pattern are the tumbler and sherbet which are pictured and an 8" plate. The plate is similar to Queen Mary with ridges on the outer rim. The center of the plate is filled with an eagle whose wings are spread as on a coin. A circle of stars is between the eagle and the ridges.

A twenty-cent investment bought all three pieces in 1942. This patriotic grouping was appropriate for the World War II households and is still well-liked today.

Above: Sherbet. *Courtesy of Michael Rothenberger/Mike's Collectables.*

Right: Tumbler. *Courtesy of Diefenderfer's Collectibles & Antiques.*

STARS & STRIPES	Crystal	Qty
Plate 8"	20	____
Sherbert	18	____
Tumbler	35	____

STRAWBERRY
(Early 1930s U.S. Glass Company)

Sherbets are extremely common, but after buying these, collectors have their job cut out for them as Strawberry is a difficult pattern to assemble in its entirety. The ridged edge is prone to damage, but even imperfect pieces are hard to find.

Strawberry is primarily collected in pink and green and they are equally elusive colors. The pitcher and butter dish are the most challenging items to find. The butter dish base is the same one seen in many other U.S. Glass Company patterns. It is void of any design except for a starburst in the center of the bottom. These butter dish bases are completely interchangeable between other patterns and yet are still quite costly.

Certain crystal (clear) and iridescent pieces are abundant as shown on the pricing lists. Except for the butter dish and pitcher there is limited interest in these two colors.

U.S. Glass Company used the same molds for both Strawberry and Cherryberry. If you enjoy Strawberry, you may want to add Cherryberry to your collection.

4.5" large creamer, 5.5" large sugar w/ lid, large creamer. *Courtesy of Vic & Jean Laermans.*

Back row: 7.5" salad plate, pitcher; *front:* butter, 6" sherbet plate, 3.5" tumbler, 7.5" deep berry bowl. *Courtesy of Donna L. Cehlarik.*

STRAWBERRY	Pink, Green	Crystal, Iridescent	Qty
Bowl, 4" berry	14	6	____
Bowl, 6.25", 2" deep	130	20	____
Bowl, 6.5" deep salad	28	15	____
Bowl, 7.5" deep berry	40	20	____
Butter dish base	75	40	____
Butter dish lid	150	100	____
Butter complete	225	140	____
Comport, 5.75"	28	15	____
Creamer, small	25	10	____
Creamer, large (4.5")	40	15	____
Olive dish, 5" w/1 handle	25	10	____
Pickle dish, 8.25" oval	25	10	____
Pitcher	250	175	____
Plate, 6" sherbet	14	5	____
Plate, 7.5" salad	20	5	____
Sherbet	8	5	____
Sugar, small	28	15	____
Sugar, large (5.5")	38	15	____
Sugar lid for 5.5" piece	62	15	____
Tumbler, 3.5"	38	10	____

Sherbet on 6" sherbet plate.
Courtesy of Donna L. Cehlarik.

SUNBURST

(Late 1930s   Jeannette Glass Company)

Sunburst is one of the least collected patterns manufactured by Jeannette Glass Company. It was only made in crystal (clear), and Manhattan and Iris are the two most collected patterns of crystal Depression Glass.

Glass companies often reworked molds from pattern to pattern. The close-up of the Sunburst candlestick clearly shows how similar this piece is to the older Jeannette pattern, Iris. Other pieces of Sunburst resemble Anniversary which followed in the 1940s. The sequence is from Iris to Sunburst to Anniversary!

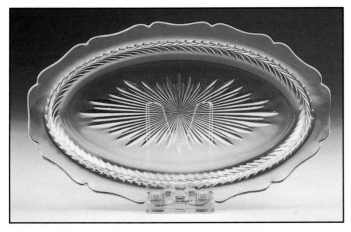

Far left: 5.25" x 8.75" oval tray. *Courtesy of Bettye S. James.*

Left: Candlestick.

Below: *Back row:* 9.25" dinner, 11" bowl; *front:* cup & saucer, 2-part relish, creamer & sugar.

SUNBURST	Crystal	Qty
Bowl, 4.75" berry	10	____
Bowl, 8.5" berry	22	____
Bowl, 11"	25	____
Candlestick, ea.	15	____
Creamer	12	____
Cup	8	____
Plate, 5.5"	10	____
Plate, 9.25" dinner	25	____
Plate, 11.75" sandwich	18	____
Relish, 2-part	15	____
Saucer	4	____
Sherbet	15	____
Sugar	12	____
Tray, 5.25" x 8.75" oval	15	____
Tumbler, 4"	25	____

SUNFLOWER
(1930s   Jeannette Glass Company)

Many pieces of Depression Glass were given away with the purchase of another product as was the case with green and pink Sunflower cake plates. So many of these were distributed in bags of flour (bake the cake and serve it on the Sunflower cake plate) that these are still available in abundance. The cake plate is the easiest item in the pattern to locate. Note that the green cake plate is darker than the other green Sunflower pieces. Because of this cake plate, many people have at least some exposure to Depression Glass.

The most elusive piece in this pattern is the 7" trivet or hot plate. The basic design is the same as the cake plate. Both are round with three feet, but the trivet is 3 inches smaller across the diameter. The cake plate is flat across the top surface; the trivet turns up around the outer rim. The price indicates just how rare an item the trivet is.

We have been told about a yellow creamer and sugar. We also heard about an ultramarine (a truly Jeannette color) creamer and sugar with Doric and Pansy designs. Let us know if you are the lucky owner of either set or both! We are able to show you a really unique creamer and sugar in a caramel/opaque mixture.

Back: 4.75" tumbler, 9" dinner plate; *front:* 10" cake plate, cup & saucer, sugar & creamer.

Hot plate (trivet). *Courtesy of Charlie Diefenderfer.*

SUNFLOWER	Green	Pink	Qty
Ashtray	15	10	
Cake plate, 10"	18	25	____
Creamer	30	25	____
Cup	18	15	____
Hot plate (Trivet), 7"	1000	1000	____
Plate, 9" dinner	30	25	____
Saucer	20	18	____
Sugar	30	25	____
Tumbler, 4.75"	45	40	—

Note: Opaque creamer, cup, & sugar, $85 each. Ultramarine Ashtray, $30, Delphite creamer, $100. Yellow creamer & sugar, $500 each. Caramel creamer & sugar, $500 each.

Rare creamer & sugar. *Courtesy of Staci & Jeff Shuck/Gray Goose Antiques.*

SWIRL
(1937-1938 Jeannette Glass Company)

"Ultra-marine" Swirl is one of Jeannette Glass Company's most popular lines. This bluish-green color, the first color issued in this pattern, is unique to Jeannette and well-received by both Depression Glass lovers and the uninitiated. Ultramarine Swirl on a white tablecloth is absolutely striking.

Similar to ultramarine is a greenish-blue variation. This color is not listed and was probably created by blending colors together at the end of a shift before closing the factory, similar to "end-of-the-day" Bakelite. Odd and unusual pieces were often created by employees: sometimes they were deliberate, and sometimes they were spontaneous. Few collectors have shown interest in the greenish-blue, and dealers report that it is a difficult color to sell. Although values of the greenish-blue color are the same as for ultramarine, there are considerably fewer pieces in this color. Perhaps, as tastes change, this will become the shade in greater demand. If this occurs, the shortage of greenish-blue will certainly cause it to become more expensive.

Pink Swirl is harder to find than ultramarine; however, for the most part, it is less expensive as the demand is considerably less. This can be very frustrating for collectors of pink. Normally lower prices within a pattern indicate a higher level of availability.

Delphite ("Delfite") Swirl is the most difficult color to locate and its popularity goes in waves. Before Jade-ite became exceedingly popular, Delphite was a color very much in demand. Currently the demand for Delphite has waned, but this will surely pass.

The prices on the lists really speak for themselves and provide an accurate indication of availability. Pitchers are virtually impossible to find. Butter and candy dishes are the next most difficult pieces to locate. Items with lids are usually a challenge as lids often got damaged or broken.

Here are a few particulars to keep in mind when buying Swirl. Many pieces are off center and a bit crooked. This is the nature of the pattern and not an indication of a problem. Plates came with two rim treatments. One is finished with a bit of a scalloped edge and the other is with the swirls of the pattern continuing until the very end of the plate. Collectors usually want one particular treatment. If you locate ribbed mixing bowls, refrigerator dishes, and measuring cups with tab handles in ultramarine, you are looking at Jennyware by Jeannette glass. For examples of Jennyware you may want to read another book of ours *The Complete Book of Kitchen Collecting*.

Salt & pepper. *Courtesy of Michael Rothenberger/ Mike's Collectables.*

Back: 4.5" flat tumbler, 6.5" sherbet plate; *middle:* 9" salad bowl, open candy w/ 3 feet, double candlesticks; *front:* 4.75" berry bowl. *Courtesy of Marie Talone & Paul Reichwein.*

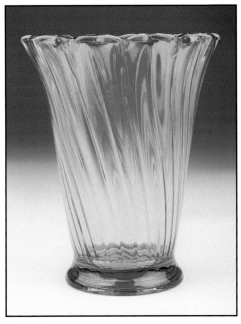

6.5" vase. *Courtesy of Jane O'Brien.*

Two candy dishes w/ lids, butter. *Courtesy of Diefenderfer's Collectibles & Antiques.*

Back: 9.25" dinner plate; *middle:* 10.5" console bowl, 9 oz. footed tumbler, 8.5" vase; *front:* lug soup bowl w/ 2 tab handles, cup & saucer, sherbet. *Courtesy of Marie Talone & Paul Reichwein.*

Coaster. *Courtesy of Charlie Diefenderfer.*

SWIRL	Ultramarine	Pink	Delphite	Qty
Bowl, 4.75" berry	18	14		____
Bowl, 5.25" cereal	18	14	15	____
Bowl, lug soup w/2 tab handles	50	35		____
Bowl, 9" salad	28	22	28	____
Bowl, 10" footed w/handles	35	35		____
Bowl, 10.5" console w/foot	35	35		____
Butter dish base	45	45		____
Butter dish lid	280	180		____
Butter complete	325	225		____
Candlestick, ea. (double)	25	30		____
Candlestick, ea. (single)			75	____
Candy dish, open w/3 feet	20	15		____
Candy dish w/lid	150	225		____
Coaster	20	15		____
Creamer	16	12		____
Cup	16	12		____
Pitcher	trtp*	trtp*		____
Plate, 6.5" sherbet	8	6	8	____
Plate, 7.25"	15	10		____
Plate, 8" salad	18	14	15	____
Plate, 9.25" dinner	20	20	15	____
Plate, 10.5"			25	____
Plate, 12.5" sandwich	35	25		____
Platter, 12"			40	____
Salt & pepper	50			____
Saucer	7	5		____
Sherbet	25	18		____
Sugar	16	12		____
Tray, 10.5", 2 handles			30	____
Tumbler, 4", flat	35	25		____
Tumbler, 4.5", flat		25		____
Tumbler, 5.25", flat	130	65		____
Tumbler, 9 oz., footed	50	25		____
Vase, 6.5"		25		____
Vase, 8.5", 2 styles	28			____

*trtp = too rare to price

SYLVAN (PARROT)
(1931-1932 Federal Glass Company)

Legend tells us that a Federal Glass Company designer developed the Sylvan motif after a trip to the Bahamas. Federal executives were unhappy with the design, fearing the abundance of blank glass would cause knife marks to be easily visible. They were concerned that home-makers would be dissatisfied with the long-term durability of Sylvan. The decision was made to arrest the production of Sylvan and create a new pattern having more design and less empty glass, while still utilizing the same molds. The result of this action was Madrid, a pattern presented in this reference.

If only the decision makers had known . . .

Today Sylvan, commonly called "Parrot," is one of the most loved patterns of all. It is collected in amber and green and equally difficult to find in either color. Nothing in Sylvan is easy to find as the production period was quite brief and competition among collectors is quite high. One could simply say that with Sylvan it is a matter of which items are just more difficult to find than the others. Topping this list in amber is the butter dish and in green the pitcher. A pitcher sold on the Internet at the end of 1998 for more than $5,000.

The green grill (divided) plate is round. The amber grill plate, as with all other plates in this pattern, are square.

Sylvan is so difficult to find that collectors are often a bit forgiving of minor damage. Berry bowls with tiny inner rim nicks are usually snatched whenever seen. This statement is not to encourage anyone to compromise a quest for top quality but just a reflection of what is actually selling.

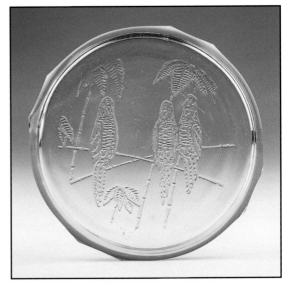

5" scalloped hot dish/coaster.

SYLVAN (PARROT)	Green	Amber	Qty
Bowl, 5" berry	35	25	____
Bowl, 7" soup	55	45	____
Bowl, 8" berry	100	85	____
Bowl, 10" vegetable	70	75	____
Butter dish base	75	200	____
Butter dish lid	375	1200	____
Butter complete	450	1400	____
Creamer	65	70	____
Cup	50	50	____
Hot dish/coaster, 5" scalloped	900	1000	____
Hot dish/coaster, 5" smooth	1000		____
Jam dish, 7"		50	____
Pitcher	trtp*		____
Plate, 5.75" sherbet	40	30	____
Plate, 7.5" salad	40		____
Plate, 9" dinner	60	50	____
Plate, 10.5" round grill	40		____
Plate, 10.5" square grill		40	____
Platter, 11.25"	65	75	____
Salt & pepper	325		____
Sherbet, cone-shaped w/foot (Madrid style)	35	35	____
Sherbet, 4.25" tall w/stem	1500		____
Sugar base	45	45	____
Sugar lid	300	600	____
Tumbler, 4.25" flat	150	125	____
Tumbler, 5.5" flat	175	150	____
Tumbler, 5.5" w/foot		175	____
Tumbler, 5.75" w/foot	150	125	____

Note: Blue sherbet:, $250.

*trtp = too rare to price

Above: *Back row:* 7.5" salad plate, 9" dinner plate, 8" berry bowl; *middle:* sugar w/ lid, 5.5" tumbler w/ foot, 10" vegetable bowl sitting on 11.25" platter, butter; *front:* 5" berry bowl, creamer, salt & pepper, 5.5" sherbet plate, sherbet.

Left: Sherbet, 5.75" footed tumbler. *Courtesy of Debora & Paul Torsiello, Debzie's Glass.*

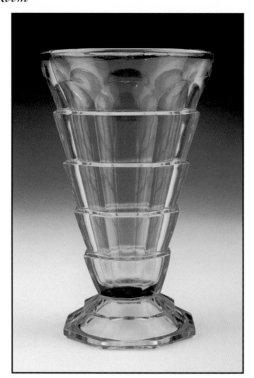

6" 11 oz. footed tumbler.

TEA ROOM
(1926-1931 Indiana Glass Company)

Tea Room was designed for use in ice cream parlors and soda fountains and the array of pieces is indicative of this. There are two banana splits, two glaces, a parfait, three sherbets, and five tumblers. Many of the other items would be useful in a restaurant setting: several creamers and sugars on trays, a variety of vases, a marmalade and a mustard each with lids, an ice bucket, and more.

So the dilemma with this dramatic pattern having many offerings is: Is it more difficult to find any Tea Room or *perfect* Tea Room? Collectors of this pattern have amazing stamina because after finding a creamer, sugar, and pickle dish the availability of pieces diminishes tremendously. The design, having many edges, is a magnet for damage. So, Tea Room collectors, take care and take heart!

Here are a few clarifications regarding Tea Room. A glace is a stemmed item similar to a goblet for use with sorbets and sundaes. Although crystal (clear) is the least collected color, the crystal pitcher is the most difficult one to locate making it quite desirable. The flat banana split resembles an oval relish dish and rests flat on the table. The footed banana split is on a pedestal. Both measure 7.5" across the longest part of the oval.

Above: *Back row:* creamer & sugar on center handled tray, 11" ruffled vase; *front:* low footed sherbet/ice cream on 6.5" sherbet plate, 8.5" pickle, tall sherbet/sundae, 5.25" footed tumbler. *Courtesy of Debora & Paul Torsiello, Debzie's Glass.*

Right: 3.25" creamers & sugars on 6.25" x 7" trays having one side handle. *Courtesy of Vic & Jean Laermans.*

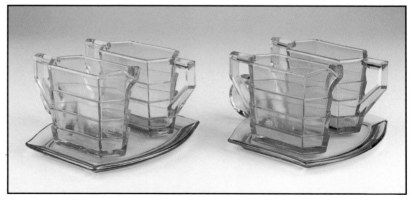

Back row: 8.5" pickle, 12 oz. footed tumbler, *front:* mustard w/ lid, 2-part relish, sugar base. *Courtesy of Debora & Paul Torsiello, Debzie's Glass.*

Creamers & sugars w/ lids. *Courtesy of Vic & Jean Laermans.*

TEA ROOM	Green	Pink	Crystal	Amber	Qty
Banana Split, 7.5" flat	120	100	65		____
Banana Split, 7.5" footed	80	70	50		____
Bowl, finger	65	50	35		____
Bowl, 8.5" w/2 handles	100	80	40		____
Bowl, 8.75" salad	100	80	40		____
Bowl, 9.5" oval	70	70	35		____
Candlestick, ea.	30	25	20		____
Creamer, 3.25" oval & flat	40	40	20		____
Creamer, 4.5" footed	25	25	10	80	____
Creamer, rectangular	30	25	10		____
Cup	60	60	40		____
Glace, 7 oz. & 6.5" ruffled	85	80	50		____
Goblet	85	80	50		____
Ice Bucket	70	70	45		____
Lamp	125	125	70		____
Marmalade w/lid	225	200	100		____
Mustard w/lid	200	175	90		____
Parfait	85	80	50		____
Pickle, 8.5"	30	25	15		____
Pitcher	200	175	trtp*	450	____
Plate, 6.5" sherbet	40	35	20		____
Plate, 8.25" luncheon	40	35	20		____
Plate, 10.5" w/2 handles	55	50	25		____
Plate, 10.5" sandwich w/center handle	55	50	25		____
Relish, 2-part	35	30	20		____
Salt & pepper	100	100	45		____
Saucer	40	35	20		____
Sherbet, low w/foot, ice cream	35	30	20		____
Sherbet, ruffled	45	40	25		____
Sherbet, tall, sundae	85	80	50		____
Sugar base 4.5" w/foot	25	25	10		____
Sugar lid (for 4.5")	200	200	50		____
Sugar, rectangular	30	35	10		____
Sugar base, 3.25", oval & flat	40	40	20		____
Sugar lid (for flat)	20	175	85		____
Tray, center handle	200	175	50		____
Tray for cream & sugar (center handle)	50	40	20		____
Tray for oval, flat cream & sugar (1 side handle), 6.25" x 7"	65	55	35		____
Tumbler, 4.25" flat	125	110	50		____
Tumbler, 6 oz. footed	45	40	20		____
Tumbler, 5.25" footed	40	35	15	100	____
Tumbler, 6", 11 oz. footed	60	50	25		____
Tumbler, 12 oz. footed	75	65	35		____
Vase, 6.5"	100	90	50		____
Vase, 9.5" ruffled	125	115	15		____
Vase, 9.5" straight	80	75	45		____
Vase, 11" ruffled	275	325	150		____
Vase, 11" straight	150	125	75		____

Pair of lamps, salt & pepper. *Courtesy of Debora & Paul Torsiello, Debzie's Glass.*

8.5" bowl w/ two handles having hand painted embellishment. *Courtesy of Charlie Diefenderfer.*

8" luncheon plate.

5.5" cereal bowl, cup.

THISTLE
Reproduced
(1929-1930   Macbeth-Evans Glass Company)

After merely one year of production Macbeth-Evans terminated Thistle. The pattern was unpopular, perhaps because the thistle motif was considered unimaginative; it had been an avidly used theme in earlier lines of glassware in the 1800s and early 1900s. Realizing a change was in order, Macbeth-Evans took the Thistle molds and created Dogwood in 1930. You can read about Dogwood in this reference.

Pink Thistle is more popular than green, and for once this helps collectors as there seems to be a bit more pink than green. Neither color is abundant because the seven pieces were only made for one year.

THISTLE	Pink	Green	Qty
Bowl, 5.5" cereal	25	25	____
Bowl, 10.25" fruit	400	250	____
Cake plate, 13"	150	175	____
Cup	22	25	____
Plate, 8" luncheon	20	25	____
Plate, 10.25" grill			
w/pattern only on rim	35	40	____
Saucer	13	15	____

Reproduction information: These items are new & were never originally produced: butter dish, pitcher, & tumbler.

13" cake plate. *Courtesy of Diefenderfer's Collectibles & Antiques.*

THUMBPRINT
(1927-1930 Federal Glass Company)

Thumbprint is one of the oldest Depression Glass patterns. The design in this pattern predates mold etching and is frequently confused with Raindrops and Hex Optic. These patterns are presented earlier in this book and you may want to cross reference any item in question. Thumbprint has a subtle imprinted texture as if someone's thumb was pressed into wet glass. The design is an oval, Raindrops is circular, and Hex Optic is hexagonal.

This pattern was only made in green and provides all the necessities to set a table and serve a meal. The pitcher we photographed was 7.25", but catalog pages from 1928 indicate there are two additional pitchers having other shapes. We were unable to locate a Thumbprint collection, so if you have one just stick out your thumb and hitch a ride to our studio. Meanwhile, we have presented what we were able to find.

Vase, pitcher. *Courtesy of Marie Talone.*

8" luncheon plate, cup & saucer.

THUMBPRINT	Green	Qty
Bowl, 4.75" berry	15	____
Bowl, 5" cereal	15	____
Bowl, 8" berry	25	____
Creamer	18	____
Cup	8	____
Pitcher, 7.25"	75	____
Plate, 6" sherbert	10	____
Plate, 8" luncheon	15	____
Plate, 9.25" dinner	25	____
Salt & Pepper	80	____
Saucer	2	____
Sherbert	10	____
Sugar	18	____
Tumbler, 4"	20	____
Tumbler, 5"	25	____
Tumbler, 5.5"	30	____
Vase, 9"	60	____

TULIP
(1930s Dell Glass Company)

From Millville, New Jersey, welcome the only pattern from Dell Glass Company in this reference. Tulip was made in a variety of colors including amethyst and blue, and none are easy to find. Tulip is rarely seen even in nearby Pennsylvania.

There are few collectors of this pattern as it has been given little attention. Perhaps as its exposure continues more interest will develop. There is a bit of a catch-22 with this pattern. Little is available, so dealers can't find examples. Few people request it because it has remained a bit obscure. When individuals meander through displays seeking to select a pattern to collect, Tulip probably won't be stacked among the offerings. Thus, the opportunity to consider this pattern is missed, and the cycle of minimal recognition for Tulip continues.

The pieces are quite cleverly designed and reminiscent of the blossom for which they are named. Edges must be examined carefully as the design of the pieces makes them prone to damage. Glassware may be found with or without texture; collectors seem to have no preference and are often delighted just to find something at all!

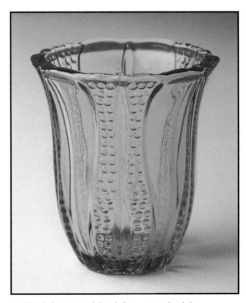

2.75" juice tumbler/cigarette holder. *Courtesy of Charlie Diefenderfer.*

Cup. *Courtesy of Neil McCurdy - Hoosier Kubboard Glass.*

Back: 9" plate; *front:* cup & saucer, sugar & creamer. *Courtesy of Marie Talone & Paul Reichwein.*

Creamers & sugars in various colors. *Courtesy of Vic & Jean Laermans.*

TULIP	Amethyst & Blue	Green & Amber	Crystal	Qty
Bowl, 6"	20	18	15	____
Bowl, 13.25"	100	90	40	____
Candle holder, 2" ea.	35	30	25	____
Candle holder, ea. 2 styles/sizes	25	20	15	____
Candy jar, complete	80	60	40	____
Cigarette holder (same as juice)	30	25	15	____
Creamer, 2"	20	18	15	____
Cup	20	18	12	____
Decanter w/stopper	trtp*	trtp*	trtp*	____
Goblet, 7" water	trtp*	trtp*	trtp*	____
Ice tub	70	60	30	____
Plate, 6"	12	10	5	____
Plate, 7.25"	15	12	7	____
Plate, 9"	20	18	12	____
Plate 10.5"	45	35	20	____
Saucer	10	8	5	____
Sherbet	25	20	10	____
Sugar, 2"	20	18	15	____
Tumbler, 1.75" whiskey	30	25	15	____
Tumbler, 2.75" juice (Same as cig. holder)	30	25	15	____

*trtp = too rare to price

TWISTED OPTIC

(1927-1930 Imperial Glass Company)

One of Imperial Glass Company's earliest Depression Glass patterns was Twisted Optic. It was made in a palette of colors but is most popular in pink ("Rose Marie") and green. There were two shades of green produced: "Imperial Green" and "Golden Green."

Confusion often reigns when sorting through the different spiraling or swirling patterns. Look at the closest side of a Twisted Optic object. The design will go up and to the right. Center handles are open, and the handle in the cup is a small circle allowing one finger to be inserted.

Cups, saucers, and smaller plates are so common that many dealers are disinterested in adding them to their inventories. The other pieces get progressively difficult to locate, and items with lids are the hardest to find. Don't let the relatively low prices fool you as they are not easy to locate. The prices are truly a reflection of the demand—low.

Back row: 8" luncheon plate, 7" salad plate; *front row:* cup & saucer, creamer & sugar.

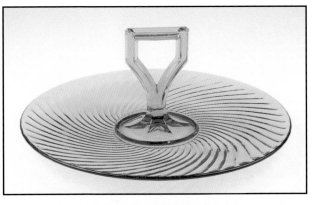

Back: sandwich server w/ two handles; *front:* two creamers, 3" candlestick, two cups.

TWISTED OPTIC	Pink	Green	Amber	Blue & Yellow	Qty
Basket	45	40	40	90	____
Bowl, cream soup	15	12	10	25	____
Bowl, 5" cereal	10	8	6	25	____
Bowl, 7" salad	15	12	10	25	____
Bowl, 9"	20	18	12	30	____
Bowl, 10.5" console w/rolled edge	40	35	25	65	____
Bowl, 11.5" console (Base in black 100)	40	35	25	65	____
Candlestick, 3" ea.	20	18	15	25	____
Candlestick, 8.25" ea.	25	22	20	35	____
Candy jar w/lid (5 sizes)	50	45	40	75	____
Cologne bottle w/stopper	55	50	50	85	____
Condiment w/lid	35	35	30		____
Creamer	12	12	8	15	____
Cup	7	7	5	12	____
Mayonnaise	25	20	20	40	____
Pitcher	50	40	35		____
Plate, 6" sherbet	5	4	3	8	____
Plate, 7" salad	7	6	5	10	____
Plate, 8" luncheon	8	7	6	12	____
Plate, 10" sandwich	12	12	10	18	____
Platter, 9" x 7.5" oval w/ indent	8	7	6	12	____
Powder jar w/lid	40	40	35	65	____
Sandwich server w/center handle	20	18	18	35	____
Sandwich server w/2 handles	15	15	12	25	____
Saucer	5	4	3	8	____
Sherbet	10	10	8	15	____
Sugar	12	12	8	15	____
Tumbler, 4.5"	12	10	10		____
Tumbler, 5.25"	14	12	12		____
Vase, 7.25",	25	25	25	65	____
Vase, 8", 2 styles	30	30	30	75	____

10.5" rolled edge console bowl, 3" candlesticks.

Above: Sherbet. *Courtesy of Charlie Diefenderfer.*

Left: Sandwich server w/ open center handle. *Courtesy of Charlie Diefenderfer.*

Creamer. *Courtesy of Charlie Diefenderfer.*

U.S. SWIRL

(Late 1920s   U.S. Glass Company)

To distinguish U.S. Swirl from similar patterns look for a starburst motif on most bottoms and bases. This is the only swirling or spiraling pattern with items manufactured in iridescent.

Green is the most popular color. However, as with similar patterns, competition among collectors is relatively low because many prefer slightly more recent patterns that have been mold etched.

U.S. Glass Company created a "generic" butter bottom that fits several other patterns including Aunt Polly, Cherryberry, Floral and Diamond Band, and Strawberry. The center of the base has only the definitive starburst, and is without other embellishments or designs. Additional similarities between the U.S. Glass Company patterns do exist. The 3.5" tumbler is only one example of an Aunt Polly mold being shared with U. S. Swirl. The 8" pitcher is the same mold used for Floral and Diamond Band. Cherryberry, Strawberry, Aunt Polly, and U.S. Swirl all share an 8.25" oval bowl.

The use and reuse of molds was a clever way to maximize production and minimize cost.

U.S. SWIRL	Green	Pink	Qty
Bowl, 4.5" berry	8	10	____
Bowl, 5.5" w/1 handle	12	14	____
Bowl, 7.75" round	15	20	____
Bowl, 8.25" oval 2.75" deep	50	50	____
Bowl, 8.25" oval, 1.75" deep	75	75	____
Butter dish base	75	75	____
Butter dish lid	100	110	____
Butter complete	175	185	____
Candy w/lid	35	40	____
Comport	40	40	____
Creamer	15	18	____
Pitcher, 8"	60	65	____
Plate, 6.25" sherbet	5	5	____
Plate, 7.75" salad	7	8	____
Salt & pepper	50	60	____
Sherbet	5	8	____
Sugar base	12	14	____
Sugar lid	28	31	____
Tumbler, 3.5"	10	12	____
Tumbler, 4.75"	15	18	____
Vase, 6.5"	25	25	____

Note: Iridescent & Crystal items 1/2 the value of green.

Comport, 4.75" tumbler.

VERNON

(1931 Indiana Glass Company)

This lovely pattern was manufactured for one year, yet its legacy continues on with strength. There are many collectors of Vernon in both green and yellow ("Topaz"); although, yellow is a bit more popular. Often Depression Glass yellow is amber or apricot, but Vernon's yellow is a true, cheerful, bright color. Crystal (clear) gets far less attention, even though the delicate Vernon detail is still easily evident and quite attractive.

Vernon is an abbreviated line with only luncheon items. Either the 8" or the 11" plate can be used as a dinner plate since Vernon has no true dinner plate.

11" sandwich plate.

VERNON	Green & Yellow	Crystal	Qty
Creamer	35	12	____
Cup	25	10	____
Plate, 8" luncheon	15	5	____
Plate, 11" sandwich	35	12	____
Saucer	10	5	____
Sugar	35	12	____
Tumbler, 5"	45	15	____

5" tumbler.

Creamers & sugars in various colors. *Courtesy of Vic & Jean Laermans.*

VICTORY

(1929-1931 Diamond Glass-Ware Company)

Diamond Glass-ware Company also produced glass as the Northwood Company. This business was responsible for lovely examples of Carnival Glass, but only one pattern of Depression Glass in this reference. Although manufactured in Pennsylvania, Victory is most commonly found in the South and Midwest and is rarely seen in its home state.

Victory was produced in amber, black, cobalt blue, green, and pink. Black is a signature color of Diamond Glass-ware and was often trimmed with gold or silver overlays. Pink can be found with floral embellishments. All colors are collected, but black and blue are the most difficult to find, enhancing their value. Trims must have survived in good condition, and scratching, which is easily visible with this simplistic design, must be very minimal.

The gravy boat and under plate are the most elusive pieces of Victory, and values shown give a good indication of availability.

We hope you are victorious on your search for Victory!

Mayonnaise comport, 8.5" indented under plate both w/ gold trim. *Courtesy of Charlie Diefenderfer.*

Back row: 12" platter, 8" luncheon plate. *Courtesy of Kelly O'Brien-Hoch.*

Above: 12.5" bowl w/ flat rim, 6" comport, 11" sandwich server w/ center handle.

Right: 3.25" candlestick w/ gold trim. *Courtesy of Charlie Diefenderfer.*

Below: Creamers & sugars in various colors. *Courtesy of Vic & Jean Laermans.*

VICTORY	Blue	Black	Other Colors	Qty
Bon bon, 7" hi-footed	30	20	15	____
Bowl, 6.5" cereal	40	35	15	____
Bowl, 8.5" flat soup	60	50	25	____
Bowl, 9" oval vegetable	120	100	35	____
Bowl, 11" rolled edge	65	50	30	____
Bowl, 12" console	75	65	38	____
Bowl, 12.5" flat rim	75	65	38	____
Candlestick, ea., 3.25" tall	65	55	20	____
Cheese & cracker set (12" indented plate & comport)			55	____
Comport, 6" tall			20	____
Creamer	55	50	18	____
Cup	40	35	10	____
Goblet, 5"	100	85	25	____
Gravy boat	275	250	125	____
Gravy under plate	125	100	100	____
Mayonnaise 3-piece set	115	90	60	____
Mayo. comport, 3.75" tall	50	40	30	____
Mayo. ladle	25	25	15	____
Mayo 7.5" under plate, w/indent	40	25	15	____
Plate, 6" bread & butter	20	18	8	____
Plate, 7" salad	20	18	8	____
Plate, 8" luncheon	40	35	10	____
Plate, 9" dinner	55	45	25	____
Platter, 12"	90	75	35	____
Sandwich server, 11" w/center handle	90	80	35	____
Saucer	18	15	5	____
Sherbet	35	30	15	____
Sugar	55	50	18	____

VITROCK

(1934-1937   Hocking Glass Company)

Recent interest in Fire-King has resulted in a renewed enthusiasm for Hocking Glass, and Vitrock has benefited from this phenomenon. Vitrock is a white glassware that often had the word "Vitrock" imprinted on the underside. It was used in a variety of glassware including Lake Como Depression Glass and a line of kitchen glass. However, this presentation concerns the pattern named "Vitrock."

All the pieces needed to set a table and serve a meal are available in Vitrock dinnerware. Thus, although the pattern is limited, it meets the needs for which it was intended. As with many Fire-King patterns, the 9" flat soup bowl and 11.5" platter are the hardest pieces to locate.

It is much easier to find white Vitrock than fired-on pieces, which is reflected in the pricing. Fired-on glass is subject to damage from abrasive cleaning and modern dishwashers, so those pieces that survived unscathed are more costly than their white counterparts.

One can only surmise that the demand for Vitrock will increase resulting in an upward movement of values.

10" dinner. (Note the slight design difference with the dinner plate in the following picture.) *Courtesy of Michael Rothenberger/Mike's Collectables.*

Back row: 10" dinner, 6" fruit bowl, 4" dessert bowl; *front row:* cup & saucer, creamer & sugar.

VITROCK	White	Fired-on colors	Qty
Bowl, 4" dessert	6	10	____
Bowl, cream soup	18	25	____
Bowl, 6" fruit	8	12	____
Bowl, 7.5" cereal	10	12	____
Bowl, 9" flat soup (soup plate)	35	50	____
Bowl, 9.5" vegetable	18	25	____
Creamer	8	12	____
Cup	5	8	____
Plate, 7.5" bread	5	8	____
Plate, 8.75" luncheon	5	8	____
Plate, 10" dinner	12	15	____
Platter, 11.5"	35	50	____
Saucer	5	8	____
Sugar	8	12	____

Sugar w/ lid. *Courtesy Of Vic & Jean Laermans.*

80 oz. tilted water pitcher. *Courtesy of Michael Rothenberger/Mike's Collectables.*

WATERFORD
(1938-1944   Hocking Glass Company)

Every few months we have a new customer approach us to inquire about Waterford with the preconceived notion that this Depression glassware is actually Waterford crystal. They see creamers, sugars, and other items for a mere $5 and think we've grossly underpriced fine crystal. Alas, this is not the case.

Waterford is the name of an Irish crystal manufacturer that produced many named patterns. Hocking Glass Company is the name of an American glassware company responsible for creating many named patterns including this one, Waterford.

Pink ("Rose") was introduced in 1938 at a time when colored glassware was becoming less fashionable. Crystal (clear) followed in 1939 and was much more successful than pink. Crystal production continued until 1944, except for the goblet that was manufactured in 1959, and the offerings were increased leaving a heritage of more crystal having been made with a greater selection of pieces. There are even two different salt and pepper shakers in crystal and none in pink. Ironically, it is the less common pink that attracts most collectors today.

The price differences between the two colors are astonishing. A pink butter dish is almost ten times the price of a crystal one, and the pink sugar lid is ten times as expensive as the crystal one. The pink water pitcher is four times as valuable as a crystal one. These prices indicate how scarce certain pink Waterford items are.

Forest Green 13.75" sandwich plates were produced to be used as part of a relish set similar to the one shown in Manhattan. The inserts along the outer circle were usually white glass (milk glass) with a green center insert. These remain fairly common and are often purchased by Forest Green collectors rather than Waterford collectors.

Back row: 9.5" dinner plate, 10.25" cake plate w/ two closed handles; *front:* sherbet, 4.75" berry bowl, cup & saucer, 5.5" cereal bowl. *Courtesy of Diefenderfer's Collectibles & Antiques.*

Back row: saucer, 7.25"
salad plate, 6" sherbet
plate; *front:* sherbet, 8.25"
berry bowl. *Courtesy of
Charlie Diefenderfer.*

WATERFORD	Pink	Crystal	Qty
Ash tray		8	____
Bowl, 4.75" berry	20	8	____
Bowl, 5.5" cereal	40	20	____
Bowl, 8.25" berry	28	10	____
Butter dish base	40	8	____
Butter dish lid	210	20	____
Butter complete	250	28	____
Coaster		5	____
Creamer, oval	15	5	____
Creamer, ftd.		45	____
Cup	20	8	____
Goblet, 5.25" & 5.5"		18	____
Lamp, 4" round base		45	____
Lazy Susan, 14"		35	____
Pitcher, juice (tilted), 42 oz.		30	____
Pitcher, water (tilted),			
80 oz.	200	50	____
Plate, 6" sherbet	12	5	____
Plate, 7.25" salad	15	8	____
Plate, 9.5" dinner	30	15	____
Plate, 10.25" cake w/2			
closed handles	22	12	____
Plate, 13.75" sandwich	35	15	____
Relish, 13.75" round			
w/5 parts		20	____
Salt & pepper, narrow		12	____
Salt & pepper, wide (flared			
bottom)		8	____
Saucer	10	5	____
Sherbet, smooth foot			
& smooth rim	20	5	____
Sherbet, scalloped		25	____
Sugar base	18	5	____
Sugar lid	100	10	____
Tumbler, 3.5" juice	120		____
Tumbler, 4.75" footed	30	10	____
Tumbler, 5.25" footed		12	____

Note: Ashtray w/advertisement in center, $20.
Amber goblet: $20. Yellow goblet: too rare to
price.

Wide, flared
bottom salt &
pepper,
narrow salt &
pepper.
*Courtesy of
Michael
Rothenberger/
Mike's
Collectables.*

16-piece boxed set consisting of 4 dinner plates & saucers
in Royal Ruby and 4 cups & 5.25" footed tumblers in
crystal Waterford. *Courtesy of Charlie Diefenderfer.*

WINDSOR
(1932-1946 Jeannette Glass Company)

In an attempt to simplify the listing of Windsor items we have used the abbreviation "zz" to indicate a zigzag or pointy rim. Keep in mind that the prices are for perfect pieces and locating perfect Windsor takes time because each surface needs examination.

Although production of Windsor began in 1932, only crystal (clear) continued through 1946. The use of colored glassware waned, but clear glass was very much in vogue. Today there are more pieces of crystal than the other colors. Several later additions are unique to crystal Windsor including the footed tumblers and comport. Green is the color in greatest demand, but pink isn't far behind. Crystal has the smallest following.

This pattern enjoyed a long period of production, and many different pieces were created. There are thirteen different bowls with the "boat" bowl being the most recognizable. It has two pointy ends along the 11.75" side and is 7" wide. The bowl does resemble a boat. In pink the 8" and 10.5" bowls with zigzag rims and the 12.5" fruit bowl are the most difficult bowls to find. Fewer bowls were produced in green and crystal. The green butter dish is the hardest one to find, and the crystal one is quite common. The pink powder jar is extremely rare and we are pleased to picture one. The three-part platter is elusive in crystal and almost nonexistent in pink. The 6.75" pitcher in pink is common, but the 4.5" milk pitcher is rare. Only the 6.75" pitcher was made in green and one will find twenty in pink for each one in green. Note the differences in the sugar lids and their respective prices.

Windsor continues to have a strong following. The more pieces placed together the more exciting the look. The play of light through all of the angles is simply mystifying, and a wonderful way to say "Adieu."

Depression Glass ends with Windsor. We don't quite go A-Z, but we hope to have enriched your buying and/or selling in some way. As stated throughout this reference, this is a start down a new road. We invite all of you to join us. And for those of you who can do so in the studio, we are anxious to meet you. Schiffer photographers travel quite frequently and arrangements might be able to be made to come to your collections. Together we can build an even better second edition!

Powder jar w/ lid. *Courtesy of Michael Rothenberger/Mike's Collectables.*

5" flat tumbler, 4" flat tumbler, 3.25" tumbler. *Courtesy of Diefenderfer's Collectibles & Antiques.*

Back: 9" dinner plate, 6.75" pitcher; *middle:* 5.5" deep cereal bowl, 11.5" platter, cream soup bowl; *front:* cup & saucer, creamer, sugar w/ lid. *Courtesy of Diefenderfer's Collectibles & Antiques.*

WINDSOR	Pink	Green	Crystal	Qty
Ash tray	42	45	15	____
Bowl, 4.75" berry	12	12	5	____
Bowl, 5" zz*	45		5	____
Bowl, cream soup	25	30	7	____
Bowl, 5.5" deep cereal	30	30	9	____
Bowl, 7.25" w/3 feet	30		10	____
Bowl, 8" zz*	125		15	____
Bowl, 8" w/handles	25	25	7	____
Bowl, 8.5" berry	25	25	7	____
Bowl, 9.5" oval vegetable	25	30	8	____
Bowl, 10.5" salad	15			____
Bowl, 10.5" zz*	225		30	____
Bowl, 12.5" fruit	125		30	____
Bowl, 7"x 11.75" "boat"	40	45	25	____
Butter dish base	20	40	10	____
Butter dish lid	40	60	20	____
Butter complete	60	100	30	____
Cake plate, 10.75"	30	30	10	____
Candlestick, ea.	45		12	____
Candy jar w/lid			30	____
Coaster	15	20	5	____
Comport			20	____
Creamer (2 styles in Crystal)	15	15	7	____
Cup	12	12	4	____
Pitcher, 4.5", milk	130		25	____
Pitcher, 6.75"	40	70	15	____
Plate, 6" sherbet	8	8	3	____
Plate, 7" salad	20	25	4	____
Plate, 9" dinner	25	35	8	____
Plate, 10" sandwich w/closed handles	25		10	____
Plate, 10.5" zz*			10	____
Plate, 10.25" w/open handles	20	20	8	____
Plate, 13.5" chop	40	40	15	____
Platter, 11.5"	30	30	8	____
Platter, 3-part	400		30	____
Powder jar complete	350		20	____
Relish, 11.5", 2-part			15	____
Salt & pepper, 3"	40	60	20	____
Saucer	10	10	3	____
Sherbet	15	20	4	____
Sugar base, 3" w/smooth rim	30	40	15	____
Sugar base, 3.25" w/scalloped rim	15	20	7	____
Sugar lid w/pointy knob	20	30	8	____
Sugar lid w/small knob	120		10	____
Tray, 4" sq. w/handles	10	15	5	____
Tray, 4" sq. no handles	50		10	____
Tray, 4" x 9" w/handles	10	15	5	____
Tray, 4" x 9" no handles	60		12	____
Tray, 8.5" x 9.75" w/handles	25	35	10	____
Tray, 8.5" x 9.75" no handles	95		15	____
Tumbler, 3.25" flat	30	35	10	____
Tumbler, 4" flat	18	35	10	____
Tumbler, 4.25" w/foot			10	____
Tumbler, 4.5" flat			10	____
Tumbler, 5" w/foot	35	60	10	____
Tumbler, 5" flat			10	____
Tumbler, 7.25" w/foot			10	____

*zz = zigzag or pointed edges

Note: Delphite ashtray, $65. Blue creamer, cup, 9" dinner, 3.25" flat tumbler, & 4" flat tumbler: $75 each; powder jar, $375; red pitcher, $500. Yellow powder jar, $375.

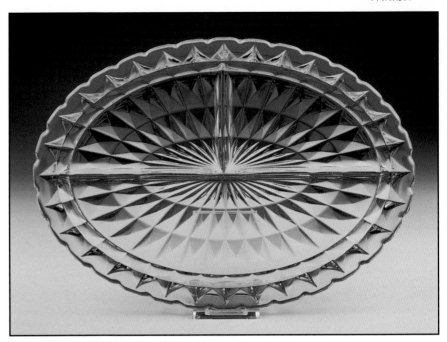

3-part platter. *Courtesy of Marie Talone.*

5.5" cereal.

Salt & pepper. *Courtesy of Vic & Jean Laermans.*

4.5" milk pitcher. *Courtesy of Vic & Jean Laermans.*

Back: 9" dinner plate, 10.25" plate w/ open handles; *middle:* 5" footed tumbler, 7.25" footed tumbler, 7" x 11.75" "boat" bowl, 8" bowl; *front:* 4" flat tumbler, butter, sugar base, creamer. *Courtesy of Marie Talone & Paul Reichwein.*

3" sugar base w/ smooth rim (3.25" inner rim diameter of lid), 3.25" sugar base w/ scalloped rim (3" inner rim diameter of lid). *Courtesy of Vic & Jean Laermans.*

Candlesticks.

10.5" bowl, 7.25" bowl w/ 3 feet. *Courtesy of Michael Rothenberger/Mike's Collectables.*

7" footed tumbler, 5" footed tumbler, 4.25" footed tumbler, 3.25" flat tumbler. *Courtesy of Vic & Jean Laermans.*

Bibliography

Antique & Collectors Reproduction News, *Depression Glass Reproductions.* Des Moines, IA: 1994.

Florence, Gene. *Anchor Hocking's Fire-King & More.* Paducah, KY: Collector Books, 1998.

Florence, Gene. *Collectible Glassware from the 40s 50s 60s...* Paducah, KY: Collector Books, 1998.

Florence, Gene. *Collector's Encyclopedia of Depression Glass.* Paducah, KY: Collector Books, 1998.

Florence, Gene. *Pocket Guide to Depression Glass and More.* Paducah, KY: Collector Books, 1999.

Goshe, Ed, Ruth Hemminger, and Leslie Piña. *Depression Era Stems & Tableware: Tiffin.* Atglen, PA: Schiffer Publishing Ltd., 1998.

Kilgo, Garry & Dale, and Wilkins, Jerry & Gail. *Anchor Hocking's Fire -King Glassware.* Addison, Alabama: K & W Collectibles Publisher, 1997.

Heacock, William. *Fenton Glass The Second Twenty-Five Years.* Marietta, Ohio: O-val Advertising Corp., 1980.

Hopper, Philip. *Royal Ruby.* Atglen, PA: Schiffer Publishing Ltd., 1998.

Piña, Leslie, and Paula Ockner. *Depression Era Art Deco Glass.* Atglen, PA: Schiffer Publishing Ltd., 1999.

Snyder, Jeffery B. *Morgantown Glass: From Depression Glass through the 1960s.* Atglen, PA: Schiffer Publishing Ltd., 1998.

Stout, Sandra McPhee. *Depression Glass.* Des Moines, IA: Wallace-Homestead Book Company, 1970.

Walk, John, and Joseph Gates. *The Big Book of Fenton Glass 1940-1970.* Atglen, PA: Schiffer Publishing Ltd., 1998.

Weatherman, Hazel Marie. *Colored Glassware of the Depression Era.* Ozark, MO: Weatherman Glassbooks, 1970.

Weatherman, Hazel Marie. *Colored Glassware of the Depression Era 2.* Ozark, MO: Weatherman Glassbooks, 1974.

Yeske, Doris. *Depression Glass, 3rd Edition.* Atglen, PA: Schiffer Publishing Ltd., 1999.

Dealer Directory

The following is partial listing of the fine dealers whose inventory and personal collections were instrumental in creating this reference. Several generous souls chose to remain anonymous, but the others are shown.

We can not thank them enough for their assistance. We invite you to contact them for any Depression Glass or Elegant Glass needs. Their integrity is outstanding and all are just down right great people!

**CHARLIE DIEFENDERFER/
WEST WALL AUCTION HOUSE**
Specialty auctions held throughout the year. Depression Era glassware, China, and pottery; Carnival Glass, Fiesta, Hall, and Blue Ridge; antiques, collectibles, furniture, and more.
Web Site: www.westwall.com
E-mail: westwall@westwall.com
Fax: (309) 887-4923
Phone: (309) 887-4726

**DOTTIE & DOUG HEVENER/
THE QUACKER CONNECTION**
Shop location:
The Pirate's Quay Shops
MP 11 Route 158 Bypass
Nags Head, NC 27959
Shop phone: (252) 441-2811
Web Site: http://www.thequackerconnection.com

NEIL McCURDY - HOOSIER KUBBOARD GLASS
Phone: (610) 346-7946
Found at the following shows:
* Liberty Bell Depression Glass Show
* Kutztown, PA Renninger's Extravaganza every April, June, September
* Brimfield, MA J & J Shows every May, July, September
* Hillsville, VA Labor Day Gun Show every Labor Day weekend
* Fisherville, VA every May and October
* Valley Forge, PA Renninger's Midwinter Show every February
* Schnecksvilled, PA Lehigh Valley Dep. Glass Show Thanksgiving Weekend
* Mt. Dora, FL Renninger's January Show

PAUL REICHWEIN
Selling in Booth 12 at Black Angus Antique Mall, Adamstown, PA (just north of Renninger's Antique Market) every Sunday. Also selling on line:
*www.collectoronline.com (Booth 115)
*www.hwcantiques.com (Booth 1)
Selling each Spring at Antlantique City Show
2321 Hershey Avenue
East Petersburg, PA 17520
Phone: (717) 569-7637
E-mail: PaulRDG@aol.com

MICHAEL ROTHENBERGER/MIKE'S COLLECTABLES
Found at:
* Weaver's Antique Mall - Booth A12
  Route 222 North of Adamstown, PA (exit 21 of PA Turnpike)
* Adams Annex - Booth J - 2
  Route 272 North in Adamstown, PA
* Collector Online - Booth 30
  www.collectoronline.com
E-mail: miker @ talon.net

STACI AND JEFF SHUCK/GRAY GOOSE ANTIQUES
Also a big part of Gray Goose Antiques:
Jerome and Donna Leamer
Phone: (814) 643-2588 and (814) 627-2639
E-mail: jjshuck@vicom.net
"Visit us on the Internet at Mega Show"
www.glassshow.com - Aisle 6
Found at: Dairyland Antiques
  (Sundays noon-5:00/ Wed.-Sat. 10:00-5:00)
  Route 655
  Reedsville, PA

MARIE TALONE/MARIE'S ANTIQUES
Found at:
* Renninger's Antique Market in Adamstown, PA off exit 21 of the PA Turnpike, north ½ mile on Route 272 in booth D - 14 every Sunday
* Renninger's Shows in Kutztown, PA annually in April, June, and September
* Renninger's Show at Valley Forge Convention Center in King of Prussia, PA annually in February
Phone: (610) 868-3702 for show dates or to transact business
E-mail: martal@sprynet.com

DEBORA & PAUL TORSIELLO, DEBZIE'S GLASS
Phone: (973) 428-4885

Collector Note:
VIC & JEAN LAERMANS
Always looking for unusual or rare creamers and sugars to buy, sell, or trade.
Phone: (309) 755-9082
E-mail: VJDep@QConline.com

MORE SCHIFFER TITLES

www.schifferbooks.com

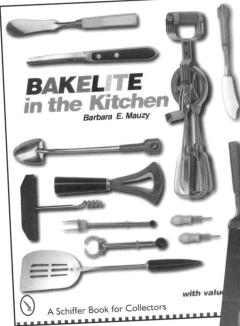

Other Books by Barbara Mauzy...

Bakelite in the Kitchen

More than 40 categories of collectible Bakelite kitchenware are presented in this appealing volume that covers gadgets, flatware, napkin rings, children's utensils, and even some related non-kitchen Bakelite examples too colorful and fun to miss. This is the one, indispensable source of information on dating, manufacturers and designs that is an absolute must for the decorator, collector and even the occasional kitchen user.

8 1/2" x 11"	573 color photos	Price Guide
192 pages	soft cover	$29.95

Peanut Butter Glasses

Decorated peanut butter glasses were made in the 1950s to sell commercially produced peanut butter. The glasses were printed with colorful flowers, birds, dogs, and specialty images. This book catalogs the known decorations by showing both front and back views of each glass. 977 color photographs and identifying text tell the whole story.

6" x 9"	977 color photos	Value Guide
128 pages	soft cover	$19.95

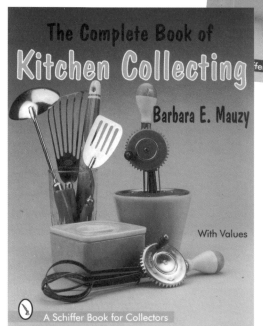

The Complete Book of Kitchen Collecting

Covers many categories of non-electrical kitchen collectibles from the 1920s through the 1950s. Over 1100 photographs depict the ingenuity and creativity of the makers of kitchenware during this period. Values, guides to the more popular designs and colors, manufacturing information, and general tips on collecting make this the complete guide for anyone interested in these colorful and inventive gadgets, tools, and dinnerware items.

8 1/2" x 11"	1155 color photos	Value Guide
240 pages	soft cover	$34.95